LIFE NOTES

Also by Patricia Bell-Scott

DOUBLE STITCH: BLACK WOMEN WRITE ABOUT MOTHERS AND DAUGHTERS
(edited with Beverly Guy-Sheftall,
Jacqueline Jones Royster,
Janet Sims-Wood, Miriam DeCosta-Willis,
and Lucille P. Fultz)

ALL THE WOMEN ARE WHITE, ALL THE BLACKS ARE MEN, BUT SOME OF US ARE BRAVE: BLACK WOMEN'S STUDIES
(edited with Gloria T. Hull and Barbara Smith)

LIFE NOTES

Personal Writings by Contemporary Black Women

PATRICIA BELL-SCOTT

W. W. NORTON & COMPANY

New York

London

First published as a Norton paperback 1995

The text of this book is composed in Sabon
with the display set in Eurostile Bold Extended.
Composition by PennSet Inc.
Manufacturing by Courier Companies Inc.
Book design by Beth Tondreau Design

LIBRARY OF CONGRESS CATALOGING-IN-PUBLICATION DATA
Life notes : personal writings by contemporary Black women / edited by
    Patricia Bell-Scott.
        p. cm.
    1. Afro-American women. 2. Afro-American women—Biography.
3. Afro-American women—Diaries. 4. Women, Black—Caribbean Area—
Biography. 5. Women, Black—Caribbean Area—Diaries. 6. Women,
Black—Biography. 7. Women. Black—Diaries. I. Bell-Scott,
Patricia.
E185.86.L498   1994
305.48'896073—dc20   93-22731

ISBN 0-393-31206-2

W. W. Norton & Company, Inc., 500 Fifth Avenue, New York, N.Y. 10110
W. W. Norton & Company Ltd., 10 Coptic Street, London WC1A 1PU

3   4   5   6   7   8   9   0

For **ARVIN SCOTT**,
who has always been there,

and for **AUDRE LORDE**,
whose courage and personal writing stand as beacons

Contents

PART TWO
SEARCHING FOR SELF

PART THREE
MEANING AND WORK

PART FOUR
LIVING LOVE

Foreword

MARCIA ANN GILLESPIE

Some of the memories I hold dearest are of times spent in the company of women, when we drop all pretense and the talk gets to the bone. Times of tears and laughter, when the silences that choke us are breached, when we speak about our fears and deepest secrets, when we let go and get free and simply say what's really in our hearts and spirits, and on our minds. Reflective, hesitant voicings of thoughts and feelings long held but priorly unspoken. We share our secret longings, let go of things held close in fear of reprisal, in fear of being ridiculed, or being held in contempt.

Unedited, uncensored womantalk. Earthily sexual, downright raunchy sometimes. Other times a bearing of wounds and hurts that have lain festering for too long: Spiritual boils in need of lancing. Tears too long damned. Feelings of shame and blame, of inadequacy, of frustration and rage. Unveilings of secret joys, forbidden pleasures, unresolved mysteries, and hidden dreams.

From these woman-sharing talks, from peeling back the layers and exposing our secret pleasures and pains, our uncertainties and doubts, our angers and despair have come transformation, empowerment, community, activism. We learn we are not crazy, or that we are the best kind of crazy. We bear witness, we affirm, we find our true voices, our true power. We heal. We are healed. We speak truth to power.

Reading these narratives of my sisters I'm reminded that often these truths are voiced silently. We write them in our diaries and journals, in letters and notebooks, and on scraps of paper. With pencil or pen, typewriters and keyboards, we give our thoughts and feelings room to breathe. And we give ourselves permission to believe that our thoughts, feelings, issues, and words are valuable. We affirm that our stories, our experiences, our impressions and opinions are important enough to be saved.

My first and only traditional diary—as in one with a lock and key —had a rosy pink cover. I remember how pleased and excited and grownup I felt when my mother gave it to me on my twelfth birthday. Before bed that night, I sat in my room and, using my favorite pen, carefully wrote my full name in it. Then I turned to the first blank page and the questions began: How do I start? What should I say? What do I want to write about? What is so important about my life that I should write about it? That diary seemed to grow bigger and smaller as it sat in my lap. Finally I entered the date, July 10, 1956, and wrote:

> Dear Diary: I don't know what I'm supposed to write in you. What do people put in diaries anyway? My mama says that everything I see, and think is important so here goes. Today is my birthday, I am twelve years old. I live at 91 Banks Avenue in Rockville Centre, Long Island New York in the United States of America. I live with my mother and father. Her name is Ethel. His name is Charles. And my big sister is Charlene. We live in a house next to Shiloh Baptist Church. My nana, my two aunts, my uncle and two cousins live down at the other end of the block. My mama was born here; my father is from North Carolina. Most all the old people are from the south, Big Foot country my daddy calls it. . . ."

Sporadically I would make entries, sometimes describing something that had happened to me, or writing about my belief that somewhere on another planet lived people who were our mirror opposites. I wrote about the white men who cruised our neighborhood looking to pick up the girls and women. One entry began:

> A white man in a blue Pontiac pulled up beside me as I walked from Marjorie's house this afternoon. I was by the school and there was no one else around. He said "I've got a big white dick, you'll like it. Get in the car I'll give you money." He made sucking noises. I kept walking and he kept following me. I wouldn't look at him, I wanted to cry. I was scared. I started to run then something said scream, and when I started screaming he took off. Nana was right you can shame the devil.

By the time my thirteenth birthday rolled around I had filled in most of the pages. My entry for that day began:

> Dear Diary, I know I haven't talked to you in some time. I got my period today, some birthday present. Mama, Aunt Vi and Aunt Hazel all said that this is something wonderful. Mama gave me a booklet which says, now you're a woman and showed me how to pin the sanitary napkin to this elastic belt I have to wear. I was hoping I would grow breasts for my birthday, but here I am no breasts walking around with this thing stuck between my legs instead. Please God, send the breasts.

In the ensuing years, I've written in notebooks, and on yellow legal pads, and have compiled a trunk full of letters that I never intended to mail. From time to time I open up one of those letters, or leaf through a notebook and rediscover the woman I was at that moment in time. Me going through my changes, me wallowing in self-pity, me kicking myself in the behind, me talking to God, me talking to myself, working out my problems. Me on the world, me in love or on love, me on me to me.

KEEPING A JOURNAL is an extraordinarily intimate activity, sharing what we write is to allow another to peer through a delicate window where we stand without covers. I sat up all night for several nights in silent communion with the women who've contributed to this book. Uh-humming and Uh-Uhing, sucking teeth and head-shaking, laughing and weeping, smiling and moaning, cussing and pshawing, agreeing and amening. I saw myself in these pages, heard familiar echoes of my voice and the voices of sister friends and sister strangers. I was allowed to share to the bone "conversating"—as the old folks used to say—with these sister journal-keepers whose writing speaks their truths to power.

Black Women Writing Lives: An Introduction

PATRICIA BELL-SCOTT

> I want to write about that battle, the skirmishes,
> the losses, the small yet so important victories
> that make the sweetness of my life.
> **AUDRE LORDE,** 1/1/80,
> *The Cancer Journals*

There is a verifiable tradition of Black[1] women who have made contemporaneous notes of their lives, though these writings almost never reach a national audience. The paucity of published journals and diaries is linked to our historical marginalization, a reality that often prevents us from acquiring the tools that make writing possible. Despite the absence of formal schooling and limited material resources, many have "written" their lives in quilts and other handiwork.[2] The fifty contributors to this book clearly belong to a legacy of Black women and girls writing for/about their lives.[3]

Personal writing is/has always been a dangerous activity, because it allows us the freedom to define *everything* on our own terms. For those seeking to defy culturally imposed negative identities, personal writing has offered avenues for resistance and re-creation. For this reason I am certain that women before us scripted their lives, perhaps in hard-to-decipher shorthand that was discounted by undiscerning eyes.[4] I also know that our diaries and journals have been lost through sabotage, and that the desire to conceal has been strongest when the writer has ignored social conventions or taboos.[5] Thus, our personal writings—unlike the autobiography written retrospectively for public consumption—have rarely been published. And against this historical backdrop, I drafted the first outline for *Life Notes* in 1985.

Since the beginning of this project, I have had four objectives: (1) to honor the nameless women and girls who have recorded lives in the face of enormous disadvantages; (2) to share the rich experiences lost when our diversity is ignored; (3) to authenticate our ability as self-defining women who can speak for ourselves; and (4) to encourage other generations to write for self-knowledge, empowerment, and posterity. With these objectives as a guide, I chose the writings presented here from a pool of approximately one hundred deserving manuscripts varying in length from two to several hundred pages.

Because I wanted to understand and share the particular contexts for these writings, I devised a lengthy biographical questionnaire which a majority of the contributors completed. Their responses revealed that they come from three continents—Africa, Europe, North America—and the Caribbean. The youngest is an eight-year-old Nigerian; the oldest is a sixty-four-year-old retired African-American telephone operator. They are a diverse group of well-known, emerging, and previously unpublished writers who self-identify as Black, environmental, and/or feminist activists; artists, consultants, editors, educators, filmmakers, homemakers, lawyers, nurses, office workers, photographers, psychologists, publicists, students, unemployed, disabled, lesbians, heterosexuals, divorced, married, and/or single mothers. They also vary widely in economic status, from those with considerable wealth to those who receive public assistance.

Most began writing at an early age (one as young as three) to ease loneliness and anxiety:

"I had no brothers or sisters to talk to and wanted a friend."

"I started to keep 'notes' at the age of ten. I was a stutterer and this activity allowed me to 'speak.' "

Some used writing as a bridge for life transitions or as a way of doing reality checks:

"Decided to write daily record of fights with first husband who was slowly convincing me that I was insane. Writing about things we fought about . . . helped me realize that I was not the crazy one."

"I started [writing] because what I was experiencing at an elite, almost entirely white college was unbelievable and unbearable. I needed someplace where I could express how I felt about what was going on without censorship. The journal validated my experiences."

When asked why they continue to write, several reasons were offered. Among the most frequent was that personal writing is a form of therapy, self-healing, and emotional release:

"The journal gives me a place to whine in peace; to spot my internal contradictions before they get too out of hand; to praise myself for purely personal victories over fear and conventional wisdom of all kinds."

"My writing is the glue that holds my fragmented self (selves) together."

"[I write] when I'm angry at my lover or confused by my daughter or scared of going broke."

Many describe their writing as a source of pleasure, creativity, and self-affirmation:

> "[It] fulfills my need for . . . freedom, adventure."

> "My writing is my way of telling myself that my life matters, and it is good. It is one thing I can depend on when everything else changes."

> "I write to stay connected to the universe, the creator, and to people."

For others writing is an act of remembering, self-defense, or survival:

> "It's the same as a picture album."

> "[It is] a form of personal resistance against the usually negative socialization I've undergone in terms of my race, gender, and sexuality."

> "[It helped] me to understand I was in a very abusive marriage and that I could not exist in it forever. . . . I wrote myself the courage to finally leave."

> "I write to keep my [illness] at bay. I write to stay alive."

To my dismay, many contributors were never encouraged to write personally and had no role models. One contributor had not known "anyone who had kept a diary" when she began writing at age eleven. There were, however, those inspired by relatives—particularly women kin:

> "Relatives encouraged me to write (relatives on my mother's side) because they said that writing was in our family's blood."

Some were encouraged by their English teachers, friends, and colleagues, whereas a few were blatantly discouraged. According to one contributor:

> "With my ex-husband, [my writing] got to be a point of contention as our marriage deteriorated."

The topics about which these women and girls write are presented in an eight-part scheme. The writings in Part One reflect the innocence of girls nurtured by love, as well as the psychic wounds inflicted by social and economic injustices. Those writings in Part Two represent the search for self-identity. The rewards and risks of meaningful work are detailed in Part Three. The delight and dilemmas of loving are the focus of writings in Part Four, by contrast, abuse and neglect are recounted in Part Five. The writings in Part Six are acts of resistance against multiple oppression. Life transitions from which new identities are claimed are described in Part Seven. Finally, Part Eight is a collage of travel notes and political commentaries.

Most contributors report that few topics escape mention in their journals and diaries. Many consciously choose to write about issues which are emotionally difficult:

> "I have found out that those topics that are most painful to write are the ones I need . . . to truly understand, so I write even if it makes me cry."

> "I don't write *anything* that I don't feel deeply connected to."

Not surprisingly, personal writings take many different forms: letters, newsletters, meditations, poetry, prose, self-dialogue, and stream of consciousness. In addition, some contributors suspend conventional rules of grammar, hoping to enhance spontaneity and freedom:

> "My hands can never wait to figure out the correct spelling since my thoughts are usually racing ahead."

"Often in my journals I don't dot *i*'s, cross *t*'s or even punctuate."

Half of the contributors maintain a routine of writing daily or weekly, whereas others reject scheduling—choosing to write "whenever the mood hits." Most write in a space of their own—in bed, at a desk, or in some special place in their homes. Those with young children write early in the morning or at night when "the house is quiet" and work can be postponed. Others with more flexibility structure writing around jobs and personal preferences. Those with demanding schedules write wherever and whenever they can:

> "I have written at the kitchen table, sitting up in bed, in the car while waiting to pick up one of my children and a number of other places that don't come to mind."

> "I write in offices, bus stop curbs, the very edge of the sea, on the bus, in bed, at the gym."

Despite a compelling need to write, a majority have put their writing on hold at least once, typically because of child-rearing, school, or work-related demands. Personal crises have, on occasion, precipitated breaks in writing:

> "I had a miscarriage with my first pregnancy, stopped writing . . . for seven or eight years."

> "[I stopped] . . . when a sister-friend was murdered."

> "When I'm being dishonest with myself—living a lie, postponing the truth, I won't write for long periods."

Personal activism and objections from significant others have also caused writing lapses:

> "I'll stop . . . when I'm concentrating more on action than thought."

> "When I was with my husband . . . I hardly wrote at all. . . . He didn't really like my writing my personal thoughts down because he thought I would be writing about him. He was paranoid."

For many, inclusion in *Life Notes* is the first time that their personal writings have been published. When I asked if the decision to submit had been difficult, some had clearly agonized over this act of self-disclosure:

> "[Sending the manuscript] was extremely difficult. . . . It's like standing before a crowd stripping . . . the writing is often that intimate."

By contrast, some felt an obligation to help others by sharing their personal records:

> "My belief was someone else might identify and see hope and joy."

> "I wanted to show . . . the depth we can go in recovery by ourselves sitting at a desk."

For the most part, contributors did only minor editing before submitting their writings—correcting misspellings and occasionally changing the names of others to protect their privacy. They rarely chose pen names for themselves, and only two deleted material described as "extremely personal" or "too explicit."

They confided that their first personal writings were done with pens or pencils in spiral notebooks, school tablets, lock-and-key diaries, or on notebook paper. When these materials were unavailable, they used whatever was at hand:

> "If I couldn't find paper to write on, I would use leaves, that's how serious the compulsion was."

Occasionally the choice in writing instruments has reflected a particular state of mind:

> "I went through a period of several years where I wrote only in pencil. I felt my stuff/writing was like words in the mind, not meant to be preserved."

> "Sometimes I feel the need to detach and use the computer; other times I feel the need for legal pads."

Among the currently preferred tools are personal computers, elaborately bound blank books, colored pens and fountain pens. One contributor makes a practice of handwriting her letters (which are never sent) with "a purple fountain pen and wonderful stationery . . . including envelopes."

Because personal writings are so deeply cherished, they are stored in private places such as desk and wardrobe drawers, cabinets, bookcases, trunks, under mattresses, in bookbags, and purses. Some writers have found unusual nooks, as did one who as a child kept her first writing:

> "under an old fashioned bathtub—there was plenty of space there. And since I had the job of cleaning the bathroom every Saturday there was no disruption there."

Most contributors have had their writings read without permission by partners and lovers, parents, siblings, children, friends, and teachers. A few have even had their writings destroyed by lovers or violated by strangers:

> "Earlier, lived with an insanely jealous man . . . who read and destroyed all my diaries for the [five] years I lived with him. . . . [He] did not want his name in them."

> "I was arrested and . . . a white male police officer read from my journal. . . . I almost went over the edge afterward. I guess like rape victims do."

Despite the risk of violation, these contributors assert that they must/ will continue to do personal writing. Most have asked family and lovers to respect their privacy. A few have issued warnings about the consequences of betrayal. One adolescent wrote in the front of her diary:

> "Get out! Keep out! Private property! Trespasser punished by fine! A dollar a page!"

Another contributor gives periodic verbal notice:

> "I've always told my loved ones, 'read my journal at your own risk, it might hurt you.' "

The contributors to this book are remarkably ordinary women and girls who, like others before them, make contemporaneous notes of their lives. In spite of isolation, multiple disadvantages, and attempts by others to stop them, they write defiantly of lives lived and dreamed in all their complexities. It is my desire that this—the first collection of personal writings by contemporary Black women—will reach a broad audience of readers from all backgrounds, including college and high school students interested in Black and women's literature, psychology, sociology, family studies, and writing. I also believe that this collection will be helpful to those involved in formal or self-therapy, as well as community-based education and mental health programs. Finally, I wish to connect future generations of Black women and girls to our wonderful tradition of life-writing. I hope that *Life Notes* will instill the faith I found on December 10, 1986, when after a night of fighting influenza induced by emotional and physical fatigue, I cuddled myself, pulled out my journal, and wrote: "Reality *can be* (re)created by one who writes."

Notes

[1] In this book, I use the term "Black" in reference to the contributors who are of African descent and native daughters of several countries.

[2] See Patricia Bell-Scott et al, *Double Stitch: Black Women Write about Mothers and Daughters* (Boston: Beacon, 1991); Elsa Barkley Brown, "African-American Women's Quilting: A Framework for Conceptualizing and Teaching African-American Women's History," *Signs: A Journal of Women in Culture and Society* 14 (Summer 1989); and Alice Walker, "In Search of Our Mothers' Gardens," in *In Search of Our Mothers' Gardens*, (New York: Harcourt Brace Jovanovich, 1983), pp. 231–43, for discussions about how Black women re-create their lives in handiwork.

[3] All are living writers, except one—Audre Lorde—who died before this work was published. I also wish to express my gratitude to those contributors who completed the detailed biographical questionnaire. Their responses form the core of this introduction.

[4] The personal writings of Black women and girls appear infrequently in biographical studies and anthologies of Black and women's autobiography. Among the few book-length works are: Carolina Maria De Jesus, *Child of the Dark: The Diary of Carolina Maria De Jesus*, translated by David St. Clair (New York: E. P. Dutton, 1962); Alice Dunbar-Nelson, *Give Us Each Day: The Diary of Alice Dunbar-Nelson*, edited by Gloria T. Hull (New York: W. W. Norton, 1984); Charlotte L. Forten, *The Journal of Charlotte L. Forten*, edited by Ray Allen Billington (New York: Dryden Press, 1954); Charlotte L. Forten, *The Journals of Charlotte Forten Grimke*, edited by Brenda Stevenson (New York: Oxford University Press, 1968); Latoya Hunter, *The Diary of Latoya Hunter: My First Year in Junior High* (New York: Crown, 1992); Audre Lorde, *The Cancer Journals* (San Francisco: Aunt Lute Books, 1980).

[5] In two groundbreaking works, *Color, Sex and Poetry: Three Women Writers of the Harlem Renaissance* (Bloomington: Indiana University Press, 1987) and *The Diary of Alice Dunbar-Nelson*, Gloria T. Hull presents brilliantly complicated portraits of Dunbar-Nelson, Angelina Weld Grimke, and Georgia Douglas Johnson. Without the personal writings Hull found buried (or hidden) in institutional archives and private collections, our understanding of these lives would be greatly diminished. In addition, several contributors to this anthology have revealed that their journals and diaries have been destroyed by lovers or partners.

Acknowledgments

Among the many people who helped to give this book life are the following:

Miriam DeCosta-Willis and Lucille P. Fultz, who spread the word far and wide—introducing me to many wonderfully gifted Black women writers,

Christine Price, my able graduate research assistant and incipient feminist scholar, whose sensitivity and attention to detail have been invaluable,

Carla Abshire, Juanita Bailey, and Stephanie Brown, all brilliant graduate students, who provided critical feedback and assistance,

Jill Bialosky and Deborah Morton Hoyt of W. W. Norton, whose editorial wisdom and artistry have enhanced the beauty of this project both inside and out,

Gloria D. Briscoe, who provided clerical assistance, often at a last minute and frantic pace,

Jane Begos, whose work as editor/publisher of *Women's Diaries: A Quarterly Newsletter*, encouraged my earliest thinking about an anthology of this kind,

Anita F. Hill, who was unable to contribute but called to affirm my efforts in a forthright and sisterly way,

Charlotte Sheedy, who believed in this project from day one,

Janet Sims-Wood and Patrick C. McKenry, who are always listening and supporting,

My mother, Dorothy Wilbanks, who for the first time shared her journal writing with me for this project, and my sister, Brenda Faye Bell, who is ever present in me and my writing,

My partner in life, Arvin Scott,

Countless women's organizations and publications, especially groups such as the National Commission for Women in Nigeria and *Canadian Woman Studies/Les Cahiers de la Femme*, which helped me connect with Black women outside of the United States,

Hilda A. Davis and the editorial collective of *SAGE: A Scholarly Journal on Black Women*, who have been so patient over the past taxing year, and last but not least,

The nearly one hundred Black women (half of whom because of space limitations could not be featured in this book) from around the world who made the courageous decision to share their personal writings with me.

PART ONE

Reflecting Girlhood

I have one hair under my armpit and lots of hair on my vagina. I'm in pitiful shape. I'm writing in my book to you from Mama's bed because I have an awful headache. That's why my handwriting is so bad.

JENNIFFER DAWN BENNETT ALEXANDER
March 20, 1989, age ten

Dear Diary,
I have a problem. My sister (it's her 12th birthday) is having a friend sp[e]nd the night. She is leaving me out of everything. When she has [friends] over she never lets me play with them.

ANNE ALEXIS BENNETT ALEXANDER
May 18, 1990, age ten

Dear Puppy,
I felt terrible today. Mrs. Beatty never calls on me and I sit right up in front and she picks ever[yone] else. It['s] like being evaluated and found you['re] not good enough. It's a terrible feeling.

VALERIE TURNER (VALERIE JEAN)
December 1, 1967, age thirteen

I lust after the boy, and if I knew him better I should love him more dearly than I do now.   **LOIS FLORENCE LYLES**
March 17, 1964, age fourteen

In Her Womb

GWENDOLYN J. DUNGY

Though I have written personal notes for years, this journal entry was not done freely. I was forced to write it when I took a class at a local university on autobiographies written by women. To my surprise, the instructor required that all students write one autobiographical chapter. I resisted the assignment and explained that I may seem garrulous and friendly, but in reality, I am a private person and would not feel comfortable doing the assignment. The instructor explained that I need not divulge any deep, dark secret. I was merely to write about some particular time in my life for my journal.

When the instructor responded to my resistance with words such as "deep, dark secret," I suddenly realized that I did have a secret. My secret was about the particulars related to my conception and birth. At that moment, everything else I had ever done or ever experienced seemed trivial and uninteresting. I felt compelled to relive the experiences leading up to my conception and birth.

Once I decided to write about my prenatal self, I became excited and wanted to talk with my mother about particulars. Fearing she would not tell me everything, I asked her about the snatches of conversation I had heard as a child and the things she had told me about her youth. I was totally surprised when she spoke easily and willingly *about her life and mine. After our long telephone conversation, I was eager to write the whole story from my unadulterated viewpoint as an unborn child. Remaking and reconstructing my life from the beginning was delicious. I smiled with each line and grinned at the end of each page.*

My body and spirit absorbed her impressions like water marks on silk. Every drop of water stains the silk but it doesn't destroy it. It marks it. Every negative imprint I absorbed during the months before I was official and certificated remains. You see my efforts to become began long before my date of birth.

Many say they can remember things that happened to them when they were as young as one and two years old. My communion with my mother began when I was inside her, in her womb. I have never been more in communion with my mother than when I lived and grew inside her.

In beginning this narrative I feel as if I have no control over the retelling of this journey just as I had no control over my origin. Relating the following experiences is like retelling a dream that has long been forgotten. A dream that floated just beneath the surface of consciousness insistent enough to entice me to recall it. It nagged me like the name of some familiar person which escapes memory for the moment and will not come forward on demand but zooms to the front of my mind when I have no need to recall it. I am pleased that I have not lost this precious and valuable memory of my life before my birth. I share this memory because it wants to be shared. No moral lessons are imbedded in this narrative and no sociological or psychological insights are intended. This is simply an autobiographical chapter.

I'm just becoming mentally alive to sensations, feelings, and thoughts. I'm aware that I'm being prepared for a serious journey. I feel, see, hear, and taste via my mother. I depend on her to keep us safe, to give me nourishing food, and to provide me with plenty of oxygen.

In addition to breathing her oxygen, eating her food, and drinking her liquids, I invade her thoughts. I tune in to them when I choose.

However, most of the time I just eat, drink, and nap, except when she disturbs me with her emotions and concomitant secretions. Then, I want to know what is going on. This is when I access her thoughts. When I first discovered my body-mate was distressed, I accessed her thoughts and through her memories discovered where she had come from and who she had been.

Mae, my mother, an only child of sharecroppers who lived in the Mississippi Delta, was extremely obedient and loved her parents very much. The way they scratched out an existence as sharecroppers was actually subsistence farming because there was never enough left over to get ahead or even to live well. Consequently, Mae had no great ambitions for she didn't know what her options were. She wanted only two things: to move her parents out of the country, and to be a writer. She was a precocious and introspective child who was seen as wise beyond her years and a little odd since the things that interested other children of her age had for her little appeal.

She was drawn to both lame and stray animals as well as lame and strange people. Her favorite pet was a pig, and her favorite playmate was retarded and disfigured. She seemed to have no jealousy, envy, or selfishness. She was attractive but didn't enjoy the full benefit of her caramel complexion, long hair, beautiful white teeth, large almond eyes, and petite figure because she was hard of hearing. Being a little quirky to begin with and also hearing impaired set her apart.

When she was very young her hearing was impaired as a result of a too-large dose of quinine for a cold. This tragedy was typical among the poor. Family and friends often made fun of her because they had to make up a sign language so that she could understand what was going on around her. She learned to read lips, and as she got older she regained a lot of her hearing.

The summer after Mae's eighth-grade graduation was a turning point in her life. She knew she did not want to stay in the country and become a sharecropper's wife, but she had not really thought about how to avoid this. During the steamy midsummer following gradua-tion down in the Mississippi Delta while on the way to church with her parents and her cousins who were staying with them at the time, the heel broke off one of her shoes. She wanted to return home, but her father, whom she loved dearly, being a Christian man could not see a broken heel from a child's shoe as reason enough not to go to worship. Shamed and humiliated, after all she was a teenager, Mae limped all the way to church and tried to slip onto a bench unnoticed. During the service, face still burning from shame, she went to the outhouse to use the bathroom. Negotiating a standing position on a maggot-infested toilet seat with one heelless shoe was enough to bring the bitter taste of bile to her mouth and the sting of tears to her eyes. While crying in this unholy sanctuary she prayed to God to help her find a way to leave the Delta and move her parents out of the country.

A lot has happened since Mae left church that day in the Delta after praying to find a way to get herself and her parents out of the country. Her prayer was partially answered before school began that September. Her father's brother who lived in Greenwood, Mississippi, sent for her to live with him and his wife where she could attend high school. They only asked for six dollars a month to help with her room and board.

While in Greenwood Mae worked for a seamstress who loved her spirit and industriousness so she gave her fabric scraps which Mae used to make ballerina-like skirts which showed off her eighteen-inch waist. Since she was industrious and needed a way to earn more money, she asked storekeepers to save the bottle caps from sodas for her so she could carefully remove the cork and sew them to cloth for purses which she sold. Since her parents only sent room and board for one month, she worked for the seamstress and also made purses and jewelry to pay the six dollars a month. Paying her own way was how Mae wanted it. It gave her a sense of independence.

Though life was not bad living with her father's brother and his wife, there was some friction. Despite Mae's willingness to clean the house and do what needed to be done, her uncle's wife seemed to resent any time Mae took to study or work outside the home. Though Mae would have preferred to live elsewhere, she did not feel as strong as, "Please God, get me out of this house."

One day while on the grounds of the high school Mae heard someone call her name. It was her cousin Little Mae who attended the grammar school across the street. Little Mae was glad to see her and immediately told her grandmother, who was Mae's great-aunt, that Mae was now living in Greenwood and going to the high school. Well that same day, Mae moved in with her cousin and great-aunt for whom she was named. So in this happy house there were three Maes. Big Mae is what they called my ninety-pound mother, Little Mae was the young cousin, and Mama Mae was the grand old lady. Mama Mae had recently moved from the Delta and was active in the sanctified church. She was a good woman with lots of friends. Being Baptist, Mae, my mother, had been brought up to look askance at the "holy rollers," but here, she fit right into the routine of school and the sanctified church.

At the end of the first term, Little Mae transferred to the high school where Big Mae attended, and they had a grand time. Little Mae was cute and real fast with the fellahs and since her cousin Big Mae was cute and new at the school, the two of them had all the boys wrapped up. Though not seriously interested in boys, Big Mae liked this new attention and realized for the first time that people thought she was pretty. In the yearbook, some jealous peers wrote, "the two Maes are cute but their heads are like doorknobs, anybody can turn them."

Mama Mae had a warm and loving house which included Little Mae's mother and father. They shared everything with Mae, though the food was not as plentiful as they needed. Big Mae ate very little and always pretended not to be hungry because she was grateful to live with this loving family and did not want to be a burden. In the meantime, Big Mae was also making a remarkable impression on the sanctified sisters at church. She taught Sunday school, sang in the choir, taught in the after-church school and wrote religious poetry which brought people from all over the area to hear her recite. "The Devil" was everyone's favorite poem.

Life was good this first year away from home, and the church women had selected my Mae as their star. They raised money and made contact with church friends and relatives in Indiana where they planned to send Mae to a special college to become a teacher. This church-affiliated college accepted bright young people who had completed the eleventh grade. Mae was bursting with excitement and almost couldn't believe that something this wonderful could happen to a poor country girl like her. As arrangements were being made, the "devil" entered to let Mae know that she was right; this was too good for a poor country girl. She was not going off to Indiana to live with a bunch of strangers who were also "holy rollers." Mae's mother's sister, Rosie, who lived in Memphis with her daughter-in-law, Anna, while her son, Eddie, was in the navy, wrote Mae's mother to warn her about sending Mae far away to live with strangers. She said that Mae didn't have to go all the way to Indiana to strangers if she wanted to be a teacher because she could come to Memphis to live with her, her daughter-in-law, and the three children since they had a big house and plenty of room while Eddie was away in the Navy.

Though disappointed about not going to Indiana, Mae was an obedient and faith-filled child who believed that this must be God's will and therefore just as good or better than the other plan. She left Mama Mae's house and joined Anna, her three children, and her Aunt Rosie in Memphis. This was really the big city and their big house was right out on a main street in a neighborhood where all the houses were close together. Stores were right down the street and people stayed up all night long partying.

Mae enrolled in Booker T. Washington High School across town and took the bus to school with the rest of the students. The school's practice was to put students back a year if they came from a school in Mississippi, but after being tested Mae was advanced to her senior year. She loved learning and the opportunities Booker T. Washington High School offered, so she quickly got involved. Home economics teachers asked Mae to teach them and the other students how to do "tatting," sewing a delicate hand-made lace, which she had learned while working with the seamstress in Greenwood. Her course work came easily, and for the first time she really felt part of her peer group. Mae felt good about how she looked and became active in school clubs. Her most happy moments were when she marched with the school band as a majorette dressed in a short-skirted uniform and boots with tassels.

The first few months at Booker T. Washington were like a dream but the "devil" still lurked near. In retrospect, the good time seemed to be a part of the undoing. Though popular in school Mae was still shy. She spent her evenings and weekends in the house. She was content, but Aunt Rosie, who had insisted she come to Memphis, now insisted that she go out with some of the young men in the neighborhood. In the meantime, Anna told Mae in secret that she should avoid one guy in particular who Aunt Rosie encouraged her to date because he was married. Mae had seen the guy talking to Aunt Rosie and the girls she rode the bus with but didn't give him much attention when he tried to talk with her. She had seen his kind before—"high-yellow" guys with the eyes, the long eyelashes, and that macho way of walking and talking.

She was especially wary of this guy they called Red because he seemed to be the leader of a gang of guys who always looked like they were up to no good. However, they were very popular in the community, liked to drink, party, and have a good time. Folks said Red and his boys were like Robin Hood and his band. They helped the poor. Mae suspected they also robbed the rich because Red had a reputation for not working for white folks. According to rumor, white folks worked for him. Mae was not sure what this meant but she had her suspicions.

In late fall, Mae decided to go to a show and card party with the girls across the street. Though reluctant to go, she dressed up for the occasion. When they arrived at their destination, she was apprehensive about going into what seemed like a tavern or beer hall. She knew her parents would disapprove because there was smoking, drinking, gambling, and a lot of cursing. What surprised her was that the cursing seemed to be all in fun. No one was angry. This was the first night she heard the "MF" word and she wanted to die! The guy Red was gambling, smoking Lucky Strike cigarettes, drinking bourbon, telling stories about white people in which he called them old "tallow faces," "pecker woods," or "MFs." He was the center of attention. When he saw Mae and the girls, he called them over real friendly-like and asked Mae to sit next to him. She was reluctant to sit, but the girls told her not to be stupid because the man wouldn't bite her. After she sat down tentatively on the edge of her chair, Red asked her what she wanted to drink, and she said a Coke, which he promptly ordered. They all watched Red play cards, smoke, and drink. After about half an hour, he asked Mae if he could hold her hand for good luck. She was nervous but wanted to fit in since everyone was having such a good time, so she let him. This guy, Red, really seemed much nicer than he had before, and he truly was the life of the party.

As I softly and quietly nestle low in the recesses of Mae's womb, I rest what's forming as my head on her pelvis while she remembers this evening. She remembers that she went to the bathroom and when she returned to Red's table she realized that the girls she had come with were not there. She was a little panicked and very annoyed since she didn't know anyone else in this place except Red now, and she had never spoken to him before this night. He told her not to worry, he would take her home. She finished her Coke and remembers nothing after that moment until she woke up the next morning in bed with Red. She does not remember any conversation with him or any physical contact, nothing. She can't recall how she got home. It's as if her mind had been taken away for some few precious hours, never to be recalled.

This episode was not shared with a soul and was shoved into the background of Mae's life as a bad experience never to be repeated. Then about two months after this episode she noticed that she had less energy than usual. She never had any problem cleaning the entire house including the yard, taking care of three young children, going to school, studying, participating in clubs, the majorettes, and still having enough energy left to go to the big Baptist church where she sang in the choir and taught Sunday school and BYPTU (Baptist Young People's Training Union). Recently, she was beginning to get extremely tired, and she was even losing some of her enthusiasm for new things. She had a bad taste in her mouth and—oh God—she had missed her period this second month! She had an every-other-month menstrual cycle so all was normal when she didn't have a period the previous month, but this second month meant something else! She was ignorant about sex because her mother had never talked with her about it, but she was savvy enough to know how one got pregnant and this nonevent of the absent period probably meant that she was pregnant.

At this realization, Mae's sobs vibrate my very core. Her sobs make her body heave and retch as her future reeled rapidly before her as history. She knew she had to tell someone but how could she tell someone that she might be pregnant, and that she had nothing to do with it. The only person she could tell was Anna. But how could she tell Anna that the dreaded Red was probably the father? Having a baby was not part of this plan! How would she be able to tell her mother and father, who were depending on her to make them proud and be the first in the family to finish high school? How could she tell Aunt Rosie, Mama Mae? Where would she live? What about school? What about her writing? Her sobbing was deep enough to jar me, as small and as inconspicuous as I was. No one wanted this child.

During the fourth month Mae had to leave school since the pregnancy had become visible. She tread through this fourth month in less than a daze. In fact, she would have been diagnosed as catatonic if she had not gone through the motions of cleaning house and caring for the children. She didn't leave the house and she spoke with no one. This thing was taking over her body. "It," as she was to refer to me until the day I was born, had begun to make itself known through sporadic flutterings. I was attempting to make contact, to actualize our relationship since we were both in this together. But Mae was much too preoccupied with herself to even fantasize about me. Though nineteen years old, she was still a child herself worried about how to be a good daughter and not how to become a good mother. She was ashamed of the way she was beginning to look and ashamed that she had disgraced herself and her family. Being an unwed mother was not the image she had of herself. Her goal was to move her mother and father out of the country and make a success of herself as a writer.

Mae could not give me love because she had no one to give her love. She did not know how to begin mothering before I was born because she could not accept the fact that she would be a mother. She wanted to die so she attempted to freeze herself. She tried to starve herself. She ate nothing but Argo starch and ice. She was totally withdrawn, ashamed, and very angry. When Red found out that she was pregnant, he made attempts to see her. She not only would not see him but planned to kill him if he got within striking range. So Red walked by her house daily with his married girlfriend, whose husband was in the Army, or his single girlfriend, who thought he was going to marry her.

When Mae became very uncomfortable with me because I was growing, stretching, and executing my daily exercise routines, she would sit in the swing on Anna's big porch where she could spread her legs and let the swing hold some of my weight. I liked it when she sat in the swing and rocked me gently. I did not like it though when that Red would walk by with one of his ladies and make Mae so angry that her adrenalin, stinging hydrochloric acid, and ugly, yellow-green bile would disturb my home. Just the sight of him made her so mad.

Mae's petite frame, my increasing size, and my constant pushing against the walls of my cramped home made her uncomfortable and irritable. But she should know that I had not been so comfortable either. Like when she kept trying to freeze herself in the park across the street, she made my little blood vessels constrict so tightly I could hardly get enough oxygen to breathe. Interestingly, though she never said a word to Red, and he never came to the house to see her because she forbade it, he and his boys appeared in the vicinity wherever she went. So every time she went to the park to try to freeze or did anything unusual, Red would show up like Superman and rescue her. These were strange birds. Really strange because though they never talked and acknowledged my presence they were forming a relationship.

Red sent messages to Mae that he was not married, and he wanted to marry her. Earlier, he had sent a message that she didn't have to have the baby because he knew somebody who would get rid of "it" for her. He then sent a message that he wanted to marry her and if she didn't want the baby she could give "it" to his mother. Of course Mae sent no response. Red also sent money to the house every week once he knew Mae was pregnant. Mae couldn't understand the contradictions she saw in him, and though she didn't like him, she deeply resented the other women he dated and hated him for parading them before her. She never considered she might be jealous.

Mae had virtually no primary nor secondary group because her shame and increasing anger, which people around her called "pure evilness," kept her even more isolated than the pregnancy did. She avoided all social contact, even church. She waited for the day when "it" would be out of her and she could get on with her life. By not choosing a name nor otherwise preparing for the baby, she never accepted the pregnancy. Her parents were disappointed; her Aunt Rosie was less than empathetic; only Anna was there for her, though there was not much communication.

Mae frequently squeezed us under the bed so she could avoid contact with people. Being under the bed was both private and cool and finding a cool place was a top priority because I was planning to be a mid-August baby in Memphis, Tennessee. Mae really gave me a rough time in these tight places. A few times, the umbilical cord was wrapped around my neck, and I could hardly breathe. I did my best drop-kicks and made Mae so uncomfortable she got the message that I didn't like it under the bed so she began to take frequent cool baths in the tin tub in the kitchen instead.

Always modest, Mae, on Sunday, August 16, 1944, decided to take a cool bath in the tub in the middle of the kitchen floor without bothering to lock the back door where friends often entered without knocking. On this sweltering afternoon, a neighbor gentleman walked into the kitchen and found himself face to face with a woman sporting a huge belly, standing buck naked and dripping with water. Dumbfounded he looked at her and quickly realized that her glaring red eyes definitely signaled danger. He immediately got word to Red that something really strange was happening with Mae. In his "bad cowboy coming to town" manner, Red dared to visit the house where Mae lived. He told her in a soft "ain't the weather nice" way that the moon was wasting away, and her time was coming to have the baby. He announced that he would sit with her until she was ready to go to the hospital. He informed her that he had a car and had made all hospital arrangements. He also told the mute Mae that the baby would have his last name so they wouldn't have to change the name later after they married.

Mae figured Red was a fool beyond saving so she let him, his buddies, and the regular "guests" sit around Anna's house watching her. She put on her Sunday white chiffon dress a lady had given her and listened to her favorite singer, Nat King Cole. Despite her size, Mae liked the way she looked in the beautiful white chiffon dress which she washed every week and wore every Sunday. She wore no colored clothes at all during pregnancy. She wore only white. White cotton was for weekdays and Saturdays, and the white chiffon dress was for Sundays. When Nat King Cole sang "Cottage for Sale," for Mae, the cottage was white. In fact, Mae had become exceedingly introspective and lived in her own white world. She wore white, ate white Argo starch, and her mind was usually like a blank white screen.

I was enjoying the soothing crooning of Nat King Cole, and all these people were sitting around watching and waiting for Mae to "waste away" like the moon. Somebody had to do something so I guess I was on. I was not exactly eager to join my mother and father who had never had a real conversation. Also, I was not sure I liked my father very much, but I was intrigued. Well, things could have been worse and anyway, I was starving! Starch was caked over my entire body, and now I was white!

I decided to get into traveling position and my maneuver was not as graceful as it could have been, so I did something like a belly flop and made a splashing sound that everyone in the room heard. They all looked at Mae and asked, "What was that?" Cool as a cucumber, Mae pointed to her stomach and said, "It." Well the run was on! The boys and Red got Mae into the car and took her to John Gaston Hospital where she delivered. Voilà!

Without belaboring the point I do want to relate the first acknowledgment Mae gave to me and my father. When the nurses brought the babies to their mothers, Mae was brought a baby girl whose mother was also named Mae. Mae insisted that this girl was not her baby. When I was being taken to the other Mae, my Mae saw me and said, "That's my baby." The nurse asked her how she knew this when she had not seen the wrist tag. Mae replied, "Can't you see she [note not "it"] looks exactly like her father" as she pointed to Red sitting next to the bed.

Chocolate Tears and Dreams

EVELYN C. ROSSER

Growing up the only girl in a family of five children in rural, South Georgia was a lonely experience. I was pampered and overprotected. I was not permitted to play football, baseball, or to box with my brothers. Therefore, I learned to entertain myself by becoming an avid reader. Through my readings I discovered a new world—ballet, Shakespeare, and opera. I found all the excitement that was missing from my real life in books. I began to write stories with characters like the ones I had read about. When I reached adolescence, my purpose for writing changed. My journal became my best friend to whom I told my secrets, heartaches, fears, and dreams. It was my vehicle of self-discovery. I could not have survived without it!

Summer 1952

I had fun today. My best friends, Shirlie and Alice, came to play with me. Mama told us to play outside. She had a cake in the oven, and didn't want it to fall. We played a game of make-believe. Shirlie was Elaine Stewart. Alice was Jane Russell. I was Marilyn Monroe! I live in a beautiful house on the beach. Every evening I took my French poodle for a long walk. I love to feel the sea breezes on my face and the surf gently lap against my feet.

Shirlie made me mad. She said I am chocolate, and everybody knows only white ladies have poodles and live on beaches. She said she could live on the beach, because she looks like Lena Horne. I started to cry. That's when Alice made Shirlie shut up. Alice said it didn't matter what color I was when I was born. I could bleach my skin. She knew it for a fact. Her cousin Betty did it. She used something called Black and White Ointment. She rubbed it on her face and neck every morning and night. Alice said the only problem was I couldn't let the sun strike me. Her cousin Betty never went outside without a hat or scarf on, 'cause if you do you'll turn blacker than you were before. I trembled at the idea. I'll miss playing with Shirlie and Alice, but I want to live in a fine house someday like the white ladies do. I'll ask God to speed up my bleaching.

Winter 1952

We spent the night sitting in Mama and Daddy's bedroom around the heater chewing cane and telling stories. Daddy's were the best. I enjoyed his stories, but he made me scared to go to bed. I think I'll sleep with the cover over my head tonight. I hope I don't dream about the headless woman walking down the railroad track or the horse that wouldn't move unless the rider gave him a drink of moonshine. Sometimes I think Daddy makes these stories up.

He ended the night by telling about the end-of-the-year program in Douglas, Georgia. Daddy lived out in the country on a farm called Huffas. To get her teaching contract renewed the teacher had to have her students entertain the superintendent and board of education members at the end of the school term. Daddy said he was in a skit about slavery.

He loved to tell this part. Daddy got up from his chair and acted out the rest of the story for us. He said he wore a straw hat and overalls with one shoulder strap hanging down. He was barefooted. All the students were lined up in rows of fives, holding rusty hoes in their hands.

The guests sat quietly staring in anticipation. The teacher waved to the pianist to start the program. Daddy said the students started moving slowly, pretending to chop cotton.

They sang slowly and mournfully:

> "Mas told me
> Mas told me
> To stay on
> The old plantation."

At this point in the skit, each student took a handkerchief from his back pocket and wiped his face. The song continued:

> "Lord I'm tired
> Lord I'm tired
> Of this heavy
> Load I keep a totin'
> Totin', totin'."

Then he said they began to chop wildly and move fast down the rows in the imaginary cotton field singing:

> "Oh, a nigger sho knows
> How to make things grow
> By marchin' down the rows
> And choppin' with a hoe."

The guests started yelling, "Ye ha! Well done, Miss Caroline. Best program ever!" Daddy said, Miss Caroline's face beamed with satisfaction. She knew she had her job for another year.

The fire left Daddy's eyes as suddenly as it had appeared. He looked sad. He mumbled something about it being wrong for her to use them like that. Daddy said, "Negroes shouldn't use other Negroes to get what they want." I didn't know what he meant, but I knew something bad had happened to Daddy. Almost in a whisper he told us to go to bed. It hurt me to see Daddy sad. I'll sleep with the quilt over my head tonight. That way no one will hear me cry.

January 1953

I loved the doll I got for Christmas. Daddy broke it today. You see, it was an accident. My brothers took my doll from me and were throwing it back and forth to each other. When I ran to one brother, he threw it to another brother. I told Daddy to make them give it to me. He came into the bedroom and told them to stop throwing my doll. They didn't. He got angry. He snatched it from my brother and threw it to me. I didn't catch it. The doll hit the trunk. Its head was broken off. I cried. Daddy promised to buy me another doll. Mama told me to stop crying, because a nine-year-old girl was too old for dolls anyway. She said dolls only make girls want babies. She doesn't know me. I don't want a baby. I want a mink coat, a red convertible, and a big house on the beach. I'll have a funeral for my doll tomorrow, and I won't invite her.

Summer 1953

Today my brothers and I went to the movies. Last week Dick Tracy was trapped in a well. I had to know whether he got out alive. On the way to the movies, we noticed a new ice cream parlor. My brother Sonny said we had enough money to buy a five-cent cone each. Edward wanted strawberry. Sonny wanted vanilla. I wanted chocolate.

A teenage white girl was standing behind the counter. When we reached the counter, she walked away. She busied herself cleaning a table. We stood at the counter and waited for her to finish cleaning the table. She turned her head to look at us and started wiping the table again. By that time my brother Sonny was mad. He knocked hard on the counter several times. The girl didn't turn around. Sonny knocked again, this time louder. The girl ran from the room. A mean-looking man came out, drying his hands on a stained apron. "What do you want?" he yelled at us. "We want some ice cream," my brother answered. The man just stared at him. "I mean we want to buy some ice cream," added my brother. The man continued to stare. Then he said, "We don't serve niggers here!" He walked away, leaving us alone at the counter.

My brother Sonny wanted to jump across the counter and smash his face in. I begged him not to. I could do without the ice cream. We went to the movies, but I had a hard time keeping my mind on Dick Tracy. Today was the first time someone has ever called me a nigger to my face. Mama was right, I'm getting too old to play with dolls. There are more important things to think about.

Winter 1954

Mrs. W. died today. Actually, she was killed accidentally. Her husband is a mechanic. She loved to tinker with cars. Her car couldn't start so she pulled up the hood and tried to start it. I don't know all the details, or the technical terms to describe what happened, but when the motor cranked, the car took off by itself. It plowed into her house, crushing her to death. I pretended to be sad, but I wasn't. I didn't like her. She was the only person who made me feel ugly and unwanted since the ice cream parlor owner called me a nigger.

She broke my heart when I was eight years old. Shirlie, Alice, and I were playing outside during lunch. Mrs. W. beckoned for us to come to her. When we reached her, she looked at me and said, "Not you, just these two."

She took Alice and Shirlie into her classroom. She was giving a birthday party for a student in her class. I peeped inside the window. Alice was standing beside her licking a cone of ice cream. Shirlie was sitting on her lap, kicking her legs happily and enjoying a cone of ice cream. Mrs. W. was playing with Shirlie's hair. I decided Mrs. W. must have thought I was a nigger too and couldn't enjoy ice cream.

Spring 1954

I played, "That's What Dreams Are Made Of," over and over tonight. I hope I don't wear it out. I'm so happy. I was kissed by a boy for the first time! There's a dark hall in our school. When the lights go out it's pitch black. Well, the lights went out today. It was only for a few minutes, but Timothy kissed me. We closed our eyes and pressed our lips together. I must admit I was a little disappointed. My toes didn't curl, nor did I hear bells the way the ladies do in the *True Confession* magazines. I must not be doing something right, but I'm going to keep practicing every chance I get. I want to hear bells and see stars.

Fall 1955

Old Acid Tongue did it again! She picks a student out every day to burn. Today was my lucky day. I wore the new dress my grandmother ordered for me from Belles Hess. I met the postman every day for six weeks! My dress is so pretty. It has a short cape that makes me think of Sherlock Holmes. I like to imagine myself living a mysterious life.

Well, anyway, I walked into Mrs. Tatum's room eager to show off my beautiful red dress. As soon as I stepped into the room, Old Acid Tongue lit into me. "How could your mother let you out of the house looking like that?" she asked. I looked behind me. I thought she was talking to someone else, but she kept staring at me.

"I'm talking to you in the red dress!" she shouted. I wanted to tell her that that was my dress and I could wear any color I wanted. Besides, that wasn't just any old red dress. It was the dress my grandmother had ordered for me, and I had filled out the order form! I didn't say anything, because I had seen her shake students for talking back to her. Whenever you try to explain yourself, you get deeper and deeper into a hole, and Old Acid Tongue just pours more acid on you. I didn't want the school to burn down!

Good Lord, Mrs. Tatum can fuss! She went on and on explaining why I shouldn't wear red. She even "for your own good" threw in a few extra colors—yellow, purple, and orange. She also cautioned me to stay away from some shades of brown. According to Mrs. T. I am chocolate, and brown does not complement my color. Within a few minutes Old Acid Tongue had eliminated four colors from my wardrobe.

I'll be glad when this school term comes to an end. I'll stay inside all summer and bleach my skin.

Spring 1956

Tonight was my shining hour. It was even better than when I was crowned Miss Pine Grove Junior High during the homecoming festivities. I delivered the first honor student's speech at our eighth-grade graduation exercises. The subject was "The Night Brings Out the Stars." I didn't understand the part about the night being a more familiar friend to me than man, but I didn't tell Mrs. S. She says I'm precocious and should go far in life. I asked her what precocious meant. She said that means I know more than I should at my age. I figure she knows what she's talking about, because I do my brother's homework. He's four grades ahead of me.

Anyway, I was real good tonight. Everybody said so. Mama and Daddy were smiling proudly, I know I'll forget most of the speech, but I wrote down my special part; "It is the dark hours of life that teach us to discriminate between the true and false, the fair-weather friends, and the faithful comrades." I'll have to remember that when I'm filthy rich, famous, and living in California.

Summer 1956

Daddy preached his trial sermon today. Mama didn't go to church with us, so I had to be her stand in. I didn't like being the center of attention, but I was happy to be able to help my daddy. He has wanted to be a minister since he was a little boy. The deacons wanted to know where Mama was. Daddy told everyone Mama was sick. She really wasn't. Daddy had been drinking the night before, and she said he ought not play with God that way. Daddy had argued that there was nothing wrong with taking a little nip as long as you didn't hurt anyone. Mama still refused because she said she didn't want to see Daddy preach his own damnation. I could never picture Daddy in hell because he is a good man.

I knew Daddy was going to be all right from the moment he outlined his hymn. "Father I stretch my hands to thee, no other help I know. If thou withdrew thyself from me, O wither shall I go." The words dripped like honey from his lips.

When I looked at the congregation, smiling old ladies were fanning and moving their heads from left to right. A few raised their fans toward heaven and shouted, Yes, Lord! Halleluiah! My mind wandered to the food that would be spread out on the tables under the shade trees. I could pick what I wanted to eat, and I was going to eat lots of chocolate cake.

By the time Daddy gave his text, he had the congregation eating out of his hands. "I am He," shouted Daddy, strutting across the pulpit like a proud rooster. When he got to the part about being Alpha and Omega, an old woman began to shout. She raised both hands into the air and spun around repeatedly. On one of her spins, her wig flew off. She stopped shouting, stooped down, picked up her wig and quietly sat down. She did not raise her head again until Daddy's sermon was over.

At the end of the sermon everybody congratulated Daddy and me. I didn't see that I had done anything of significance, but Daddy said I had saved the day for him. I felt a little guilty because I had winked at several boys while I pretended to be wrapped up in Daddy's sermon. If you ask me, Mama should have been sitting in the chair facing the altar. She was the one who vowed to God to love, cherish, honor, and obey Daddy, not me. I'm just a child. Besides I wouldn't marry a preacher anyway. Preachers' wives can't smoke or drink. If I'm going to live in California, I'll have to have champagne parties and smoke cigarettes in long fancy holders like the ladies do in the movies.

April 1957

Dear God, please teach me forgiveness. I was wronged today and I responded bitterly. I've grown accustomed to seeing "For Whites Only" signs on public facilities, sitting in the balcony in movie theaters, being served in the kitchen in restaurants, and sitting in the rear on buses. I'm used to being mistreated by white folks, but how do I deal with discrimination within my own race?

I was proclaimed the best speller in the school this year. To get this honor, I sacrificed many hours of recreational time. Whenever I jumped rope or played hopscotch with my playmates, I would mentally spell words to a rhythmic beat. I was obsessed with one idea—

bringing the first place trophy for being the best speller in the district home to my high school.

However, I did not get the opportunity to compete in the district spelling bee today. A new girl named Katie had moved to town after I had won the intraschool competition. Her father is a principal, and her mother is a teacher. In contrast, my mother substitutes and works in the school lunchroom. My father preaches and works at a local lumberyard.

When I got to school this morning, Mrs. S. told me that I would not be the one to represent our school at the district spelling bee. She explained to me that she, along with other teachers, had decided that Katie would have a better chance to win the spelling bee because of her family's academic background. She further explained that I was culturally disadvantaged. I asked her what she meant by this. She said I had not been exposed to many books and had not traveled extensively. I told her I bet I had read more books from the school's library than anyone else in the school. She said that didn't count. The decision had been made.

I tried not to cry, but tears trickled down my face. Lord, I tried not to be disrespectful, but I had studied so hard. When I cried about the months I had wasted studying, Mrs. S. just patted me on the back and said, "Now dear, we must not think that way. No learning is ever wasted!"

In my frustration and anger, I wanted to slap her; but most of all, I wanted Katie to lose the spelling bee. After all, she had not earned the right to compete in the first place. I had! She had stolen my opportunity to be a winner.

Mrs. S. allowed me to attend the spelling bee. I sat alone feeling dejected, thinking about how my mother had sacrificed her money and time to dress me for the occasion. She had made a beautiful skirt and blouse for me at night, after cooking and washing dishes all day. I knew my disappointment would break her heart more than it did mine.

I sat anxiously with fingers crossed, praying for Katie to lose. When she misspelled the word chrysanthemums during the second round, I cried tears of joy. Sweet vengeance was mine.

Please help me to understand what happened today. Help me to understand why I feel so rotten. I felt inferior today with my own race. Lord, help me to understand what this incident was trying to teach me.

Dear God, help me to become Katie's friend. She didn't have anything to do with what happened today. Give me the strength to keep on pursuing my dreams. Obsess me with fiery passion to succeed. Give me the courage to face life unafraid.

Dear God, bless my mama too. Help her to forgive my teacher. Mama called her tonight. She didn't apologize for what happened to me. Perhaps she thinks the incident is trivial. Perhaps she does not realize that children have feelings too. Perhaps she does not know that culturally disadvantaged people can be heartbroken too. When will she learn?

Fire and Snow

DEBORAH E. MCDOWELL

Why do I keep a journal? Next to sewing, keeping a journal helps both to keep me centered and to relieve the various stresses, frustrations, and anxieties that inevitably mount in the course of a day. But, quiet as it's kept, journal writing keeps me out of jail.

Because this is writing done solely for myself, with no concern for sound, sense, or the approval of others, I think of it as freer writing. In my journal entries I am able to close my mind and ears to that bloated, overfed superego, that disgusting internal critic and censor who finds everything I write for "scholarly" and "professional" audiences wanting and "unfinished" in some respect. Just after my first yawn and stretch of the day or just before I turn off my bedside lamp at night—my two favorite times for journal writing—I can express fragmentary, petty, happy, melancholy, evil, obscene thoughts and fears without fear of ridicule, judgment, or neglect.

Thursday, 15 August 1985. 10:35 A.M.
The Villager Restaurant, Waterville, Maine

Two inches of snow can paralyze the city in Bessemer, Alabama. Banks close, stores close, but, most important for a nine-year-old, schools close. So rarely did snow fall back home that no child with a day off from school could possibly stay inside, especially not on a day when a house was burning.

The story goes that it was Miss Eartha Mae Tubbs who first saw the blaze creeping up the side of Miss Hazel's kitchen window. Since she didn't have a phone, she ran next door and pounded on first the front door, then the back door, then the window of Miss Hazel and Mr. Alf's bedroom. When nobody answered, she ran the three blocks to Blankenship's store to call the fire department, but it was too late by then. The flames had already swallowed the house. I remember being frightened by the piercing sound of the sirens which brought bodies, wrapped in quilts and blankets, to their front porches up and down the block.

When there was a fire in our neighborhood, everybody's greatest fear was that it would spread to the next house if the fire department didn't get there in time, because the houses were built so close together. Grandma soon saw that the fire was still blazing with an intensity that showed no signs of stopping, and so decided it was time to wrap us all up—my brothers, Reggie and Boodie, and me—and take refuge at Mama Lucy's.

Mama Lucy's was the last place I wanted to go, because her house always stank of camphor and strong medicines and was too crowded to let me roam. She dipped snuff and kept a spit cup by the side of the bed. I always wondered who emptied it or why she never changed it. Of all the times we went to visit her, I never saw anything but this Trellis Peas can with its fading label. When Grandma used to take me there with her on the way from the store, or after church, she would always say, "Now you set still, you hear?" knowing that that was one of the hardest things for me to do. But who would do anything else at Mama Lucy's? Every which way you turned in that little shot-gun house, you were bound to bump into something or knock it down.

Mama Lucy had suffered from diabetes for many years and the sore on her right foot, always swollen and running with pus, made my stomach turn. She lived alone and spent much of her time making paper sculptures from old newspapers and aluminum foil—crosses, trees, snowflakes—that she would pin to the wall over her bed. Every time I would wrap up a watermelon rind or scraps from the dinner table in newspaper or unwrap the Goo Goo Clusters which were rotting my teeth, Grandma would say, "Don't forget to save some paper for Mama Lucy."

I was determined not to go to Mama Lucy's the morning of the fire. I wanted to see the fire, to stand with the other children and grown folks who had gathered in the street in front of Miss Hazel's to watch her house burn down. But Grandma had this other plan. "I don't want to go to Mama Lucy's," I pleaded, "I want to go see the fire."

"Well, you ain't going to no fire," she scolded.

She ordered me to put on my old green corduroy coat with the quilted lining that Mama had made, and since I could not find my cap, she gave me one of hers—an old, dusty, ugly, dimpled felt thing. "I don't want to wear this old hat," I complained. "It's a hat for old folks."

Grandma gave the Look that said, "Put that hat on gal," then growled, "I can't have you catchin' your death in cold."

While she was wrapping my little brother Boodie in his snow suit, I escaped through the back door to catch the excitement of the fire. I was hypnotized by the flames that melted the tar shingles and swiftly left the house nothing but a charred stump standing pathetically in the middle of the block. Neighbors kept asking where Miss Hazel was. Had Mr. Alf gone to work? No, he was laid off. As the questions ran through the growing crowd, someone spotted Miss Hazel at the corner with a bag of groceries in her arms, Mr. Alf's old army coat flapping around her legs. As she got closer, she saw that it was her house on fire and, dropping the bag, she ran toward the house screaming, "My baby, my baby, did anybody get my baby?"

I don't know what stunned and shocked me more, Miss Hazel's

piercing screams or Grandma's backhand up side my head. "You gon' have your way, do what you wanta do anyway ain't you, Little Miss? Well, a hard head makes a soft behind. I tole you to wait while I put Boodie on his clothes, but nothing do you but act like you grown folks, like you ain't got to mind nobody." The words came out to the rhythm of the licks on my arms, my legs, around my shoulders. But Grandma stopped beating me when somebody yelled, "Hazel is trying to get in that house." It took all the strength that Mr. Ed Mitchell had to hold Miss Hazel back. For months after the fire I could hear her screaming in my sleep, "My baby, my baby, oh my God, my baby's in that house."

Well, we didn't get to Mama Lucy's that day, because the fire didn't spread. The neighborhood was in somber mourning for little Ruthie Pates, barely eight months old. It was around that time that Grandma became both feared and respected, because she had prophesied that little Ruthie would not be long for this world.

"That child is too pretty," Grandma said when little Ruthie had lost that generic baby look and her face had taken on its own mark of personality. "She don't even look real. Look at her," neighbors marveling at her perfection were heard to say. She was the envy of every woman who had ever had a baby in the history of Pipe Shop—short for the U.S. Pipe and Foundry, which gave our neighborhood its name and the men of Bessemer employment while the steel industry was still hanging on, and could pay an almost livable wage to Daddy and the other neighborhood men who worked there.

Anybody could see that little Ruthie was going to be "bright," that is, light-skinned. Grandma used to say that the telltale sign was the baby's ears. If the outer rim hadn't turned dark by a certain month, then it was certain to be fair-skinned and marked for success and the pain and satisfactions of others' envy.

Ruthie was the only baby that Miss Hazel had been able to carry to term, and so everybody understood why she worshiped the child and spent every penny of the money she got for taking in ironing on her little outfits—booties with satin ties, panties with rows of ruffles on the seat, pink dresses smocked and embroidered, and dainty cro-

cheted sweaters ornamented with rosettes. Oh, how she would roll
Ruthie around the neighborhood in a carriage she had gotten at the
secondhand store. Mama had helped her to fix it up. When she wasn't
pressing and mending clothes at Dixie Dry Cleaners, Mama sewed to
supplement the chicken feed Daddy brought home from the plant. She
always had scraps of fabric left over from somebody's outfit, and
scrounged around until she found a navy canvas to re-cover the ripped
and faded carriage top. I was always one for matching colors and
noted that the new top did not match the sun-bleached blue of the
sides, but Miss Hazel didn't care. The show was not the carriage, but
Ruthie.

One day when Miss Hazel brought Ruthie by our house, Grandma
called to her from her lookout on the porch. "Come here, Daughter."
"Daughter" was the name Grandma gave many women younger than
herself whom she selectively favored with a motherly caring and concern. Some thought she was just a plain old busybody. Miss Hazel
came through the gate and Grandma began without interruption:
"You look on this child too much, Daughter. The Lord done seen fit
to open up your womb and give you this child, but he don't intend
for you to put it before him. You know the Bible speaks against worshiping other gods, so don't make this child your god."

Miss Hazel replied with a simple, "Yes, ma'am, Miss Edie."

Because everyone knew how much little Ruthie was Miss Hazel's
heart, nobody could figure out just how or why she could leave the
child in that house by herself. By nightfall there were at least a dozen
conflicting accounts of the fire. Mama had come home exhausted from
a day of bending over a sewing machine and darning clothes often too
threadbare to hold a patch. Sometimes she brought them home in the
evening, muttering while she mended, "Now whoever this coat belongs to oughta just give this up. It won't even make a good dust rag."
Or one of my favorites, "Don't these men know a crotch ain't no toilet
stool? I'm tired of smelling their piss."

The evening of the day of the fire Mama knew the mending had to
wait. Miss Eliza B. Vicks; her sister-in-law, Miss Honey; Mr. Herbert
Burns; Miss Sadie Madison; and Mrs. Cleo Sturdivant, the Avon lady,

sat in our living room giving Mama all the details of the fire. Miss Honey, who sold bootleg whiskey, started in:

"I know the people's been saying that Hazel came and asked me to watch the baby while she went to Cox and Autry to get some milk, but that's a lie. She couldna' no way and no how, 'cause I left home 'fore day this morning and Cox and Autry don't open that early. I left to catch a ride to Cippio with Eugene. He said they might be doing some hiring at a plant there, and we wanted to get there as soon as we could, so we could be up close to the front of the line." I wondered why Miss Honey went, 'cause they didn't hire women at Cippio. Mama told me later it was so Miss Honey could fill out the forms for Mr. Gene. He couldn't really read and write.

"I heard Hazel left Alf in the house to watch the baby, but Old Man Garvin came by and asked Alf if he wanted a day's work laying some sheetrock." That was Mr. Herbert Burns who cut all the men's hair in our neighborhood. His wife was an invalid, suspicious and afraid of everybody and everything coming into her house from the outside, especially anybody who might need to pee. She took no chances on anybody sitting on her stool. Somehow, one day, Cleophus Diggins got in there, before Mr. Herbert could stop him. He kept us laughing for days about the pink tile, pink tub, pink commode, pink curtains, pink toilet paper, pink soap. "Who wants to piss in a pink toilet, anyway?" said Cleophus.

Mr. Herbert kept his version of the story going. "Since Hazel only went to get some milk for the baby and a few odds and ends, Alf thought the baby would be all right till she got back. Mr. Garvin was in a hurry to get started, 'cause his wife was trying to fix up the house for Thanksgiving. They was having company and he only had three days to finish the room." Mama cut him off, I guess because she always used to say that Mr. Herbert belonged to the iron butt school of storytelling. You had to have an iron butt to sit long enough for him to finish talking. And don't let him reach into his shirt pocket for that red can of Prince Albert tobacco. That was a sure sign that he was settling in for one of his epics.

All the while the others talked, Miss Sadie Madison sat still, her dress pulled down over her knees, her face turned off to the side to hide the bluish-gray birthmark that covered the length of her right cheek. She drew on her cigarette and blew the smoke in my direction, unmindful of my presence at the table in the corner where I always did my lessons. "Now I can't say who told me, but somebody said they saw Alf up by the ball diamond this morning, and y'all know who lives over there."

Mama, who had no patience for gossip, interrupted Miss Sadie, but she kept rattling on. "The truth is the truth and it shines in the dark," countered Miss Sadie. "And if Alf care more about his woman than he do his own flesh and blood, then ain't nobody got to cloak him in his sin." When Miss Sadie's loose and judging tongue broke its silence, I no longer pretended to be tracing the boot of Italy and penciling in its cities for geography class. Just why I, a girl of nine, was so fascinated by talk of a husband and his "woman," I was not to discover for a long, long time, but I remember finding this turn in the conversation so arresting that I stopped and did what no child was allowed to do: look grown folks in the face while they were having "grown folks conversation." My mother looked at me and said, "You, go to bed Little Miss."

There is no irritation, no injustice like that of being ordered from the room just when a conversation is getting good, especially when you have to get called out of your name besides. Everybody called me Debbie, short for Deborah, except for my grandfather, who called me "Miss Priss." He gave me the name, he said, because I was always prancing and being prissy. When Papa called me Miss Priss, it was always with a loving tone of voice. The rest of the family and most of the substitute mothers in the neighborhood who stood watch over me and any other child within their reach, took this name, a name that marked my specialness, and vulgarized it, nastied it up. "Little Miss" was derogatory and associated with everything punitive.

"I gave your Little Miss a few licks for you," said Miss Ophelia as she led me by the hand up the front steps where Mama sat on the porch shelling crowder peas.

"What was she doing, this time?" Mama asked. "Mouthing off again?"

Miss Ophelia nodded her head.

"Did you sass Miss Ophelia?" Mama asked.

I answered, the tears of public humiliation welling up, "Cleophus Diggins was bothering me, so I told him his mama had one titty and she carried it in a holster."

"Where did you learn this kind of talk," Mama wanted to know, barely able to keep from laughing.

But I couldn't answer her, 'cause I didn't know. I guess it was something I had heard in the lunch line at school.

Although I didn't like the name Little Miss I could take it as long as it wasn't preceded by the epithet for every verbal female child, "womanish." "You are a womanish Little Miss," Grandma used to say with that deep guttural tone of voice that she would summon for mention of anything distasteful. It almost sounded like she was expectorating when she said it, and I was reminded of the sound my brother Reggie made after gagging on the cod liver oil Grandma made us take every spring to clean ourselves out and prevent what she called "caustive" bowels.

We called her Grandma, but Edith Johnson McDowell Lucky Crawford was actually my great-grandmother on Daddy's side. She and her last husband, Leslie Marshall Crawford, or Daddy Les, lived with us in a duplex on Long Eighteenth Street, one block over from Short Eighteenth Street. No Crescent View Lanes or Cedar Park Circles graced my neighborhood. I was Grandma's namesake. She wanted me to be named Edith and my mother compromised and gave me that as a middle name. I never thought "Deborah Edith" had the right ring, but at least it kept peace in the family. She had marked me, she said, with a mole just above my upper right lip. She had one in the same spot, so that as much as justified her insistence that I bear her name. She and I were always on-again, off-again. I thought she was old-fashioned and meddlesome. She thought I was womanish and would certainly come to a bad end for giving sass and listening to "reels" like "If Loving You Is Wrong" and "Who's Making Love to Your Old

Lady," and "Steal Away," not to be confused with the spiritual about stealing away to Jesus.

I had always discounted her prophecies and dismissed them as the superstitions of an old lady, grown more feebleminded by the day, but when her prophecy of Ruthie's death came to pass, I started to believe her. Whereas, before the fire I would grumble and complain when she asked me to read to her the Ninetieth Psalm, after the fire, I would take that Bible from the mantel where Grandma said it had to rest, and handling with care its leather backing cracked and dried with age, I would begin in the most sonorous tone my childhood voice could muster, "Lord, thou hast been our dwelling place in all generations." Whereas, before the fire I thought she forced me to read First Corinthians, Thirteen to complete the work of her hands, after the fire I read with understanding, "When I was a child, I spake as a child, I understood as a child, I thought as a child. . . ." Before the fire, I dreaded the trips that Grandma made me take with her to Mama Lucy's, but after, even when deep down inside myself, I wanted to color or play jacks or cut paper dolls from the Sears and Roebuck catalog, I walked the blocks with Grandma and served my apprenticeship to this witchy good Samaritan who had marked me with her mole. I sat still in the corner beside Mama Lucy's metal chifforobe, the picture of Jesus Christ on the cross looking down on me as I tried to hold my breath to block the stench of Sloan's liniment.

Myself

TINUKE OLUYOMI

In May of 1992, this Nigerian girl, then eight and a student at the staff school of the University of Ibadan, was involved in an automobile accident resulting in the loss of all her teeth. While in the midst of a long recovery, she started to write at home. She sent the following narrative, along with a color photograph of her beautiful toothless visage, for this book.

[1992]

My name is Tinuke Oluyomi. I am eight years old. I like my father because he throws me up and down which makes me laugh, giggle and chuckle. But there is nothing I would love him to do more often—tha[n] . . . to talk to me as a friend rather than a daughter. I like [my mother] because she talks to me as a friend. But what I do not like about her is that her face frightens me when she is angry with me. I like [my oldest sister] because she is gentle and responsible. One thing I do not like about her is that when they tell her to rest, she would not rest. I like [my oldest brother] because he is kind-hearted. He pampers me a lot and of course gets angry at me a lot. [My second older sister] is intelligent and hopes to become a lawyer. I like her because she behaves like a mother to everybody. But she can be harsh. I am the last born of the family and will be nine on the 28th of March 1993. My parents are not divorced but they live separately. I feel sad about it. I wish there was a children's court, where all the children will give their points and I would be the judge.

SOMETIMES I GO to the balcony and listen to the birds sing, look at the squirrels jump around on the trees which are in front of my house—watching them makes me feel happy. When I don't have a test and I don't feel like reading a story book then I go to the balcony. Alone [on] the balcony, I start living in the world of my own which is quite different from the world that is going on around me. Sometimes I pretend to be a farmer planting some beans, maize and vegetables on a farmland using the flower bed as the farm land; I use stones and sticks as tools and I make my own artificial gum (made of sand from the flower pot, water from the bath room and the edible from farm school). Some other times I pretend I am mummy by using my aunty's eye pencil to put old age lines on my face—the types that are on mummy's face. I also use the traditional brain pow[d]er called 'ERO' on my face the way my mummy uses it. [When I] get tired of using the powder and the eye pencil . . . I tiptoe to her room, pick up from her dressing table her best perfume to a place where no one can see me use it and spray it all over my body. By this time the whole house will be filled with the fragrance of the perfume.

Normally, the first thing mummy does when she wakes up from her nap is to call me and try to find out what I have been doing while she was asleep. . . . [B]ecause of the amount of the perfume I have used, by the time I get to my mummy she would immediately sense that I have used her perfume and of course get angry with me. By this time, I will feel nervous and try to cover up with a lie and at the end I get a thorough beating not because I used her perfume but for telling a lie.

There are times when I go to the balcony and think of some things like when mummy has just given me a good spa[n]king, I think she is wicked and unkind and most of all she can't understand a single thing; but in another minute I am playing with her.

I sometimes go to the balcony with mummy and my aunties—we tell stories, sing songs, tell riddles and jokes and poems. Sometimes, when I a[m] there alone with mummy, we talk like age mates.

I THINK the president of my country could do better than what he is doing and people say the same thing. I think they should start giving children news in the way they can understand [it] because I don't see why children should listen to something they don't understand.

I heard about two countries that were at war—throwing bombs and killing people. Though I can't remember the countries I don't like it. When I hear of wars I'm usually afraid and it gives me nightmares.

While some countries are rich, others are poor. In the poor countries children . . . starve. I feel sorry for them.

I THINK I am very beautiful. I love being a girl . . .

Weeds

The "Weeds" entry was an autobiographical exercise I tried in response to a friend who was taking a correspondence writing course. She promised she would share each of the exercises with me. The first was to write a creative autobiographical statement. This entry became a compilation of autobiographical thoughts and existing poems I had written that looked at my development.

It was difficult for me to make these admissions about my impressions of myself and what I find most interesting about who I am. It is always easier to talk and think about what makes other people interesting. Still, I view these statements as "hard to share" revealings of my essential self. But what good is sharing that doesn't touch the core? One of the joys of writing journals is how it puts me in touch with my personal spirituality, that god-self in me that exists in all of us.

I used to imagine myself a racing car, steadily gaining speed. I would watch the roadside flying by until I reached a point of such velocity that I simply exploded into a million pieces. My spirit, (other self) would go on looking as the fragments scattered. I've often tried to unravel that day/night dream. What was it that traveled so fast—my thoughts? (That's all I can come up with.) I feel less and less that way though. I think I finally slowed down enough to start looking for road signs—needing some direction.

When I was a child, my uncontrollable fine and curly hair would work its way out of braids, pigtails, and bobby pins, casting its fate to the wind. My mother would insist that I wear bangs, saying my forehead was too prominent. My hair was like my grandfather said my brothers and I were—weeds, without direction.

My voice has always impressed me, less so now that lower respiratory problems have altered its sound, resonance, tone. And I have always wanted to sing. Or in some way be musical. When I was young I used to envision myself a prima ballerina, what poetry of movement I thought the ballet. How exquisite, magnificent, and whole. We could not afford lessons. I comfort myself now with the metaphysical reassurance that most assuredly in another life or perhaps on another plane, I dance, danced, and will dance. Perhaps because I did not dance or sing, I wrote. At first to ease my own confusion with life, living— me. Later to share some of the information I had miraculously gleaned from my experiences regarding the marvel of survival and the wonder of growth.

Once in a poem I wrote of myself:

> Born of the humidity in a below sea level land
> Bred on the moisture therein
> Fed the food not thought fed to champions
> Growing on grits, shortenbread, pork chops,
> chicken, mashed potatoes and sometimes greens . . .

> Movement necessary as it came
> one town, one city, one state
> not really all the same
> stays shortened by the restless need
> like ants in the pants
> hot coins in a pocket

having to be moved or
needing to be spent . . .

Being but so young in age
so ancient to newness . . .

My life has been one of screamed secrets and convoluted emotional exchanges. I was borne of one. All of these things I once regretted, I now embrace. In another self-revealing poem I quoted my grandfather in a chorus: "Just like weeds, just like weeds, like weeds, he said . . ." And I added, "or are weeds the only really strong things there are."

Arrival

The writing of this autobiographical piece was an unusual experience for the author, as it is one of only two examples of "personal" writing she has done. However, she wants to make clear that to her, personal writing is public writing. She does not and never has made a distinction between the two.

When I was a kid, growing up in Tucson, Arizona, I believed in the cowboy code of behavior. It involved acting honorably and being kind to women and children. I was not particularly kind to other children, but I loved my mother and my grandmother. I don't remember how honorably I conducted myself either. After all, I was only four years old. My prairie consisted of four acres of mostly rocks and dirt and assorted nasty critters, who occasionally got into the house. Once we found a Gila monster climbing the dining-room drapes.

My mother, grandmother, and step-grandfather had moved to Arizona from San Antonio, Texas, in 1945. In Tucson, my mother met and decided to marry a man the family considered beneath her. When she threatened to run away with him, my grandparents gave their consent. She was sixteen and had graduated from high school when she was fifteen (she kept her diploma on the wall beside the bed). However shallow my grandparents' objections about the man—he was not of our class, nor (of all things) was he multiracial, which we were, and (worst of all) his family had picked cotton—they were right in that he was the wrong man. My mother ended up having an affair with a Japanese man. She got pregnant with me and when my natural father, the Japanese, found out, he told her to go home to her family. Finally, after the man she was married to beat her and she tried to abort me by throwing herself down a stairway, she called an uncle and he took her back to Arizona.

I was born barely seven months later, on October 21, 1947, in my great-grandmother's house in Albany, Texas. My mother had gone there to keep from losing me. My great-grandmother Maggie was Irish and African-American. My great-grandfather was Dutch and Choctaw Indian. My mother's father was African-American. My great-grandfather's mother, who was Choctaw, and his father, who was Dutch, had moved to Texas from Oklahoma, where many Choctaws had been relocated by Andrew Jackson. The Cherokees, Choctaws, Creeks, and Chikasaws all made the trek along the Trail of Tears. In the 1860s or 1870s, my great-grandparents moved to Texas. We now think because his family was there, but we have no proof. All I know is my great-grandfather's family name was Waggoner, but when he was born, the birth certificate was changed and his last name became Smith, because they said Waggoner was a white man's name. My own birth certificate lists me as the child of my mother's husband, with a C I assume for "Colored" under race.

When the doctor came to see me, he told my great-grandmother, "Maggie, she's not going to live," but my great-grandmother said, "Yes, she will." She put me in a shoebox by the heater and fed me hot toddies. Someone told me that happened to Willie Shoemaker, the jockey, too—the toddie part, that is. They always said my great-grandmother was a nurse. I don't know if that was true, but she knew how to keep me alive. When I was well enough to travel, my mother moved back to Arizona and returned to her husband, but by the time I was eight months old, he'd tried to strangle me because I wasn't his, and when my mother became pregnant with his child, he said he wasn't the father and kicked her in the stomach. She lost the baby. My mother left him for good and we went to live with my grandparents in Tucson, where my memories begin.

I remember being strongly encouraged to read and aside from coloring, which was my favorite activity, reading gave me the most pleasure. I had two books of Japanese fairy tales that contained haiku. I loved those books. One had a red cover and one had a blue cover. I used to sit for hours looking at the drawings and being read to, until I could read on my own. I also learned to spell. A detergent commercial on the radio soaps spelled out the word *Tide*. I'll never forget. I nearly drove my mother crazy spelling that word. I think that's really why I learned to spell and read so early. In the interest of preserving her sanity, my mother made sure I learned to spell some more interesting words, and to keep me occupied, she taught me to read. We got our first Siamese then, too. His name was Lately, because he was born last. He was a good companion and even kept a scorpion at bay while I stood on a chair, until my grandmother came and killed it. We had chickens, pigeons, pigs, dogs. It was a great life for a kid. Alas, that came to an end when my mother met a new man. When I was five, they got married. He was in the army and stationed at Fort Reilly, Kansas, so we left my grandparents. My mother had a baby girl and I saw snow for the first time. I also started school. My stepfather had been stationed in Japan and had had a Japanese girlfriend, who'd had a son by him. My mother showed me a photograph of her once. She was wearing high heels and white socks. Later, I saw a photo of a little boy. He was fat and cute and my mother said he looked like my stepfather. I was far too young to know. In fact, I think I only know about the little boy because I heard my mother and grandmother discussing it.

I was always listening in. They said you had to watch what you said around me, and since I could spell, they couldn't get away with that much anymore; although even if I could spell, I didn't know what half the stuff meant. Finally, they started spelling backward. I learned how to do that too, so things were just not said with me around after that. But if anyone was discussing me, I never heard even a whisper. I did not know I was half-Japanese. I thought that fellow she'd divorced and whom I did not remember was my father. It's hard to believe now that I would be twenty-six before I knew the truth. Although I realized as I got older that that man couldn't be my father, I was never able to confront my mother, and she never volunteered anything until I was seventeen, and she did it in such a way that I still couldn't question her. If only she had told me all when I was a child, it would have saved me a lot of confusion and pain.

I didn't know I was half-Japanese, but the fifth-grade African-American girls at Sacred Heart in San Francisco knew. We went there after my stepfather came back from the Korean Conflict, and after we'd spent about a year living in Las Vegas with my grandmother and her new husband, who was in construction. Day after day, the girls would say, "Get away from us, Nigger Jap, you can't play with us, Nigger Jap." Finally, I told my mother and she went to school and told the nuns I had Indian blood and that the kids were mistaking that for Japanese. I suppose it was acceptable, because the taunting stopped. I used to beg my mother to let me go to the Catholic school where all the Catholic Asians went.

By now, I was reading about the lives of the saints and the knights of the Round Table. I liked Saint Teresa best, then the Blessed Virgin, but even so, they came well after the Mickey Mouse Club. I guess I didn't read poetry that I remember, although when I was about six, my mother read me Gray's "Elegy Written in a Country Churchyard" and "The Road Not Taken" by Frost. She also liked Langston Hughes and held him in very high esteem. She wanted me to be an English teacher, because that's what she would have been if she hadn't gotten married. She told me again and again how important it was to get an education, so that by the time I entered high school, I was set on the path to college, at least in my mind. I think if she had not held literature in such high regard, I might not have become a writer, but I can't say that with any real certainty. What I do know is that, by the age of ten, reading was a major activity of mine. I preferred to read rather than play, and when I was twelve she signed me up in a book club, but it took a couple more changes of residence from California to Arizona and back to Los Angeles before I actually wrote something I made up.

IN 1959, we moved to LA from Tucson. My stepfather was in the California National Guard by then and we were enrolled in Holy Name School. One day, Sister told us to go home and pretend that we were martyrs and that the next day we'd be fed to the lions, and to write our last letter. She had me read mine to the class. I was mortified. Now I realize she thought it was good. After that, she had us memorize "Captain, My Captain" and some of the Gettysburg Address. Another assignment was to write our own version of "Jabberwocky." She also had us write poems. I don't have them and I don't know what I thought about them. I do remember feeling pleasure when I was writing. I felt a kind of satisfaction I hadn't before. Unfortunately, my mother removed me from that school because of problems my stepsister was having with a lay teacher, so I never got my poems back and I didn't write a poem again until I was thirteen. The shock of going to public school and all was too much for me.

But one day, I saw a flyer announcing a poetry contest. The poem had to be about something historical and I remember failed efforts, especially one about Abraham Lincoln. My mother and stepfather had split up and we were having a difficult time financially, so we moved back to Tucson and I enrolled in Tucson High School. I was miserable, lonely, and given all these absurdly easy courses because my mother had not brought my files from school in California. What a wasted, boring semester. Luckily, my sophomore year, I took World History, my straight-A course, the only one I had in high school. I got a good English class and teacher, and the next time I saw an ad for a poetry contest, I entered it. The poem was very Edgar Allan Poeish. I called it "Le Mort." The teacher asked me why French and I told her I thought it sounded better (I was studying French). I didn't win, but I kept on writing. I would request extra assignments so I could do some creative writing. I discovered the Romantics then and began to imitate Shelley and Keats. Around that time, a Mormon spiritualist my mother and grandmother were friends with gave me a tiny leather-bound set of the Shakespeare plays, and I spent one whole summer reading them. I especially loved the tragedies. I also read the Catholic Bible every night before I went to bed. I watched TV a lot, there being no restrictions on that activity. My mother had given up trying to control me that way, partly because I was the family brain and I would someday become an *English Teacher*, make a decent living, support my mother, and be a credit to the family and the race(s). So I was accorded certain privileges like watching TV till all hours, not cooking, and doing a minimum of housework, whereas my stepsister learned to cook, clean, and sew, and had to pick up the slack whenever I had extra studying, etc., etc. Although my stepsister is a working woman, she is rather traditional. I guess those roots are hard to kill off, or maybe she really was more domestic than I.

I wrote some fiction, but it didn't interest me as much as poetry. I must say that I developed my interest in moral ambiguity from fiction, though, and also from *film noir*, which my mother loved and which I also came to enjoy and love now that I am older. I was fascinated by *The Scarlet Letter*. As I didn't know about my own illegitimacy, I can't say that that had anything to do with it. No, I was just fascinated by the story and the characters and the judgment meted out to them by society, acting as God's henchmen. I have never lost that desire to understand how certain people can set themselves up as guardians of morality. Illegitimacy *was* an issue then, though. There's such a high birthrate among young unmarried African-American women now that nobody seems to remember a time when it was unacceptable, but believe me, it was. In Tucson, there was a caste system among African-Americans too. The Mexican-African-American mixtures, Filipino-African-American, and Indian-African-American, as well as a few very well-off full-blooded African-Americans, comprised the African-American upper class in Tucson. That's the class I come from. We were better off financially, at least in how we saw ourselves, though really we would be called lower-lower-middle class today. The closest thing, I think, to my family and the society they inhabited was probably the Creole society of New Orleans. Needless to say, welfare was a no-no. Only the most pathetic people were thought to need welfare and people on it were disapproved of, if not downright shunned.

My mother was quite strict and I could only go out on double dates (once in a while) with my cousin John. I never had a single date until I was a freshman in college, so one can't totally judge the scene by me, and indeed by my freshman year in college in 1965, the social stigma against out-of-wedlock pregnancy had eased enough that several young women got pregnant and dropped out. They got married, though, because things hadn't changed quite that much yet.

College was a terrible shock for me. I didn't write at all my first year. I missed my friends from high school. I hated science. I got a *D* in typing. I failed biology, which I hated. I dropped botany and finally found my niche in geology. I did not like my freshman English class, but I loved my major, which, surprisingly to some people, was Japanese. One night before registration, I'd been reading the college catalog, assuming I'd be majoring in English, when I happened on Oriental Studies. I can't explain the feeling that came over me when I read the description of courses in Japanese. I can only describe it as a kind of peace. That night, I made my decision, not knowing whether in the end it would make a difference because I had not been able to save enough money for registration and my latest stepfather, a barber, would not lend it to me. The fee was $125!

In those days, I barely had five dollars a month to spend. My mother did housework and I worked as a janitorial assistant for the Neighborhood Youth Corp. Right after graduation, someone stole my purse at Woolworth's and my last paycheck for $90 was in it. That was all I had for the summer and I couldn't find anything else. There weren't all these fast-food places then and such. It was tough, especially if you were a minority, and of course it still is, probably more so. If I couldn't afford college, what was I going to do? Finally, I applied for a job as a Playboy Bunny. They were interviewing in Phoenix and I figured I could work and pay for school. Ha! After looking at myself with the blinders off, I had to admit that I did not have the boobs for it. There I was looking just like the stereotypical flat-chested Japanese woman. They'd never hire me, I thought. Anyway, I was only seventeen.

Looking back, even if I had had boobs, I would never have lasted among those chauvinists, but remember, it was still only 1965. My consciousness hadn't been completely raised yet. It's funny too that my mother, who was so strict, only smiled when I showed her the card from Playboy, inviting me to a get-acquainted party. She knew I'd come to my senses, as moms often do, but if she'd railed against it, I'm sure I would have gone. I'd never thought of doing anything but teaching. What would I do?

On the last day of registration, I was lying in bed depressed when my grandmother came over. "Get up," she said, "I got the money for you." I couldn't believe it. I jumped up, dressed, and rushed to campus. I still needed books and such and I don't remember now how I got them, but I did. The second semester, I tried to get on work-study, but they said my stepfather made too much money, and although he gave me nothing (my mother bought our food), they would not accept me, so I started to do housework. My grandmother would drop me off on her way to work and pick me up on her way home. I was quite timid and I remember my grandmother asking me what the woman had me do. When I told her, she was really angry, because I was doing more than I was supposed to for the money. One day she said, "You don't have to do this." She dressed up in her uniform and took me to the work-study office. She practically begged the director to let me on the program. He was from Georgia and kept calling my grandmother girl, though they were about the same age. She was at her most humble, most subservient, and she got me on work-study. Later, we went home so she could, as she put it, take off that goddamn uniform. It was her day off.

PART TWO

Searching for Self

Rodjie,

It rained & thundered just beautiful. I got soaked, but I love to walk and play in the rain, except my hair doesn't. I wish it would be alright for us Negro[e]s to wear our hair natural. I think it looks good but it's not [ac]cepted by society. Any way I got soaked anyway, hair & all and mommy nearly had a white child.

VALERIE TURNER (VALERIE JEAN)
June 12, 1968, age fourteen

If you're not happy with something it's best to let it go. I've been complaining for too long, bitter over nothing for too long. I've sent my depression way into me, I think it is in a safe place—the rest of it evaporates through my poetry, when the safety container is overfilled.

PAULA OBE THOMAS
1991–92

. . . While we are becoming more of what we always imagined we really wanted to be, we steadily become less of who we are. The process is so subtle, deception is easy.

QUO VADIS GEX-BREAUX
1974–75

Whenever I follow my gut, there is always a reward even if that reward is simply refuge from chaos.

PATRICIA BELL-SCOTT
6:19 A.M., October 18, 1992

At an Artist's Colony

TOI DERRICOTTE

This selection of autobiographical prose is taken from The Black Notebooks, *a book which I began writing in 1974 when my family became one of the first black families to move into Upper Montclair, New Jersey. I began keeping journals in order to understand my inner responses to living in this environment which some part of me had been taught to think of as ideal, my feelings of depression, shame, anxiety, self-hatred, fear, isolation, as well as my desire for love and intimacy. Part of the complexity to my situation had to do with my appearance as a white-appearing black person. I hoped that writing my feelings down, especially the ones which were the most disturbing, would exorcise their power over me.*

Though the writing began strictly as a personal document, after several years, I came to think that the work probably had value for others too. Perhaps hidden fears and longings are under the surface of much behavior between blacks and whites, and many people are either unconscious or too ashamed to bring these parts of the self to light. Further, I came to believe that racism, and all its manifestations, is a reflection of deep psychic structures that have to be uncovered, addressed, and altered before changes in the external world will be lasting.

Black Arms

Agroup of us are sitting around the TV room. Ray, a painter from the South, is talking about how hard his mother works. He says: "I told her all you need is a pair of good black arms." The others snicker.

I am new here. All I want to do is get along. I say nothing, though now I know there is a part of me that is a joke to this man—my washerwoman great-grandmother, my cook grandmother.

I will be silent. I want him to like me. I want to tell him how he hurts me. I want to speak. But then the colonists will say: "You know how sensitive they are." I will be labeled. And for six weeks, the only black person, I will never be able to sit at the dinner table without "Black Arms."

Dinner Time

Last night at the dinner table, John, a man who didn't know I'm black, noticed the book of women's diary writing which has a section of *The Black Notebooks* in it.

He asked me to see the book, and when he took it, I could see he wasn't going to just skim over the table of contents. He went directly for my story, putting down his fork, and began to read. I felt a coldness, like a breeze ruffling a curtain on a line. The other dinner tables were quiet; many of the colonists don't know I'm black. I could just hear him blurt loudly, "I didn't know you're black. You don't look black. How did you get that color?"

I don't like to lose control of my identity that way. I fear being questioned or attacked, like an animal in a cage, prodded and poked by onlookers.

The man, fortunately, kept his comments to the quality of the work. "This is great. It sent a shiver up my spine. It's dramatic."

The other people at the table didn't know the content. Not that I mind every person at the colony knowing I'm black. I don't care, and I am proud of my work. But when several come at me from all sides,

I don't know which way to turn. And heaven help me if I should show anger or be defensive.

John wouldn't let it alone. Later, as several of us were sitting around the fireplace, he said, "You should read this article in the *Times*. You'll like it. It reminds me of your book." I hadn't seen the article, but I knew it must be about black people. As soon as he knew I was black, I became a category, and anything he reads by or about a black person reminds him of me.

A Chinese man who has also read my book said, "This article is nothing like the writing in Toi's book." I was glad he spoke, defending the uniqueness of my experience.

Later, John was playing pool. I was sitting twenty feet away and noticed him staring at me. I thought he was thinking I was attractive and was beginning to feel flattered. Suddenly he yelled across the room. "You really should read that article. You'll find it interesting. It's really timely."

Another man in the room called: "What's the article about?"

"Racism," he yelled back.

The people in the room looked up. I felt the conversation go out of my hands.

The other man said, "That isn't timely. It's ongoing and eternal."

I was glad somebody spoke. And it wasn't me.

The Testimony of Innocence

Last night I went over to Marty's studio to share my work. She read some of my diary entries and I read some of her poems. She said she felt my diary entries were extremely important. She asked me who they were addressed to, and I read her the diary entry which describes my audience: ". . . all the people in my past, black and white, who represent the internalized process of racism within me." I want to recount those experiences through which I have internalized racism and which surface in behavior that rebuilds it in the world.

In 1976, when I began writing *The Black Notebooks*, I wrote mainly to myself, although at the back of my mind was an idea that maybe someday, I would get the courage to make it public. The idea was to tell the truth as deeply as I could, however painful, but also to write for the larger human community—the world. I know that sounds ridiculously grandiose, but I felt an honest confession would have merit. My negative self-concept made me trust myself more than writers whose descriptions of racism make them seem removed from blame and responsibility—testimonies of their innocence. I have always distrusted that, both from whites and blacks.

My skin color causes certain problems continuously, problems which open the issue of racism over and over, like a wound. These openings are occasions for reexamination. My skin color keeps things, literally, from being either black or white.

I know where I would like this all to end. I would like it to end, as all confessions, with a sense that I am starting over. I would like to be finished with shame, to know I love myself and my own people, that I believe I have something positive to contribute, that I am not disloyal, weak of character, and unlovable—not because I am black, but because there is something intrinsically wrong with me.

In my writings I wanted to catch a process in myself, ongoing, continuous, private, and deeply rooted. I wanted to stumble on some answer, some illumination that would make me see myself and the world in a new way. Then I would put the triumphant closing chapter on the diary and publish it—with pity, even disdain, for that woman who had written it.

My decision to make more of my entries public comes from my meeting at the colony with a Chicano woman and political activist, Pat, who, when I showed her my most scary black hatred entries, still loved me, showed me the mirror of acceptance. How I love her for that!

I'll publish. I'll make a name for myself; I'll make money. I'll win the love of my relatives and get a professorship at a university. I'll win a movie contract and play the heroine of my own story. It seems awful to hope success will come out of such disaster.

Not to worry, Pat says, writing about racism doesn't make you successful, it makes you ignored.

Ray

Yesterday, after breakfast, I saw him lumbering toward his jeep. He looked a little lost; several of his close friends have left the colony. I had heard him say another gem this morning, "I wish I had ten little black women to sew the holes in that canvas . . ."

Every time the opportunity comes to talk to him the time doesn't seem right. Either other people are around or there's another problem. After his art show last night, I stayed longer than anyone, but he seemed depressed with people's reactions. It would have been piling shit on top of shit if I had tried to talk to him; and I don't think he would have heard what I was saying. I found myself listening to his worries, reassuring him, and kicking myself for being a coward.

But this morning was perfect. I know he often goes into town for doughnuts. I had been on my way to my studio, but I turned in my tracks.

Sitting in the doughnut shop, I waited for a relaxed moment. The comforting cups of coffee were placed before us. He lit a cigarette. "There's something I have to tell you," I said. "I'm black, and last week when you made that comment about black arms, it made me feel bad. And this morning you said something else about little black women sewing holes in the canvas." I didn't say it in a mean voice, just a human voice, one on one. (Inside, I'm saying, Why can't I just blurt it out? Why do I have to be so careful?)

I tried not to look at his face so I could get my words out, but I caught a glimpse and saw a muscle twitching in his cheek, his mouth was slightly open, and he was listening to me intently. I went on, "You see, I wanted to say something to you when this happened last week, but I didn't want to say something that would make people look at me as if I'm different. Sometimes when people find out I'm black, they treat me differently from then on. So when people say things that hurt me, I don't know what to do. I want to tell them. But, at the same time, I'm afraid I'll be hurt even more if I do."

He started to explain, "When I said that about 'black arms,' I was repeating something my mother-in-law said, and I was repeating it because I was horrified by it. What you feel must be similar to what I feel at my wife's house, because I am the only goy." I was happy he was identifying, but I hate it when, after I let a white person know they've said something racist, I end up having to listen for hours to their life. "Please, I don't want to put you on the spot. I just want you to understand my feelings. Do you understand? What do you hear me saying?" He said, "I hear you saying that certain comments which other people make without sensitivity have great poignancy to you because you are black." That wasn't exactly what I was saying, but it seemed close. Besides, it had taken all the bravery I could muster to come this far, I couldn't press him further.

In the past, I have left conversations like this empty, not getting what I wanted. I thought it was rage I wanted to vent. But today, because he listened, because I had waited for the right moment and asked for what I wanted, I thought, maybe I've found the answer. From now on, if I just wait, if I just talk about my feelings honestly, if I don't expect the person to say something to take my pain away, if I just ask him or her to repeat back what I said until they've understood, then everything will be fine.

I want so much to find a formula! Of course, there is none. Sometimes it will come out OK, like yesterday, and sometimes I will walk away with a hole in my heart that all the black women in the world cannot sew up.

Saturday Night

Several colonists sat around trying to have fun on a Saturday night. We miss New York, movies, Chinese restaurants. We talked about feminism, about how, these days, many of the young girls have babies while in high school.

A Southern lady said, "That's what black girls have been doing for years. They have babies and their families raise them. Maybe it's catching up with white girls." This is the same woman who three days ago was talking about how black people have "funny" names. "They name their kids the strangest things." I thought about the twins in New

Jersey whose mother had honored the doctor who had delivered them by giving them names he suggested: Syphily and Gonorra.

This woman loves to talk about black people. She's our resident expert. She said, "There aren't any black people here. I haven't seen any."

"Yes there are," I said, smiling.

"Who?"

"You're looking at one."

"You're not really black. Just an eighth or something."

"I don't know how black I am, but I am black."

"Was your mother black?"

"My mother, my father, my grandparents. They are black, and they look just like me."

"How do you know you're black?"

"I'm black because black people were the first people I touched and loved."

A woman at the table said: "Did you read the article in the *New York Times* that said if they were strict about genetics, sixty percent of the people in the United States would be classified as black?"

I looked around the table. I was laughing. The others were not. They were worried about how black I was when they should be worrying about how black *they* are.

I thought of all the little white children, the light of their mothers' and fathers' eyes, in Montana, in flat Wyoming, in Idaho, in lakey Michigan; I thought of that "funny" blackness inside of them, a kernel in each little heart put there, somehow, in the night, like a visit from the tooth fairy.

I thought of the layers of lies of the first generation which covered that mystery up, the layers of repressed questions in the second, which decomposed into layers of unconsciousness. Layer after layer, till one day little children walk around with unconsciousness laid over their minds like shrouds, pretty little children in pinafores with a nigger maid who has a funny name. Somewhere babies are popping out of women and no one understands where they come from.

I smile at the little heart of darkness in sixty out of a hundred babies.

The drop of blood that can't lie to statistics, that will be bled out, measured, and put in a crystal tube.

That blood gives those little ones a special light. Wherever I look I see brothers, sisters, who want to break out of their cramped skins, singing with love.

That

Marty said yesterday she was surprised that Pat had called the colony a "white establishment," and said she was uncomfortable with some of the people. Marty hadn't noticed any of "that." Had I noticed any of "that"?

I was on guard. So many times if a black person admits discomfort, the white person then says that the black person must be "sensitive, paranoid"—not responding to the present environment, which is safe and friendly, but responding to something in the past. They want to hear that the white people in this environment (themselves) are fine. It's the black person who is crazy.

I was nervous about continuing the conversation, but, at the same time, I have set myself up as an "expert" by sharing my journal. It's about time I try to handle conversations like this, stop withdrawing in anger and fear, resenting the hot seat. I said to myself, "I'll tell the truth in a way that creates better understanding rather than alienates." So I didn't get my back up or skillfully change the subject, I spoke from myself as if I *am* an expert, I *do* know something she doesn't. I had a certain tone, not a put-down, but a tone of self-confidence. I was proud hearing myself speak. I was humble in not attacking, but I was determined to tell her what I know, to assert my authority.

I said, "It is not something that is done consciously; but most of the white people here have had limited exposure to blacks; there are bound to be great problems in communication. There are some people who hate and fear blacks and don't want to be under the same roof. For example, Jan told me that Sandra said, when she saw no black people in the dining room, 'Good. I'm glad there are no black people. After New York, this is refreshing.' "

Marty said sometimes when she is with black people, she doesn't know what to do; no matter what she does it seems to be the wrong thing.

She told me how she had invited a black woman, a lawyer, over to her house for dinner and during the dinner conversation, the guests at the table started talking about Arabs raising the price of everything in England. Marty said she didn't think they were saying anything racist, and even if they were, what did the Arabs have to do with this black woman? But the woman stood up from the table and said, "I'm sorry, I find this conversation extremely embarrassing." Marty asked me did I think the woman was right to do that?

I told her, "Marty, frequently white people who have been made uncomfortable by something a black person says or does, go to another black person to try to ease the pain, to feel vindicated. First of all, I wasn't there, so I don't know what she responded to. Secondly, there would be no way to find out unless both of you could sit down and really talk to each other."

Marty said, "That will never happen because she has never asked me out, and when I called her she was cold."

"Black people don't like pain either."

I thought of how sad it is, how there are so few true friendships between whites and blacks in which the people are really themselves. Even when white people are trying, they are often operating on stereotypes and, though the black person might want to accept them, the only way to break the stereotypes is to tell the truth, which causes pain. A black person and a white person are not just two individuals who have to decide whether they like each other, but representatives carrying huge expectations, beliefs which they must scale like dangerous mountains trying to reach each other.

Jan's Studio

I visited Jan yesterday. I went there feeling greatly honored that she had asked me, since most artists prize their time alone and don't want to be disturbed. I had just come into her room, sat down on the mattress, received a cup of tea, when she took off Mozart and asked me if I wanted to hear one of her favorite records, a record about the New York prison Attica. The hair on the back of my neck stood up. What connection had she made between me and Attica?

Give her a chance, I thought, calming myself, maybe it's just a coincidence.

It was atrocious. A white band had taken the departing words of a prisoner and repeated them over and over as if we were certain to catch the significance. Atonal music played in the background; everything got louder and crashed to an end.

I sat there embarrassed, feeling the need to receive her gift with enthusiasm. She waited. The only word that came to my mind was "interesting."

After she took the record off, she started flipping through her collection of classical music to find something else especially for me. "I have a record by Paul Robeson. Would you like to hear that?" Oh God, I thought, it wasn't a coincidence!

"No, thank you."

She seemed puzzled and at a loss. Finally, she asked, "There is a picture around here of a black man I liked. I slept with him. Would you like to see that?"

I gaped at her innocent face: Jan, the woman whom I head toward at dinner time because she is not pompous or intimidating, one of the only people here I feel comfortable with.

I told her that just because I am black doesn't mean I am one-dimensional. I told her that I am interested in many things, just as she is. I like classical music and know quite a bit about it. She said, "But my other black friends like it when I play those records." She looked genuinely hurt.

I told her all black people are different. She said, "But I've tried so hard. I'm tired of always trying to please them." She looked at me in anger. I was one more proof of her inadequacy, as if I should have taken whatever was offered and let her feel generous and good.

I left abruptly, sorry for my anger, sorry for what I had learned about her, sorry that she had lost her feeling of closeness, however illusory, to black people—sorry, sorry, sorry—and somehow to blame. I had felt close to her, now I distrusted my instincts, and dreaded a deeper isolation here than ever before.

Jazz

Now that I am the "known" black, everything with a tinge of blackness on it is delivered to me.

Mark, the composer, who has been talking about Mozart at the dinner table for days, comes running up to me this afternoon when he sees me on the path, his face lit like a beacon. He doesn't even bother with a greeting.

"Guess what I've been doing today?" he blurts out.

I can't imagine.

"I've been writing JAZZ," he presents, as if it is a Cartier jewel on a silver platter.

What am I supposed to say? You must be a really nice white guy? Thanks for taking us seriously?

"Good for you," I answer, and walk on as quickly as possible.

Crazy Thoughts

How beautiful the view from my desk of wild flowers through the cathedral window. I watch the lovely black birds. How kind the lunch on my doorstep, the vegetable torte with white cream sauce, the chocolate cake. How pleasing the flower on the table, the yellow Victorian sofa, the barn of colorful chickens. Kind and specific the words in the office, the locks on my doors. I am treated like a queen. But when the lights go off, I face my fears.

Why is my stomach in knots? Why do I fear that during the night I'll be smothered? I think poison gas will come out of the register. I think the people are monsters, not artists, and during the night they will implant a small radio in my brain. How can I think this? Memory of my father being smothered by a pillow my grandmother put over his head when he was three? In the morning I am ashamed.

I try desperately to make friends, hoping I will actually feel that trust that makes the knots in my stomach loosen. I was terrified to come here; I always feel frightened, except when I'm near home. I trust no one—especially not myself.

I try to do my work. This is a perfect environment. No cleaning. No cooking. I needn't even go to get my lunch; it is placed in a basket outside my door by a man on tiptoes. Wood is stacked. I make a fire. I sit in the sun. I want to be grateful. I am grateful. But the sickness of fear backs up in my throat like phlegm.

In the kitchen the cook speaks softly. I want to sit by her all day and stay away from the roads on which I have been hurt by a word. But she is cooking and I don't want to bother her. Please, let me not bother anyone or anything. Let me leave the tub without a hair. Let me not speak to those who turn their bodies slightly away from me. I must notice this.

No one can help. Only I, myself. But how can I let go? My face is a mask, like Uncle Tom's, my heart twisted in rage and fear.

After

After I came back I was sick for several weeks. I felt completely wrung out, run down. I had left smiling, beaming, thanking everyone—the kitchen help, the office help, the yard help, everyone—for their kindness. My friend came to pick me up. The night before we were to drive home, I sat with her in the restaurant—the first black face I had seen in weeks—and, for an instant, I felt my body falling under me, as if I had slipped under the wheels of a train. I had almost made it until the last minute, keeping a stiff upper lip, and here I was, so close to the end, finally about to lose it.

They were so sorry to see me go they offered me a stay of two more weeks. If I stayed I would prove my desperate bravery to myself. But I declined. I was tired of feeling frightened and wanted to go home where I felt safe.

A Jewish activist friend returned from the colony shortly after and asked me to please write a letter telling them how hard it was to be the only black person there. She had found the same token black during her stay. I postponed it and postponed it. I didn't want to do it. I had been a success—I had gone someplace far from home and stayed four weeks without having a nervous breakdown. And they had tried to do everything to please me—cook, clean after me, put wood in my fireplace. I didn't have the heart to tell them I had been miserable and frightened all the time. Besides, I wanted to be a "successful" black person, a person whom they would ask back, a person who would ease the way for other blacks. "See, we're not as bad as you thought."

The day my friend returned from the colony she was full of news about how she had written a letter to the board, sent names and addresses of black artists. The president had talked to her for a half hour about how pleased he was with her efforts. The next day she called me, despondent. Her editor had called her from her large publishing house—they were remaindering her last book. I felt so sorry for her. I told my husband about her efforts at the colony, and how she had come home to this big disappointment. "I'm not surprised," he said. "Somebody from the colony must have gotten to somebody at her publishing house and they iced her." I looked at my husband angrily. "Oh, that's silly," I said. "One has nothing to do with the other." But I felt the ground under me sinking.

A Sistah Outsider

SHAMARA SHANTU RILEY

On and off since the fourth grade, I have recorded my thoughts and daily experiences in a diary or journal. I think my grandmother bought me my first lock-and-key diary at age eight partly to encourage writing skills. At first, my diary only revealed my youthful social activities. But as I grew older and more politically conscious, social issues became infused in my journals.

The inspiration for the title of my selected journal excerpts is from Audre Lorde's Sister Outsider *because the term typifies much of my life. Because of my multifaceted identity as a Black lesbian, I have often simultaneously felt like a "sistah" and yet still an "outsider" in the Black, lesbian, and womanist communities. In this contradictory space of sistah-outsiderhood, I am often expected to negate some component of my identity in the name of "unity" or in order to pass someone's litmus test of acceptance. In order to deal with these conflicts in my life, writing has increasingly become a hobby of mine. Writing gives me some sort of voice to articulate my thoughts about my identity in a world where people constantly try to deny me the right to have my own identity. Writing in my journal is also cathartic because it enables me to survive, to heal many of the wounds that have existed in my life.*

As my journal excerpts reflect, much of my undergraduate social life was spent trying to fit into some crowd to the detriment of my identity. Nevertheless, college, especially my later years, served as the catalyst of my increased consciousness and understanding about my relation to others in the world.

As I reflect on my journal writings throughout my undergraduate years, I think about how much I've grown in my consciousness about the isms affecting not only my life but the lives of others as well. I also think about those who've helped me with this ongoing process of transformation—the women at the YWCA, the writings of various womanists, and my queer friends.

First Year of College

After I graduated from high school, I decided to leave the sheltered, middle-class sanctuary of St. Petersburg, Florida, for Chicago in order to be more independent. Even though I had decided to major in political science back in tenth grade, I still lacked a political consciousness. In my first year at the University of Illinois at Chicago (UIC), I was much more preoccupied with fitting in than about eliminating world oppression.

September 15, 1988

I am finally in college. Today was the first day of classes. College seems so much better than high school. It seems much easier for me to make new friends here in college than it ever was in high school. I guess that's because I live on this floor with about fifty other freshmen who are also trying to fit in. I'm going to try to make a new life for myself here in college. . . .

October 12, 1988

. . . I keep getting these feelings for other females. I kind of have a crush on ———. Am I a lesbian simply because I find her attractive? I still remember how I used to look at other girls in middle school, and I was attracted to ———— in high school. Maybe it's just a phase I'm going through. But are these feelings I keep experiencing even normal? . . .

October 18, 1988
Today I accidentally went to a lecture about homosexuality. I was goofing around in the student union with nothing to do and encountered a large poster with this strange symbol that looked like two stick people joined in hands. When I later asked what the symbol meant, a woman told me that it was the symbol of womanhood and two of those symbols meant lesbianism. The lecture was about this white woman who was trying to gain custody of her disabled lesbian lover, but because lesbianism isn't recognized by law, the disabled woman's family got custody of her. The lecturer discussed how the case involved homophobia. I've never heard of this term before, but it's supposed to mean hatred of people who are gay. I feel sorry for her situation because it doesn't seem fair that she can't see her lover because of who she is. Why should it matter what people do in the privacy of their bedroom? I wonder why Julia and Sherrie looked at me funny when I told them how I had gone to the lecture? . . .

December 1, 1988
. . . My feelings for other women are getting stronger. I'm so confused about my sexual preference because I kind of like guys too. But I think I like women more because they're much easier to talk to and they're more serious about stuff. . . . People are starting to ask me why I'm not dating any guys, so I just make up stuff to change the subject. . . .

May 16, 1989
. . . Marcus asked me to go out with him and I said yes. Everyone else but me knew he liked me, and didn't even tell me. He's an OK-looking guy and isn't nearly as concerned about getting the panties as some of these other UIC guys. Maybe he'll help take my mind off the

funny feelings I keep having. But I don't want to be intimate with him anytime soon. . . .

Sophomore Year

During my sophomore year, I started to have an inkling of race consciousness. I began attending more lectures on Black identity (which always connoted Black heterosexual male identity). I was even active in a campus group called the Black Student Retention Program (BSRP). However, I was still oblivious to a consciousness as a woman and queer. Sophomore year was a year where I continued to privately struggle with the social consequences of being a lesbian.

October 10, 1989

. . . Sherrie finally decided to sit down and talk to me after avoiding me for three days. Ever since I told her that I thought I might be gay, she has been squeamish. I'm not even sure if I am or not. When we talked, she said that she avoided me because when I told her that I liked someone female, she automatically assumed it was her. And to think that our friendship could have been ruined because she assumed wrong! But I hope that this news doesn't jeopardize our friendship. Sherrie's my best friend and she's like the older sister I never had. I don't know what I would do if she decides that she doesn't want to be my friend anymore because of this. Why should it even matter? I'm just like everyone else, except that I might be gay, that's all. I'm not even sure if it was right to tell her. . . .

October 22, 1989

. . . ——— asked me to go out on a date with her this afternoon, but I turned her down. How in the world did she find out about my sexual preference? I do kind of want to get to know her better, but I can't afford to let everyone know my business. I can't jeopardize my hard-built image by dating someone who also goes to UIC. If word gets around about this incident, I don't know what I'll do. . . .

December 13, 1989

. . . I think that I may be bisexual. In some ways, I kind of like guys, and in some ways, I kind of like girls. How does one determine what preference one has? Is it by whom you've dated, slept with, had a serious relationship with, or a combination? I don't know what my preference is. I wonder if anyone else feels the same way. . . .

February 4, 1990

. . . During halftime, the 1990 Homecoming Court all came out onto the court like we did during rehearsal. I was first runner-up. I was so happy that I called my family right after we got off the basketball court. I got a lot of votes from BSRP and Black Students for Communication. I finally feel accepted at UIC, but if people find out about my sexual preference, they won't want to hang with me anymore. . . .

February 8, 1990

. . . Sherrie told me that Brian asked about my sexuality. He asked her why I was never seen with any guys whom I am romantically involved with. Sherrie told me that she lied and told him that I had no boyfriend because I was busy with my studies. She also told me that Shawn was in the room and said that she also thought I was "strange." What do I do now that people are beginning to suspect about me? After all, I am dating ——— and she comes by my dorm room sometimes. . . .

March 10, 1990

. . . Tonight I was walking home from work and these Alphas harassed me in front of my dorm. . . . One of them said "Hey, baby," but I just ignored him. They started making sexual comments about how they wanted to [have sex with] me and make me into a real woman. One of them said, "We don't like dykes around here. All you need is a good man and you'll come around." When I tried to move past them and enter my dorm, they blocked the door. I was so scared and felt so helpless because no one else was around. I didn't know what to do. Then they came away from the door and just started laughing at me. . . .

Junior Year

During my junior year, I transferred to the Urbana-Champaign campus of the University of Illinois. I publicly claimed that I had transferred because the Urbana-Champaign campus had a better political science program and more prestige. However, I now think that I transferred from the Chicago campus partly because of the rumors surrounding my sexuality. Because I pledged a predominantly white sorority, much of my junior year can be characterized as the year of the assimilation approach. Much of the year was spent trying to assimilate into mainstream society with drastic results. In the process, I ended up negating my identity as I sought to fit into my new school. Although I privately realized that I was a lesbian, I still dated men publicly because I saw myself as having an image to uphold as a Greek.

By March 1991, with a women's health conference as the catalyst, I began referring to myself as a womanist and reading womanist books. I had always believed that females should have equal rights to males; however, before the conference, I was part of the "I'm not a feminist, but . . ." group of young women. With this identification as a womanist, I began coming to terms with my Black womanhood as I sought information not only on the legacy of Black women, but on Black people in general.

Working at the Daily Illini (DI) *as a features writer and later as a columnist gradually enabled me to reclaim my own voice since I constantly had to defend my views on a conservative campus. In the end, these experiences made me more willing to speak up for myself and demand—not ask—to be heard.*

August 23, 1990

Today was the first day of classes. I'm glad I transferred from the Chicago campus because I didn't like its commuter-campus flavor. I like this campus much better. Unlike UIC, these surroundings make me feel as though I'm really in college. I will definitely be able to make a new life for myself here and put the past behind me. . . .

August 28, 1990
Today was the day all of the rushees were to pick up our bids at Illini Union. . . . I got a bid from Pi Beta Phi . . . Some Pi Phi seniors picked me up to take me to Sisterhood Night . . . I'm the only black person in my pledge class of forty-eight girls. We hung around the house and took pictures with the actives. I found out that there are 142 of us in all. My new sisters are really nice, although I do wish I weren't the only Black person. . . .

September 15, 1990
Ever since I pledged the Pi Phis, I've been gaining more friends although I now wish that I had decided to live in the dorms instead of an off-campus apartment. However, the Black kids on this campus look at me like I'm some traitor whenever I wear my Pi Phi attire around campus. The Black Greek Council members tease me even more than the independent ones do. They're just jealous because I didn't pledge any of their groups. Already, people have called me "Aunt Jemima" and "wannabee" behind my back. . . .

October 2, 1990
Today Rachel introduced me to this Black guy named Claude during lunch at the house. I guess she invited Claude to come over because she suspected that I wanted to get to know other Blacks in the Greek system. Claude is the Phi Delts' VP and was our sorority's Arrowman last year. We sat in the dining room and talked for a little while, and then he suggested that we go for a walk. Claude said that he wanted to take me out of the house so we could really discuss our experiences in the Greek system. We walked along the Quad and discussed our experiences . . . At least I have someone who I can talk to about being the only black in a white Greek group. . . .

October 11, 1990

... Tonight was our Halloween exchange with the Delta Sigs. I knew I shouldn't have gone; I should have stayed at home. ... By midnight, I couldn't take it anymore and just left the party without saying good-bye to anyone. While I was walking along Armory Drive, Susan and Lesen saw me crying and wanted to know what was wrong. I didn't tell them about how I felt so left out with all of those white people because I didn't want to hurt their feelings. No one in my sorority would understand. I tried to call Claude, but he wasn't home; he must be at some party. I just feel so left out right now; I definitely don't belong in this sorority. ...

November 1, 1990

... Tonight I went to Impromptu at Cochrane's with Claude. I had a really great time. Claude is a really nice guy. We sat in my apartment and talked for a couple of hours. ... While I was looking at Claude, ——— flashed across my mind. I'm just not that interested in having an intimate relationship with a man. ...

November 7, 1990

... Tonight I depledged from Pi Phis. ... I can no longer attempt to be something that I'm not. Who will be my close buddies now? Now that I'm out of the group, my sisters and I will not be as close, if they speak to me at all. And most of the black people on campus seem to hate my guts. ... At least I can still hang with Claude; he's under-standing about my decision. ...

March 21, 1991

Today was the state conference on women's health at Jumer's. Since it was free, I simply went by myself to get more information about health issues. But I learned a lot today. ... There was also a workshop on racism in the health-care system and virtually every woman of color in the room had an experience. I also told about my experiences with racism in the health-care profession when I went to the doctor at UIC that one time. . . . The conference really inspired me to learn more about women and their contributions to America. . . .

April 14, 1991

. . . Tonight was the Betty Friedan lecture in Illini Union. Just as I expected, she was very exclusionary in her speech. . . . She talked about how "our" mothers lived in the suburbs and were housewives before the 1960s women's movement began. . . . If this isn't a typical case of racism and classism in the women's movement, then I don't know what is. At least half of the women of color in the room left by the time she finished because she totally made us feel invisible. . . . I think I'm going to write a staffer's comment in the *DI* about how she basically implied that we made no contributions to the women's movement and how the women's movement must be more inclusive if it is ever to accomplish its goals. . . .

April 28, 1991

Today I found out that I will be one of the *DI*'s columnists next year. Now I will finally be able to speak after people have ignored what I have had to say for so long. Now they will have to listen to what I have to say. . . .

Senior Year

By far in my twenty-one years of living, my senior year in college has been the most challenging and positive. During my senior year, I started to believe that I had value, I had worth. With this increase in self-esteem began my process of coming to terms with my multifaceted identity. I began seeing the interlocking nature of oppression as I started to analyze my internalized racism, sexism, and homophobia.

I also began to realize that I was not simply a passive victim of oppression, but that I could actually help make change and empower myself in the process. I became involved with a campus multicultural women's organization called Women Working for Progress (WWP), I also participated in one of WWP's support groups for Black women, the Womanist Circle.

By reading more about Black women through the Womanist Circle, I also learned more about my life as a Black lesbian. With increased political consciousness, I also realized that lesbianism is more than a bedroom issue and the people usually don't have a problem with queerness when it is kept so privately, but when it is just as out in the open as heterosexuality. A lecture by Kwame Ture served as the catalyst for my coming out on campus while the Second Annual Graduate Conference in Lesbian, Gay and Bisexual Studies, better known as the Queer Conference, served as a catalyst of my learning more about queer history and identity.

September 8, 1991

Today I did an article at work on my experiences as a Black lesbian, but later decided not to print it in the *DI*. So I have to do another one tomorrow. I decided not to have it printed because deep down I still don't have enough courage to come out to seventeen thousand people. I still don't want everyone to know my personal business and I'm afraid of how people will react to me when they read it. . . .

October 17, 1991

Today was the breakfast for Angela Davis to end her visit at the U of I. . . . I am totally in awe of this sister. She commands such a presence. I wish I had that effect on people when I speak. After breakfast, we all sat around and expounded on some of the issues that were touched upon in her lecture yesterday evening. I asked her about how we can deal with many Black women's misconceptions of womanism. . . . After she left to catch her plane, a bunch of us sat around and discussed political issues. While we were on the subject of homophobia, I managed to get enough courage to publicly state I was a lesbian for the first time—and to women who I didn't even know! . . .

October 30, 1991

. . . I've been catching a lot of flak for my article about how there can't be a Supreme Being. One woman wrote me and expressed anger that I would call God "It" instead of "He". . . . I just don't believe God exists. If there is such a thing, then the world wouldn't be in such a bad shape. And if this God is supposedly so good and kind, then how come It allowed slavery to happen? Why are people starving every day? . . .

November 7, 1991

. . . Tonight was the first time I entered Chester Street Bar, although it was so-called straight night. Will I be able to meet other sisters here? C Street is about the only place in the county where I'll have an inkling of a chance of meeting other women, so I hope. . . . I didn't dance with any women because I still haven't told Tahtia, Larry, and Meridee about my real sexual preference. I don't want to lose their friendship. . . .

November 27, 1991

. . . I also lied about my sexuality to Larry when he told me about the rumors floating around after I wrote the article about homophobia in the black community. I told the women at the Y because they looked like they would accept me anyway, but I don't know how Larry would react to it. Sabrina also told me that people have asked her about my sexuality. I purposely wrote the article to make my sexuality ambiguous because I can't deal with rejection right now. . . .

December 21, 1991

Tonight was the first time that I went to C Street on a gay night. . . . I wanted to ask some of the women there to dance, but I was nervous. I've never danced with another woman in public since my past girlfriends were even more closeted than I. While I was there, the question of whether I was nervous to ask other women to dance because of my shyness, fear, or both flashed across my mind. I think it might be a combination of both factors. . . .

December 28, 1991

. . . Today Grandma, Wes, and I were talking at the kitchen table and Grandma mentioned how her Bible study class had an interesting discussion yesterday. When I asked her what the topic had been, she said homosexuality and I immediately froze. While we had different views on the issue, I still tried to portray myself as a hetero who was just expressing a progressive opinion. I kind of wanted to come out to her since we were on the subject, but the "don't mess things up" message constantly came into my head. They've got to suspect by now. . . . I just wish they would just come out and ask me if I'm a lesbian so it would be easier to tell them. . . .

February 7, 1992

. . . Tonight I asked another woman to dance when I went to C Street. . . . I have finally overcome some of my shyness and fear of other people knowing my identity. . . .

February 8, 1992

. . . Tonight while I was at C Street, this guy named John asked me to dance. Because I had nothing better to do, I said OK. While we were dancing, this Black woman passed by and gave him a dirty look. He asked me if I knew her, and I said no. . . . Then he made some comment which I didn't hear because of the loud music. Then he said, "That was just a joke. But I know that you can't be a lesbian." When I told him that I was, he was astonished. "But you don't look like a lesbian, you look good," he said to me. I asked him if he thought that just because I was a lesbian, I had to be ugly too, but he had no response. It's funny how people have all of these stereotypes about lesbians. . . .

February 11, 1992

. . . Tonight was the Kwame Ture speech on Black liberation. Although he made some good points, some of his claims were very flawed. . . . Kwame claimed that because heterosexism was nonexistent in the Black community, homophobia was not an issue that needed to be addressed in the movement. He claimed that homosexuality was "tolerated" in the Black community and there were no incidents of gay-bashing. . . . I was one of the first people to get to the mike and challenge him on his views. When it was my turn, I outed myself in front of all of those people by questioning how he could claim to be for the liberation of all Black people and not even acknowledge heterosexism in the Black community. . . . He challenged me to name one gay-bashing incident in the Black community. When I proceeded to tell him about my experience at UIC, he tried to cut me off. . . . As we went back and forth, Dino tried to cut me off. But I wouldn't let him and basically told him to move aside because I had something to say . . . Now every Black person on campus will know about my sexual orientation, but oh well. I felt like a burden was lifted off my shoulders when I outed myself tonight. . . . My challenge obviously affected him, because he talked about the issue for a long time at the [African-American Cultural House] reception. At the reception, people looked at me funny, but I didn't care. . . . People probably think I'm crazy for daring to challenge the Black power man, but he is not exempt from holding misguided views. . . . I'm proud of myself for standing up to Kwame and Dino tonight. This is the first time I have stood up for myself.

February 23, 1992

. . . Tonight was the Black Women's Achievement Dinner. . . . Camille came up to me to tell me that she supported what I did at the Kwame Ture lecture. I've gotten a lot of support for standing up to him, but I've also gotten a lot of criticism. During dinner, Tahtia told me how she had to defend me several times against people who didn't like what I did. I have gotten flak for having been "disrespectful" to an elder like Ture. But when he dismisses the existence of me and other lesbians and gays in the community, am I just supposed to be silent? . . . The presentations at the dinner really inspired me and made me feel proud to be a Black woman. . . .

March 3, 1992

. . . This evening I read Suzanne Pharr's book in one sitting. . . . This book really has me thinking about how I've internalized negative imagery of myself, how I've been trying to achieve the good lesbian role so people will accept me. . . . We've been very lax at the YW about attacking the isms. . . . I'm going to approach Imani about doing that heterosexism workshop this semester. . . .

March 24, 1992

. . . Tonight Susana, Christy, and I facilitated the first part of the workshop series on heterosexism and homophobia. It went along OK, although we were all very nervous at first. . . . We defined heterosexism and homophobia, and discussed the different ways it manifests itself. . . . We also discussed internalized homophobia. . . . Although I know the language on how to move beyond internalized homophobia, I just wish my personal life would catch up with my politics. Facilitating the workshop made me realize even more how much I've internalized the oppressors' values and how I still have stereotypes of what a lesbian looks like. Ever since I started dating again, I seem to have backslid. . . .

April 4, 1992

Today was the last day of the Queer Conference. . . . I guess the conference was OK overall since I did learn about different people's queer identities. I learned the most from the Black men who presented papers at the conference, and their papers really made me start liking my identity. However, I am disappointed about the fact that not one sister presented a paper at the conference. When I asked some of the coordinators why this was the case, they told me that no Black women sent in an abstract. . . . I'm definitely going to make sure that I send in an abstract for next year's conference so there will be no excuse for this blatant exclusion of our experiences. . . .

April 12, 1992

Today Steve and I were the guests at WBML's show on gays and lesbians in the community. . . . I still didn't like the format of some of the questions, and I told them so. The typical questions like when did we realize that we were gay were on their list. . . . I hate when people try to address our experience without addressing the larger issues that affect that experience. Although the DJs were willing to ask us about racism in our lives, they didn't want to get to the deep issues of how heterosexism affects our lives. And they certainly didn't want to get into the issue of heterosexism within the community because they probably would have to challenge themselves on some of their assumptions. . . .

April 25, 1992

. . . Tonight was Tahtia's Q Sweet Ball in Illini Union. . . . After the ball was over, these Omegas were trying to talk to ——— and me. This one Omega from Nigeria tried to squeeze my phone number from me with these tired-ass pickup lines. . . . He asked me if I had a boyfriend, and my negative response was in such a way that he could tell that I was not the typical female he's encountered. "You've got a girlfriend?" he asked in amazement. I said yes. "Then you're, you're a lesbian? But you don't look like a lesbian," he said. I asked him what he thought a lesbian was supposed to look like, but he couldn't respond. For some reason, I get a pleasure out of messing up hetero men's world who try to stereotype us lesbians. . . . He then proceeded to ask me all of the stereotypical questions I get whenever I tell men about my sexuality. He asked me how lesbians make love, when I realized I was a lesbian, and all of that. When I asked him when he realized that he was heterosexual to show the absurdity of such a question, he was flabbergasted. He then pointed to ——— and asked if she was my girlfriend since we came together. Since ——— was giving me that don't-tell-him look, I lied and said no. I hate having to deny our relationship because ——— is fearful of what people will think of her. . . .

May 3, 1992

. . . Tonight was the Sistah Souljah speech in Krannert Center. Just as I expected, she was tripping hard. Many people left the auditorium, she was so outrageous in her male-identified views. . . . While she was supposedly discussing Black liberation, she made a statement that feminism was only for white women. . . . Then she stated that one of the keys to Black liberation was the family and emphasized the necessity of everyone being in hetero relationships . . . I was so angry that I made sure I was the very first person at the microphone. I didn't even think about the consequences of my coming out to a packed auditorium of two thousand people who wanted to vent their frustrations over the Rodney King verdict on some scapegoat since she had fired everyone up. . . . I told her that as a lesbian and woman-identified woman, she was denying my reality and stated that she was in no way for Black liberation because of her comments. . . . She tried to bust me out and make me look stupid by claiming that what a person did in "his" own bedroom was "his" business and thus didn't need to be spread around. I wanted to tell her that people's problem with homosexuality is when it is out in the same level of visibility as heterosexuality, but she cut me off. . . . She also claimed that she was woman-identified also because she was a woman, which was downright ludicrous. . . . I left Krannert so mad! I am so hurt, I can't believe that my own people rejected me so much. . . . They booed me when I stated my case and cheered as she vented her homophobic outrage at me for daring to challenge her views. . . . Tonight makes me wonder whether I should even bother doing social justice, whether we can have a true movement or just a spectacle. . . .

May 6, 1992

. . . Today ——— and I discussed various social issues. Because she is so apolitical, she rarely wants to discuss such things . . . It was obvious that my challenge for her to analyze how she has internalized heterosexism and images that white is better irritated her. She said that all I see is politics, that I always see things as a Black-and-white issue. But everything is political . . . This is the first time I've had a girlfriend who is overall much more closeted than me, and it's hard to deal with. . . . When will she understand that holding my hand, kissing me publicly is in itself a political act because of the way society is structured? . . .

May 14, 1992

. . . I also found out that I got into the Ph.D. program in political science at the U of I. I got a "minority fellowship." It's funny how with all of the women in grad school, the financial aid is still referred to as a "fellow"ship. And which minority group are they talking about? . . . I have no idea what my Ph.D. thesis will be on, but at least I don't have to decide right now. Maybe I'll just expand on my senior thesis and go into more detail about statehood for D.C. But I kind of want to do something about Black women and their political activism. Who knows? . . .

May 15, 1992

. . . I went to the beauty shop today to get my hair done for graduation. While I was there, I saw Dauri, who was also there to get her hair done for graduation. We talked for a while about our families and I told her how I wanted to come out to my family. She told me that all the coming-out books say to never come out to one's family during a momentous occasion like graduation. She advised me to wait until a regular time to tell them. But when will be the right time to tell my family? Because my family lives so far away, whenever they visit me or I visit them, it will be a momentous occasion. When I told Rhonda about my thinking about telling my family, she told me that they don't need to know anyway, but if I do tell them, I should wait until they ask me. I wonder what I should do? . . .

May 16, 1992

Today was the LAS graduation in Krannert Center. I have the distinction of being the first person in my generation in the family to graduate from college. . . . —————— also came to my graduation and sat right next to my family members. I'm sure they assumed ———— was just a good friend of mine. If they knew the nature of our relationship, I don't know how my family would react. I guess they would be disappointed. I feel kind of guilty about not telling them that I'm a lesbian. Someday I've got to tell them. . . .

As I begin my graduate studies at the University of Illinois, what I've learned the most from my college experiences is that constructing one's decolonized identity is not a one-step but rather a continuous process. The next step in my process of undoing internalized homophobia is to come out to my family in order to remove myself from the mask of half-truths I've told in order to be accepted and keep the peace. In my process of transformation, I've also learned (albeit slowly) that organizing with others is also necessary in order to change these conditions and that a transformation of my individual self alone will not alter the structures of society. I'm trying to challenge others to learn more about themselves and rethink the negative imagery of themselves, to challenge dominant groups on how they negatively relate to others, etc. In the process, I continue to learn more about myself as I continue down the road of self-empowerment.

The Sins of Our Father

DAKOTA WELLS

In the course of a lifetime there are occasional, momentous events which shake our seemingly solid foundations. The following journal entry, written in the form of a letter, is the reconstruction of one such crisis which stimulated a sense of disintegration in the author but developed into an invaluable opportunity for the transformation of her self and her relationships, and a resettling of her own worldview.

November 3, 1990

Dear Lee-ann: When you called me for the first time in November of 1987 it was a crisp and colorful New England autumn, and I was immersed in the wonder of my new baby girl. Forgive me for my hesitation; I didn't even know your name really, so it took a moment. I connected your last name with your mother's and then I realized. You were my sister.

There was an incredible synchronicity in your calling at that particular moment in time. There I was holding Toni in my arms and in my mind the most salient image I had of you, my younger sister, was of a tiny newborn, an infant no one seemed to know anything about after her birth. As we spoke did your mind travel back as well? Did you also think about the circumstances of your birth?

We talked about our children. I told you about my recent adoption of Toni and about my two older children, my son, Che, who was then fourteen and my middle daughter, Nia, who was eleven. I remember you told me about your two sons who were a little younger than my older children but relatively close in age to them. You asked about my brother, Doug, and I appreciated that concern so much. As we spoke, we discovered that we were both divorced and remarried. We seemed to have so much in common. We were both professional women. You'd gotten your master's at Harvard and I had done my psychology internship at Yale. I don't know exactly how we came to talk about our common interest in languages. I could not believe we had both majored in Spanish. But still, I remember stammering, "Incredible! My father, . . . our father speaks four languages; his father spoke eight." I didn't know what to make of it. My mind spun fanciful ideas. Genetics? Spiritual phenomena?

I liked talking to you that day—sitting on the bed in the curtainless guest room looking out at the yellows, oranges and reds. We had a warm conversation; we both seemed so pleased to speak to one another at last and we were clearly so happy that we had so much in common. I remember we talked about meeting someday. If I ever went to Washington or if you ever came to Massachusetts . . . And we said good-bye.

So it began—my newborn relationship with you, a woman I'd never met, a woman who was my sister. Did the fact that your adoptive father had died recently, in some way clear the way for us to make contact? You told me you had grown up as an only child and that your mother wanted you to meet your sister. Were you a lonely child? Did you wish you'd had a sister? You told me about your grandmother and her half-sister who had come to have such a close relationship. Did your telling me that story mean that you wished that for us?

I first heard about you, Lee-ann, more than twenty-five years ago. You were nameless to me then. The year was 1960 and my parents were divorcing. It was an angry, frightening, acrimonious time. My mother was so filled with anxiety and dread that she sought to turn me against my father and to enlist my help in protecting her from him and from the world she would face alone. So I heard about my parents' sex life and about his philandering. I heard much more than I can ever put into words, much more than any child should know. I listened to the story about you, the daughter he'd had by the teenager who had been my baby-sitter, the daughter he had neither seen nor supported. The revelation of this infidelity came only one year after I had met my father's son, Jules, who was conceived out of wedlock many years prior to his marriage to my mother. That had been hard enough to deal with! It had been difficult to imagine the man I knew as the most loving of fathers having forsaken a child to be raised in an orphanage. But a baby, a baby girl conceived while he was married, while I was a baby myself? I was a young girl in 1960. Only sixteen years old and beginning my senior year in high school, I had not yet begun to date and had never even kissed a boy. I understood next to nothing about the nature and politics of male/female sexuality so I'm not sure how I put this all together in my mind then, or how I pushed it out. There was so much to cope with at that time. Who would I live with? How would I finish high school? How could I be safe and secure?

For days after you called, Lee-ann, I vacillated between joy-filled dreams and doubts and fears about the possibilities of sisterhood. My mind and heart were filled with pale, unarticulated anger at my father who had presented me with the responsibilities of yet another sibling and with the tortuous questions which were taking shape in my mind. But I was happy to hear from you. I pushed the disquieting thoughts aside and focused on the positive. I had a sister! I'd always wanted one. Didn't every girl? You had wanted one too you'd told me. You were an only child, and now, for all intents and purposes so was I. As you knew, my younger brother (*our* younger brother), Doug, had been permanently disabled by a head injury eight years before. He's more like my child now. He barely knows me and does not recognize his own children. So I welcomed the idea of having a sister.

When I was a young girl, before I knew anything about you Lee (do you mind if I call you Lee, I've always loved that name) I had worried about what had happened to you. You had been the illegitimate child (how I hate that word now) of a teenage mother. Were you given up for adoption or did your mother keep you? I imagined you as poor and disconsolate in the world without a father. I prayed that you were all right.

Your phone call revealed that you were fine, educated, married and with children of your own. I was relieved. Now. I wondered whether we would look alike? We both loved languages and traveling. What other passions would we share? Remember how you said you'd thought of adopting a child—a girl you said, because you only had boys. Remember my eager response? "Oh, do it!" I'd said. The more in common the better. I imagined that I had finally found the best friend I'd always longed to have. We'd plan trips together —to the theater, to the Vineyard, to inns here and abroad. We'd go shopping together and gossip all day long. I'd send you letters and gifts through the mail and we'd share the books we'd read. When other relationships didn't go well, I'd remember you. I'd know there was someone I could depend on. In all your trials you could depend on me.

But these fantasies drifted away, just as my worries about you had when I was a teenager. You know how life intrudes. In fact, as the weeks went by, forgive me, I didn't think about you very much from day to day. I had a new baby, a relatively new husband, a new house and a new job. Not too much time to think about an unknown sister, although I know the reality of you never left my preconscious mind.

Nine months after your phone call, I went to Washington for a conference. I intended to call you and tell you I was coming, but I guess I was ambivalent. Nervous. So I waited until I got there and I called you from my hotel. A woman answered to say that you were out of town. Could she take a message? Your husband would be in soon. I left my name and number and without asking or being told, I knew it was the maid.

Your husband, Marvin, called me after I was back at home. He sounded friendly, and explained that you, your mother, and the boys were on a cruise in Alaska; he said he'd tell you I'd called. When I didn't hear from you for six months, I wondered if you'd changed your mind and didn't want to go further with our relationship.

When you called the following February to say you would be in New York for a wedding in April and wondered if I could meet you there, I was delighted. I didn't ask why it took so long for you to respond, perhaps you needed time to think things through.

When would we meet exactly? Where? "How about my f . . . , Pa's house?" I volunteered. You said you'd like that. Of course I knew, but I felt so dreadful when you said you had never met him. Remember how you worried about what you would tell the boys? How you tried to decide if you'd bring your mother along? You were so worried for the two months before we met and when we spoke on the phone to make further, more concrete arrangements you shared those fears. Do you remember? I suppose you were seeking some expert advice from your psychologist sister about things you may not have felt comfortable discussing with friends. It was at that time that I began to tell some of my friends about you.

And me? My weight was the first thing that came to mind. I had seen a picture of you, one that your mother had recently sent my father. You were so beautiful, trim, sophisticated looking—every inch the Washingtonian! I had never been slim and there I was then with the ten extra pounds I'd gained after I'd adopted Toni. I tried to laugh at myself. I did laugh at myself in fact. There were so many issues to be concerned about, the secrets, the beginning of a connection with you and, most of all, my feelings about Pa. How to continue to love him in the face of this transgression? What would my mother say about all of this? All these things to be concerned with, and I thought about my weight. Probably safer than thinking about the really big questions!

But I thought of other things too, Lee-ann. I worried. I worried about my mother and how she would feel about this meeting. Would she be angry, jealous? I decided to wait and tell her after I'd met you. At first I didn't worry too much about my children; I'd told them the embarrassing and painful story about their grandfather a short while ago, but, of course as the date got closer I realized that this meeting would make this rather sordid story come alive for them. I thought about my father's house—the place where we would meet. How could I have suggested we meet at Pa's house? Then ninety-two years old, with cataracts, living alone, Pa could not see the decay of my childhood home. He was competent—sharp as a whip. He could overhear anything I tried to whisper in his presence. He cooked for himself, cleaned, washed his own clothes. But still. The cleanest things were covered with a coat of dull gray dinge. Everything else was filthy.

All of these fears, I suspect, were really about whether you would like me. In the face of an actual meeting with you, my concerns sifted to the differences between us. I thought of you as a Black Washingtonian. Your husband was an attorney and you were the director of a major government agency. What did you think about me? What did you know or imagine? I was a former flower child, later a Black power radical, and now a psychology professor, teaching in a nontraditional college and living with my husband and three children next to a sheep farm in western Massachusetts. Although slightly gray and mellowed, I was certainly still far left of where I imagined you to be politically. I wonder now why it never occurred to me to consider that I might not like *you*? But of course I did like you.

When the day arrived, I cooked at home and brought food along. I arrived early and cleaned the dining room as best I could. We used the good dishes from the china closet after I washed them. Of course, you arrived while I was still in my work clothes. Drove up in your top-of-the-line Mercedes, which was equipped with a telephone and who knows what else. You and Marvin were gorgeous, tall and lithe and your sons were wonderfully handsome. Superficial differences, the struggles with my own self-esteem pervaded my mind, but I also saw that you were lovely people who could have been spending a summer day at an airy cape on Martha's Vineyard, so relaxed were you all, so graciously oblivious to the dirt.

Remember how the older kids took off together, to play pool in the basement, to talk and laugh and look at pictures? The rest of us sat around the dining room table, you and Marvin, my husband, David and I, and Pa and Toni. You probably wondered why my first husband was there. He'd come to drop off my two older children, and just stayed for a while. I was grateful. Anxious as hell, I needed the extra support. We ate lunch and tried to make conversation. We tried to find common ground. It was awkward and a little strained, but it was sweet and heartwarming too, this coming together of people who had never met, who wanted now to acknowledge their family ties. We took pictures: Everyone together; the five grandchildren alone; our father with his two daughters. And when it was time to go, I knew you left with a one hundred dollar bill from Pa pressed in your hand. "What should I give her?" Pa had asked me. "I'd like to do something for her; I never have before." We all said good-bye and promised to stay in touch. Perhaps we'd come to visit you in Washington. Perhaps . . .

The next days were hard. My friends were eager to hear about our meeting. All of my woman friends, without exception, had been thrilled when I'd announced I was going to New York to meet a sister whom I had never met before. A sister! "How wonderful!" "How lucky you are!" they'd said, not knowing the whole truth about the shameful roots of this kinship. "She doesn't really care about your father. It's you she wants to meet," they had said. And so on. I'd been awed by the uniformity of my friends' responses. They didn't share my personal history, but as if responding to some archetypal need, they found this story of sisterhood as appealing as I did. Indeed, as appealing as you seemed to. Their responses were entirely different from those of the few men I told. Men seemed to think it was interesting or nice, but they were essentially unmoved. Even my husband asked "Who?" again and again, whenever I mentioned your name. Women, on the other hand, were strangely moved as if some primitive longing had been answered, some primeval void filled. Did you find that too?

I'd been excited about our meeting as well. In retrospect, I was overly romantic, the (re)union was clearly too idealized. Perhaps because of that, for days afterwards I felt inadequate. Less than. Not quite a failure, but an underachiever. You seemed so rich and beautiful, and for some days I ruminated about what I could have had. What I *should* have had. Why, I agonized, had I made the wrong choices?

Meeting you forced me to remember the sense of derailment I had had at the time of my parents' divorce. (What did it stir up in you?) My parents' divorce had shattered my world. The pain of their separation and the subsequent breakup of my entire extended family had prematurely ended my childhood. It had taken away a sense of safety and specialness. Most painful of all, in my father's mind I became fused with my mother. Fused, through a crazy process of projection and distortion, in such a way that I, my mother, and, indeed, all women were defined, by my father, as unfaithful, wanton and betraying.

It had always been assumed I would go to college. There were no questions about how this would be paid for. Though we were certainly not wealthy, both my parents worked and college was not so unaffordable in those days. I would have had a relatively easy time financially; my father had always managed to give me anything I really wanted. In my early childhood I had dreamed of becoming an attorney. It was not a fleshed-out, grounded vision. No one in my family had gone past high school, but one of our family friends was an attorney, a district attorney who was honored and revered in our community and in our home. I was considered bright. I read all the time, was articulate, and perhaps a little sharp tongued. I was not interested in science, nor in teaching, so in our lower-middle-class household that spelled a-t-t-o-r-n-e-y.

The divorce, and my father's rejection of me changed all of that. He refused to pay my tuition unless I lived with him and I couldn't live with him because his anger forced me out. I was a senior in a Catholic high school where the nuns had no sympathy for my plight; they demanded that we pay up or leave. So my mother got a second job—washing toilets. She sat in the basement of Jack Dempsey's Restaurant and handed towels to ladies in the rest room and provided needle and thread and hands to sew torn hems and ripped sleeves. The tuition was paid and I graduated. She worked and I worked, delaying my college entrance so that I could earn enough money to go.

I waited on tables during college and more than a score of years later my almost constantly aching shoulder still carries the strains of that era. I worked my way through college and afterward I became an investigator for the welfare department and then taught in poor ghetto schools. It was during those years that I realized that the rupture of my family had also brought me a gift—perhaps all the more worthwhile because it had been unsought and undesired.

The divorce had generated the gift of empathy and understanding. It forced the racism of my childhood to become painfully apparent. Save for my brother, Doug, I had been the sole Black child in my Roman Catholic elementary school, the only child I knew in my all-white neighborhood whose mother worked. Working outside the home was akin to a mortal sin in the nuns' eyes, for even though our neighborhood was working class, it was also white and thus more caught up in the feminine mystique. Having a second income was the only way my family could have afforded that neighborhood and that school. Later, the combination of being Black and a child of divorcing parents must have marked me in the eyes of the nuns in my high school; they certainly could not help one so sullied. Working my way through college and then teaching and doing welfare work in an inner-city Black and Hispanic community, once again I was the only Black and was thus "privileged" to hear the racism and invectives directed at the students and the welfare recipients.

It took a while but I finally opened my eyes to the racism which had always been directed at me. I joined the movement of the Sixties. Like many others who were fortunate to come of age in that era, I became a militant, both angry and visionary, and later a clinical psychologist with a goal of working with families in community mental health. I became a helper and a change agent, seeking to heal myself and the world around me.

I rethought all my past choices in the wake of meeting you. Did you question yourself or your life-style at all? Only three years younger than I, your experience was different. You'd never even had an afro you told me. When you were still a toddler your mother married a man who was in the military. What was that like? Wasn't the "illegitimate" child supposed to appear hungry and ragged and in need of saving, I wondered. In the stories of yore was not the rightful heir the one who had been privileged and had accomplished? Was it not she (actually he) who could in her (his) beneficence right the wrongs of the past and reinstate the unacknowledged child? I laughed again, this time at the way in which fate had turned tragedy on its head. You were certainly no child to be pitied or rescued. Here you were, a woman who despite the early hardships of her life had come out on top. I laughed at myself and my newly discovered arrogance and wished for noblesse oblige, and I honestly cheered for you, Lee-ann, and for what you had become.

Still, my own sense of myself was shaken. I should have been an attorney or at least married one. How I would love to have a magnificent home and a live-in housekeeper. The ex-radical now liked fine clothes. I could have been elegant and sophisticated like you. I looked at my life as woefully inadequate. Were you shaken at all by meeting me? I remember I stayed inside that self-pity for a while, but being a psychologist I knew that talking about it would help. I spoke to my family and friends about my doubts. I even discussed them with you, remember? Everyone supported me and thankfully a few folks kicked me in the butt. My son assured me "Really, mom you're much prettier than she." (He's prejudiced, of course.) On one occasion, he looked at me in dumbfounded amazement and said "Mom, when did you get to be so materialistic?" (I'd done a good job with him.) Remember when we spoke on the phone after our visit and I said, "You're so beautiful and so rich!" "First of all I'm not that rich," you responded. "And you're the one with the Ph.D." Thank you for that affirmation.

The world turned right side up again when my friend Mary, after attempting to reassure me, asked me straight out why I didn't go make money if that's what I really wanted. "You're an organizational consultant and a good one. You could build that business if you wanted to. Why don't you do it?" There was something in her voice, a kind of confrontation and challenge that made me feel empowered again and helped me to remember that there are always other possibilities. I was still making choices every day. Nothing was set in stone. It would be nice to have more money, but God knows, by any reasonable standard, I have more than enough. I had never wanted making money to be my goal. And I still don't! Mary helped me to see that I was still choosing, based on my values. I felt better about myself. But then, again, there was the more difficult matter —my father.

When I thought about Pa during those months after you and I first met, my thoughts reeled dizzyingly back and forth, in and out of the murky memories and imaginings of the past and the feelings and questions that assaulted me in the present. Each time you and I talked, new information crept in and more questions were raised. What had Pa done? Now as a mother, a woman in her forties, I knew that you had become my sister as the result of an undeniable and terrifying transgression. Now that I had met you, many realities could no longer be denied. Your mother had been fourteen years old when she'd given birth. It could have been me; it could have been my daughter.

But the voice of Daddy's little girl cried, IT COULD NOT HAVE BEEN MY FATHER! *This father* I did not know. There had to be some mistake. I knew my father would never knowingly hurt any-one, especially not a child. He loved children. My daddy's pockets were always full of coins for the taking, candy for the giving. He made magic for children—pulling coins and dollars and lollipops out of their ears. When I was a child, my daddy washed my hands for dinner by slowly soaping them between his own. He warmed my hands on winter days by holding them in his. As I write this now it seems somehow tainted. It never did before. Lee, he sat up with me when I felt ill, held my head while I vomited, told me stories, wonderful stories, of obiyah men and bound coolies and trunks full of silver dollars. He called me Lady Wells and told and retold the story about the time he shook hands with the Duke of York. We spoke Spanish together just the two of us, talking with half-made-up words so that no one else could understand.

I thought of every reason, every excuse. Was this baby-sitter per-haps a troubled teenager, a little too needy, a little too pushy? Was it not just an inappropriate choice of someone who was a little too young? Perhaps my father was lonely, unhappy. I even tried to blame my mother just as I tried to blame yours. Like the young American woman in the film *The Music Box*, who could not accept the possibility that her father might have been a Nazi in his youth, it was incomprehensible to me that my father could have raped a child. (Even now I cannot speak those words and it has taken me several years even to write them on paper.)

Is that what I should call it? Is that what it was? A girl fourteen, a man fifty-two? Any fourteen-year-old child's mother would call this RAPE. I wrestled with these voices. I drew and redrew alternating portraits of my father in my mind. Which voice to hear? Which vision to accept? How to integrate these antithetical perspectives? By slow degrees I was able to discern the convergence. My father's personality was both loving and winning. He had always been a flirtatious man. Women were constantly flattered and praised in the inimical style characteristic of this colonized British West Indian man. No matter their age, their appearance, their marital status, they were always so beautiful, so young, so desirable, or so my father told them. I had always seen these affirmations as innocent, even sweet, gallant and charming. He chose to see it that way too. In fact, I know he still does.

I'm glad you had a talk with Pa about what happened with your mother. You told me he said it was a mistake. He's told me that he thought your mother was older, about sixteen or so. To say it was a mistake was important, but what an understatement! Is it aging memory or denial that obliterates your mother's real age? It clearly escapes him that if she had been sixteen it wouldn't have made a damn bit of difference!

I told you I stopped talking to Pa for awhile. Don't blame yourself. It was not your fault. It was all about the realization of my father's misogyny. I finally saw it, or saw it once again in full and blazing color: how he'd abused my mother, how he'd put me in her place, how he'd spoiled me in the beginning and then cast me aside later. Even now at ninety-four, he has a forty-two-year-old neighbor, a woman whom he says takes better care of him than anyone in the family ever has. According to him, I have always taken my mother's side anyway. I'd even betrayed him when I was a child, he said.

So I didn't call him for months. Of course seeing the pictures of our family "reunion" didn't help. In the pictures where you and I were photographed alone together with Pa, he was leaning away from me, kissing you. The little note he sent thanking me for "getting the family together" helped, but after you'd left he'd said, "Don't worry, she won't take your place." If this was a loving remark, why did I hear it as a threatening statement of his sense of male prerogative and power?

Even though I have ended my silence with him, I am still angry. But how can I consciously express my anger to a ninety-four-year-old man who lives alone facing the daily decline and humiliation of age. I had stepped back from him just a little, I thought, but it was far enough for him to say, "You feel so far away now, just when I need you most."

What guilt this stirs up inside me. I remember the bedtime stories, the seemingly endless gifts, treats and pleasures, the black puppy adorned with the big red ribbon, the one he'd hidden in the barbershop until the birthday moment when he presented it to me. I remember dancing with the best dancer in all the world, my little feet sustained by his bigger ones. I remember the card games, the picnics, the parties.

Now Pa tells me he can't make out a will, because he doesn't know who to leave his money too. What can he be questioning? Who can he be thinking of? You? His neighbor, most likely. I'm embarrassed to admit, even to myself, that I feel entitled to the things he will leave behind. Entitled as his daughter and caretaker over the last twenty or thirty years. Entitled because of the times when during and after his two surgeries I sat by his hospital bed tending to him, negotiating, pleading, and at times threatening the nurses and doctors who seemed to take such little care of this treasure of a man, my father. I loved him despite his blaming of me for the rupture of that marriage, and I continue to love him still, even as I serve as a target in the never-ending conflicts between him and my mother—conflicts that disrupt my life and the lives of my children, even now.

I'm glad you and I have stayed in touch since that first meeting at Pa's. Remember, after that first meeting, how we talked about your son's difficult reaction to the news of a new and different grandfather? Remember how we spoke of my older son's and your younger son's academic struggles? How we struggled to figure out what is happening to our young Black boys? Had we done something wrong? How did this "new, subtle racism" work? If even relatively privileged children like our own had such problems, what would our people's future be? Over and over, in our conversations, our connection as mothers comes to the fore.

Inching along cautiously, we continue to meet and move closer. Remember the wonderful time we had together in Boston? Remember how we talked about our ages and how you tried to erase three years from yours forgetting for a moment that you'd told me your real age before and of course being your sister I'd be able to figure it out. I smiled to myself then, me, the feminist, who would never lie about her age. Of course you couldn't know that since childhood one of the things I'd always said was "No matter what age you *say* you are, you're still the age you are." Don't worry, you're still beautiful and will certainly be at any age.

As I drove home I thought about you and about sisterhood. I thought of my mother, who had been so pleased to hear about my first meeting with you and so genuinely delighted that things had turned out so well for you and your mother. (She mercifully did not reiterate how my father's sin had destroyed their marriage years before it actually ended.) My mother knew all too well that this could have happened to her. I thought about my girlfriends, how I'd come to treasure them over the years. In my youth, like many in my pre–women's liberation generation, I preferred male company. "Men make better friends," I'd said. Girls are so . . ."

But I had gradually been forced to rely on women. At first I clung to men, desperately trying to replace the father who had turned against me because he mistakenly believed I had turned against him. But soon and very soon I realized men often failed to commit themselves and when they did they often left. My first husband had left me with two children, no job and no place to live. After having another relationship with another man who refused to commit, I gathered the strength to move haltingly along. I chose to work at a women's college, to live in a community in which women's presence was strong and central. I knew I had to learn to depend on myself. I thought that being around other women would help. And it did.

When I remarried later, I learned that despite being a wonderful husband in many ways, David often didn't really listen. Too much talking for him. So time and time again I felt alone and had to reach out for my friends/my sisters. Sisters I'd forgotten, sisters I didn't know I had, sisters who were available, because they understood. Little by little I discovered the unparalleled value of women friends. Girlfriends. Fellow mothers. Little old ladies. Together. The special, unique ability to feel and talk and work and share and talk about it all some more. And so I began to work on these relationships and came to love and cherish their uniqueness and their power.

When you entered the picture, Lee, I wanted this "sisterhood" very much, but, of course, it is more complicated than that. In our subsequent meetings we have continued to move closer, in small babysteps. As in the game of our childhood, we have not yet been caught forgetting to say, may I? We have said, not yet, but we have definitely not said no.

You and I have come together in neutral spaces, restaurants, hotel rooms and our father's house. We have not yet revealed our own spaces. We are afraid no doubt. Of having more or having less? Of judging and being judged? Of being envied or distanced and perhaps rejected? Afraid at deeper levels that we will love and be unloved? Afraid that we won't be sisters truly? But perhaps we never are, at least not in that idealized way. Real relationships are infinitely more complex.

Is it too painful to think about the experiences of sexual abuse and rape that we have in common as women? I have my experiences with these. Have you? Certainly there are the joys we share as mothers and as women whose work is meaningful to us. But we have our differences too, don't we? Differences in politics, in style, in interests, in talents. I suppose true sisterhood involves sharing the commonalities and appreciating the differences, if not for ourselves, at least for what they mean to the other. At best our differences enrich us.

You have been a blessing to me, Lee-ann. You reinforced the hard-won conviction that sisterhood is powerful indeed. Sisterhood can overpower the sins of our fathers. Through linking we can reclaim ourselves. We have this possibility, if we choose it.

I, for myself, welcome you as my sister and hope to move closer to you as time goes on. At last the agonizing questions regarding my own self-worth have been pushed aside; pushed aside is the internal jockeying for meaningless position; pushed aside is the wish to trade places which had been fed for a moment by the feeling that my place had been usurped. For this is a story, in part, about my own becoming, about learning to focus on who I am and what I do rather than what I have. After all, it is only I who can write this story in just this way, this story about coming closer to another woman despite the diminution of a relationship with a man, this story about deciding to connect despite the pain of acknowledging and remembering. And it is also a story about love and relationship. For those are truly the only really important things worth striving for. I write because I want us to become close, to make up for lost time. There is something special here Lee-ann!

About the men? I'm still not sure. I am no longer concerned about the will. It is completely unimportant to me to be concerned about men's worldly goods and whether they choose (or choose not) to bestow them upon us.

You seem to have made your peace. I hope I will. For after all, there are our sons to think of, all of our sons. Perhaps Pa's story is an old, old story. Perhaps it belongs to another century, just as he does. At least I hope it will soon become so.

But for right now, I feel that I am defined more by your existence and my relationship to you, than by our father's acts. I hope you feel that too.

Love always,

Your sister Dakota

Oreo Blues

CAROLE STEWART MCDONNELL

It is very hard to be one's self in this world. The cost is heavy: loss of friends, status, livelihood. But to not be one's self is in the long run a lot costlier. I firmly believe that "fitting in" kills people in the long run because in order to fit in they have to deny and kill certain aspects of themselves.

These are the notes I worked from when I was working on my novel, Black Girls Have Always Loved Cowboys (and Other Oreo Blues)*. I like that title. The word "oreo" is beginning to lose its ability to shame me. I grew up with only white, mostly Jewish friends. I'm black, the abused granddaughter of a Methodist minister. I know what it's like not to fit in. I've had it from every side. Jews, Christians. Blacks, whites. Men, women.*

I try to be me. What am I? An Orthodox Jamaican-American woman raised in a Jewish neighborhood and married to an Irish-American son of atheists. I've hidden all my life. Like all black women, I'm a great observer of the games folks play in life. Yet, I am not like all black women. I have been told that often enough. Black women, like all minorities, try to dictate what the right mode of behavior is. It is a habit of minorities to "rein in" other members of the minority. Blacks speak of "not acting black." Jews speak of "not acting like a real Jew." Orthodox Christians speak of "behaving like a Christian." Feminists speak of "being a true woman." Frankly, I'm sick of trying to be what others want me to be. God will defend us to the end to be ourselves because he has made us to be ourselves. God hates falseness.

From elementary school through high school, kids hung out with the same crowd. There was no crossover; there was no moving up; there was no getting "in." If you were a laughingstock in elementary school, there was no chance to emerge from under the shadow of everybody's sneers for the next eight years. You waited silently at home watching for graduation five, four, three, two, one year away. After graduation your life would start.

My sister and I called them the MBKs—the Mean Black Kids. Around six grade, they decided we were the enemy, although we ourselves were also black. We always got As. We spoke too "white." They hounded us up and down the halls of Andries Hudde Junior High School and Midwood High. They beat us up in the girls' bathroom. We were always ten minutes late for our classes, as we always took the circuitous route of avoidance. Up the stairs, around the corner the long way, down the stairs again, class at last.

We pressed into the white world and never looked back. I married an Irish-American artist from California. Sis married a British attaché to the UN. Gentry from Wales.

We didn't fare well with the white kids either. Sis and I stayed at home and watched Masterpiece Theatre and everything else on PBS. We could name every tortured male artist of the Western world and list every scene from "Of Pure Blood" Parts One and Two. We knew the details of the slave trade inside and out. And became addicted to stories of pain and oppression. That's when I fell madly in love with Jesus, the man of sorrows, acquainted with grief.

My white friend Katie says she detests white male arrogance. She finds the strutting of black men "cool." I, on the other hand, dislike black male arrogance. But am absolutely enraptured by white male cockiness. One wonders about stuff like this. Katie is a social worker. I'm a poet. Black male pain just isn't romantic. A Black man in pain on television usually has some tangible or political problem. I've always hated politics.

This morning I heard Bill Moyers on the radio discussing hate crimes. I wonder if I should go on with this catalog. How important are personal crimes in an America faced with white supremacist groups?

When I was young and impressionable, I saw a movie called *Sweet Hostage*. It starred Martin Sheen. He was poetically crazy and crazy in love. He read his sweet hostage poetry and hoped to be her knight-errant. Very Sixties. I've been a fan of Martin's ever since. I blame him. I told my teenage women friends not to go see *The Fisher King*. I wanted to save them before it was too late.

I recently saw the Estevez/Sheen brothers on a TV interview. I wanted to be their sister. Two months ago, JR at the hardware store gave me one of "those" smiles. He has four brothers. I stopped going to the store. I believe we should avoid temptation. God gave us wills. Know thyself, I always say. Know what you have to lose.

I have three brother-in-laws. They wonder about me. The real American family, I've discovered, is profoundly screwed up. Inherited and passed-on generational pain. Something in the genes. Something like original sin, I expect. Dysfunctional relationships dating back to God's rejection of his son, Adam.

I don't know if Americans are basically "prejudiced" or "clannish." All those tired, poor, rejected masses yearning to breathe free coming to the New World to fight life and each other for the American Dream. Love can be eerie with all this baggage.

The only sweet pain is the artistic kind. Don't let anyone fool you. Sweet sorrow is only sweet when we experience it secondhand or in far hindsight.

Brian was Italian, Irish, and Native American. Lonely, new to the neighborhood—his senior year. Not part of a set. He didn't know me from Adam. It was not through jaundiced eyes that he looked at me, but through rose-colored glasses.

Brian always complained of his "neuroses." He was, he said, intensely screwed up. He thought me very pure, good, true, altogether lovely. Now, is that a good idea? The kindest male figure I met while growing up who showed me unconditional love was a neurotic white boy? Did this bode well for my future? I wrote him love poems ("O Brian, what XTC when IUC") daily and slipped them to him while moving through the hallways. He treasured them humbly as if they were diamonds. He was too amazed at my love to be offended or nervous. The dear boy had a gift for taking a crush in stride. I never met his mom, dad, or twin sister. We talked every day on the phone and met at local parks to discuss life. But I never went to his house; his dad hated blacks. I lost him when he went to California to find himself. I wish him well wherever he is.

Paul was Jewish. I nagged him to read the Bible, Old and New Testaments. You've got to be fair, I told him. He hated all Christians because of the Holocaust. We knew each other from elementary, junior high, and high school. He didn't care what other people thought about me. He'd be my friend anyway. He told me once I was very vain. The world did not revolve around me, he said. Sounds shallow now, but it opened up a world of health for me. Paul was the first healthy male friend I had. Kind, wise beyond his years, he pitied me. His was the only boy's house I visited during my teenage years. In some ways, I was his mission field.

My relationship with Douglas intimated horrible things to come. Douglas had long hair and dressed like a rock star. The television! The Sixties time of rock and roll saviors! The long hair that looked like Jesus!

Lon sat me down in the middle of homeroom. He told me he was honored at my attentions but he couldn't love me. He couldn't love me because he was Jewish. And what if he loved me and fell so in love with me he had to marry me? It would be awful for him to wake up and to find no more Jewish people left in the world. He thought I would understand, seeing I was black. It was painfully obvious he had carefully thought about this problem of my long-lived (from fifth grade) crush. It obviously disturbed him to break my heart.

I had four women friends in those days. Beth, Jan, Lisa, and Emily. All white. Three Jewish and one Unitarian. Faithful to me, no matter how odd things got. And things at times got odd. They tried to persuade me to fall for "some black guy, please." But, too late, my fate was already sealed. The black kids had already decided I was not "really black."

Question: Why is blackness defined as a certain urban way of being? Why is it defined as a low grade average? Why do black kids treat smart black kids so badly? I spent six months in sixth grade seriously wondering if I should try to fail. Maybe I could win back my black friends.

Question: Why do black folks habitually begin negative statements with the following: Black men are . . . Black people are . . . We are always defining ourselves. And in front of the kids. One more person who comes to me with a "Black People . . ." comment in front of the kids and I'll hit the roof.

The universe was very perverse to me in high school and junior high. It was uncanny how humiliation tended to seek me out. I was a magnet for embarrassment. This made me realize that evil, personal and malicious, existed. When I tell people I believe in the devil, they think I'm kidding. I get around it by reading them post-Holocaust Jung. That kind of satisfies them, in an intellectual way.

I told my friend Ben—who is white and only falls in love with black women—that I had found stories about black women who were done in by black men, Jewish women who were destroyed by Jewish men, but nothing about black women who are done in by white men. He asked me if there were any books about white men destroyed by black women.

I blame *Imitation of Life* and *Rebel Without a Cause* for certain aspects of my crazy mixed-up love life.

I had a problem with Westerns, though. A kind of love/hate thing. How am I, a black woman in the U.S., to relate to cowboys, the "Great Forbidden"? The object of a cowboy's affections was usually blond, virginal, and sought after. I was virginal but not blond. And I wasn't domestic. I couldn't cook my way out of a tin can. I had no chance of nabbing Gary Cooper. My vagina was not worthy of worship.

Sometimes, there'd be an Indian squaw or a Spanish senorita lingering sadly in the background, pining away, her heart enclosed in a cage of tarnished gold. You knew he'd never love her. He might sleep with her but he'd never fall absolutely in worship with her. Her hair had no sheen and her vagina was not of Puritan stock.

Two days before my graduation, John (white)—one of my chief menacers—came over to me.

"I'm sorry," he said. "We've treated you like shit. I won't be able to live the rest of my life properly if I don't apologize to you. Please forgive me."

What's this, I thought to myself, conversion experience? The next day, Patti came over to my desk for similar absolution. "I'm so sorry," she began. "I just wanted to fit in with everyone else so I was mean to you. So many times, I wanted to tell them not to hurt you but I couldn't bring myself to." I told her I wasn't going to forgive her for being a coward. I hate rationalizations.

Far outshining the usual yearbook doggerels, an eternal gift from Dom glows. "Do me a favor," he wrote under his yearbook photo, "become famous."

Black women have always had a problem with my choice of lovers. Especially the light-skinned ones who were so proud of their tannability. I finally figured it out. It's all right to have white blood in you if your lightness was a consequence of your great-grandmother being raped. But if you chose, actually chose, to sleep with a white man, that wouldn't do.

One black woman (very light and addicted to comparing her skin color to the white priest's tan and to my children's skin) actually said to me, "When I saw you standing over there, I said to myself, 'That woman is married to a white guy.'" A. I must have some kind of permanent mark of Cain that even now isolates me. B. Happily married folks used to warn my husband and me: "Why did you choose each other?" They, however, were always blessing God for "bringing them the perfect mate." God chose for them but Luke and I had simply chosen each other. C. She had rationalized and psychologized away any apparent love she encountered between my husband and me. Moral: Humanity has deeply imbedded in its soul a deep desire to meddle with other people's love affairs.

My female friends from high school and I had guts, loyalty, and a keen, intense dislike of anything "shallow." We called ourselves, the no-clique clique. Later, after college, I called Lisa. We went to a Japanese movie about three sisters. It left us both cold; its message, apparently lost on us. Sometimes things are so well-lit, you can't see. I told her it was she and Emily who had given me my taste for bizarre off-Hollywood movies. She was honored. All in all though, it was a bad day. I couldn't find the self I had to be. I didn't know who or what I was. She thought I was obnoxious, I could tell. That was that. I lost her on the same day I had again found her.

I met Ken after graduation under the local movie theater marquee. *Woodstock*, the movie, was playing. That should've tipped me off. Ken was riding the cosmic rainbow to enlightenment. He took LSD precisely once a month. Only. He could handle it, he said. No mere dabbler, he. This poor guy with half-fried brains was desperately in love with me. My pain exploded unto him. I played on him every dramatic lover-destroying mind-game I'd seen on stage or screen. More than Hamlet psyched out Ophelia I psyched this poor guy out and crushed his heart under my heel. In the movies, cruelty is dramatic and powerful. Real life is different. I still haven't forgiven myself. Never with all the rationalizations in this excuse-seeking world will I forgive myself for my cruelty to Ken.

Orientation week at college. Daniel. Brooding Welsh-Armenian. My type. Free at last from my hometown, I was bold. I leaned against the red, white, and blue metal sculpture in the middle of the campus mall and told him to kiss me. He did.

I also met Neal during orientation week. The oddest relationship of my college years. Neal's nickname among friends was "gay-bait." My bisexual lovers were always checking him out. I was madly in love with him and he was always trying to gently dissuade me. I was always pretending I'd finally gotten over him, that I'd met the man of my dreams. He'd buy this piece of propaganda and calm would reign between us again. Again, we'd be the best of friends. Then he'd meet some guy I was dating and all signs of his former relief would disappear. If the guy was straight, Neal would peg him as a creep and worry about me and tell me to drop the guy. He was always right. If the guy was bisexual, Neal would scram. Sooner or later, the guy would start checking him out. Poor Neal, handsome, gorgeous, whose deepest desire was to be eternally free of my erotic attachment to him, could never resist the urge to protect me from myself. Neal was astute, if homophobic.

He was Jewish, respected the historical Jesus but worshiped Thomas Mann and kept trying to show me what Mann was trying to say. I wasn't about to read *The Magic Mountain* to please anybody.

He was always talking about his Japanese sister-in-law. One year, he fell in love with a beautiful black dance student. He actually fell on the floor at her feet he was so nervous. It made my year. They were my twisted role models, my real life Romeo and Juliet. I could love vicariously.

He often tried to paint me, but—although he was an excellent painter—he couldn't. Artists, he explained, have trouble seeing the features of those they're really close to. That made me immensely happy. I had made it to Neal's mind.

Sometime after I had met Luke, a few months after my college graduation; a year and a half after his graduation, Neal telephoned out of the blue. I told him about Luke. He asked me if Luke loved me. Yes, I said, offended. Of course Luke loves me. Do you think I'm fantasizing this? "Okay, fine," he answered. "Bye, then, see you one of these years. I'm off to California to learn architecture." California swallows all my friends.

There is always so much unsaid in strange middle-of-the-night out-of-the-blue phone calls. A few years later, a different interpretation of that call subtly stole into view. Could it be, I asked myself, child in arms, that in the year after his graduation Neal realized he had fallen in love with me?

Jamie I also met during that first year. He was involved in a cat-and-mouse gay relationship with his roommate. Jamie was profoundly sexually confused. We had as perverse a platonic relationship as could be endured by two people who mean each other well and who never thought of being honest with each other.

Nor was Jamie a happy bisexual. His predicament he lay squarely at the penis of a sicko scoutmaster. I understood, being the victim of a sicko cousin myself. Perhaps, he countered, that's the reason for your white male obsession. I responded that my problem was I'd seen too many paintings of sorrowful WASP Jesuses in my time. He said he understood.

"What would your daddy say?" he once asked me, "if he found out you were going out with a white boy?"

"I don't have a daddy," I answered. "Never did. He divorced my mother and never cared to see how things turned out with us." Jamie was more disturbed by my answer than I was. He thought I was an innocent little wuss, not at all connected to my pain. He looked at me as if I were crazy to be so light-hearted about my father's deserting me. He lightened up after a while and threw one of his many humorous cracks my way, "My dad," he said, bursting out laughing, "would freak if I came home with a white boy."

Once I looked through his window and saw Marie, another black woman kneeling in front of him, rubbing his feet. She seemed so needy, so pliant. I can not describe the look on his face. It was a look of intense spiritual detachment mixed with an urgent oppressive need to have her there.

Once I sat in his room across from Michael, an unbearably flaming gay acquaintance. And very promiscuous. If you were gay and on campus, Michael had slept with you. While awaiting Jamie, Michael gushed about Jamie's auburn pubic hair. Good grief Jamie, I thought to myself. I know you're needy, but Michael? Couldn't you have held back just once?

Once I saw Jamie crossing the mall in the distance. He wore a yellow mid-length raincoat. It hung on him like a little boy. I wanted to cry.

The physical beauty of these men must not be underrated. I am awed by physical beauty. Consequently I have been at times very shallow. But 75 percent of these perfect physical specimens had major screws loose. And these screws inevitably ended up rattling around near their penises. It is excusable and understandable in our culture that a black woman should fall for the supposedly unattainable white male. But why she should pick so many troubled souls is a thorny question.

Once, walking along the campus green, I heard someone call my name. I turned and looked far down the green. I waved back but was uncertain to whom I waved. From far away the waver metamorphosed into four or five different men. Was it Neal? Jamie? Tim? Topher? Tad? Craig? I was profoundly confused. I wondered about myself. It was an epiphany. They all looked like each other and they all looked like Martin Sheen.

I don't know how I feel about need as the springboard of attachment. Nor am I discussing the everyday generic brand of need, the pain in the neck who will not let one go and who is an abyss of complaints. The folks I wonder about have the tragic potentiality of sooner or later falling into alcoholism, or double suicide. Jamie and I were perfect for each other. We just didn't know it. Thank God.

Question: Am I really all that different from the black women I grew up with? They were all married to black men. And spent bitter days talking about their "screwed-up black men." Yet, I think they would have preferred my dating screwed-up black men instead of screwed-up white men.

It is very hard to find dates if you're the only black woman among your set of friends. I once asked myself: If I were the only black person in a college, and a black guy enrolled in the college, was it my racial duty to try my best to go out with him. Was that the right thing to do? Or should I stay celibate all during my college years? I learned the hard truth about this more than once: I am decidedly odd. I still can't handle my hair. I paint and write stories all day. I'm not house-proud. In short, I'm too unconventional for black guys. Most black men can't deal with artistic black women or unconventional black women.

From age ten, I listened to the romantic woes of black women. Battered women, celibate women, "cold" women. Sometimes I saw their creepy ex-lovers, ex-husbands. Self-dramatizing, self-destructive.

They showed me wallets filled with photos of their children; kids they never visit. One man I met had a wallet with fourteen baby photos in it. He was twenty-seven. I didn't know who I respected least: him or the women who had slept with him. I couldn't figure out who I pitied most: the men with no way to prove their manhood but wallet-sized photos or the women—as caught up in their romantic self-destruction as I was.

My relationship with Jamie ended rather abruptly. At a dance he placed his hand on my thigh. I removed it. "No, Jamie," I told him. "I can't sleep with you. I love you too much." Then followed one of his looks and a noncommunicative chuckle. The next day he called me to his side as I stood above the cafeteria hall. We looked down at the feeders below. "You do not love me," he said, "You've been watching too much television. I'm troubled and you're hooked on 'troubled.' I am your mission field. You want me because I am unattainable."

Looking back, I am amazed at my scruples. I wanted to say, "Unattainable? You? Jamie if it breathes and has an ass, you'll sleep with it." I didn't though. Destructive, cut-them-down-to-my-size zingers always come to my brain but they stop at my teeth. It's not in me to hurt my attacker, no matter how tight their grip on my throat. Though black, I am the quintessential American woman.

I resolved at that time to always be myself. I had been a mirror to Jamie for three years. If he wanted me wise, I was wise. If he wanted raucousness, I was raucous. Cynicism? I was cynical. I had thought he wanted chastity. Therefore with him, I had been chaste. All Jamie had wanted was me, whoever that was. I realized the Wrong Me had lost him. From that moment, I decided that if anyone was going to hate me, he or she would have to hate the real me. All the guesswork had made me tired, had made me lose who I was and still hadn't gotten me my man.

Warner, the only black guy I ever was friends with, trembled in my presence. I thought of him as a brother. Notice that I have not mentioned my great absentee good-for-nothing belittling father. I think somewhere I made an inner spiritual vow never to be hurt by black men.

Greg was my randy friend for randy times. We slept together when we had nothing better to do. He was arrogant, handsome, and supremely ingenuous. Everyone said there wasn't much to him. And I pretty much thought the same. He didn't know from taste, nuances, connotations, or mind games. If you needed a dollar, he'd give you three. I could never have fallen in love with him. He was not even remotely complicated or intense.

He arrived at my dorm room one misty moonlit night, tears in his eyes, a can of beer in his hands: Could we sleep together that night? I told him no. I was dating someone (don't exactly remember whom, might have been Topher or John). How was he to know I only had thought of him as a brainless stupid howbeit handsome clod?

He smiled what to me seemed and still seems a sudden smile of recognition, as if in facing me he had just become acquainted with true human evil. This was not the kind of look one expected from a brainless hunk like Greg. The word spilled out of his mouth, forever tainting me, "cockteaser." He punched me in the face two or three times and burst into tears. He punched me in both breasts and gave me such a blow to the stomach I fell against the wall. He pulled me up and with one hand restraining me against the wall, he used the other to unzip his fly. Visions of my sicko uncle rushed to my mind. "Greg," I screamed. "Please, no." He pulled away from me, called me a cockteaser once more and ran off into the night. Three weeks later, they sent him to a mental institution. Moral? Sex is deep bro', even handsome macho brainless white males are affected.

Or maybe this is a better moral, the old cliché. To be man (or woman), is to judge by appearances. Who ever realizes the extent of his or her projections? I, a black woman, victim par excellence had victimized. I had acted as a man, used someone as a mere vessel for my own enjoyment, thought of him as a mere tool, deprived him of a soul. Consumerism is what physical lust is really about.

I dated Topher on and off for three years. His name is used among my friends as a byword for emotional and psychological cruelty. He branded me stupid and never let up. I was the brainless thing he used to "get off."

When I ponder the seven deadly sins, I have a soft spot in my heart for lust. Not the active physical kind. But carnal concupiscence, sensual longing. I can understand judging gluttony. No one should choke down inner pain with food. Tell your pain. And anger, especially righteous, justifiable anger. I can understand God's judging that. Anger, especially righteous anger consumes. One gets so bitter one becomes absolutely useless in life. But sensual longing, the need to be held physically and loved inside and out, why should God judge that?

We all are searching for the hug of God, our ultimate true love. Sometimes we realize this. Usually we forget and fly to weak human hearts, and powerless human beds which cannot heal us. Perhaps that is the sin in lust, the forgetting of God's own beauty and his own ability to comfort.

Once, watching my eyes, Neal saw me worshiping Tad from afar. The next day he introduced me to him. He was handsome and kind, and being shy had no girlfriend. Neal locked the door of Tad's studio, exiting with the line, "You two are perfect for each other." I couldn't stop trembling. My teeth chattered. I perspired till beads of sweat rolled down my arms. "I'm human," he said, and smiled a game smile. Tongue-tied, I got up and left. I avoided his presence from then on. Two years after his graduation, he visited the campus, he waved to me from his place near the campus mall. "Hi, Carole," he shouted. I was floored. I had spoken to him only once but he had entered me into memory.

A cellist from South Carolina, Jeffrey would rise from his seat and remain standing until I sat down. I was tremendously honored. His ancestors I am sure did not rise for black women's femininity. They ignored us as we dusted their silverware and made their beds. His sister came to visit. I told her her brother was a southern gentleman. She chuckled, then added. "A southern gentleman is a man who will sleep with a black woman at night but won't sit on the bus beside her the next morning."

Lately, I'm listening to country and western music. All those cowboys, skinny, romantically oppressed with some intense world sorrow. White poverty, unlike black poverty, is romantic. Dear Lord, obviously I, a black woman in the nineties U.S. am still not sane.

I tell my hubby I find him useful. But he shouldn't worry, although he's useful (like all those polysyllabic words I affect when I go to the tonier parts of town) I really do deep in my heart of hearts love him. He says not to worry. He's sure he uses me too. The man is too understanding for words. I don't remember knowing or meeting any understanding black men when I was growing up. Somewhere along the line, I missed the perfect black male role model. Last night, at church, the minister prayed for me that I should forgive my father. I burst out laughing, "That'll be the day," I said.

John visited his friend twice a month at college. We met at the Halloween party and he seduced me on the dance floor. Assured, he raised his right hands and signaled to his friend. His friend threw him his dorm key. We went to Wally's room and John "worked around" my virginity. He visited two weeks later. And two weeks after that. And again, two weeks after that. And finally, one night, we spent all night making love, my having on the spur of the moment the week earlier tossed away the burden of my virginity. John did not mention my loss one way or another. He gave me his address and telephone number. I tried not to look as if I were in love because I figured men didn't want you to be in love with them. John would sit staring at my face. You think too much, he said once. I'm sorry, I answered. Don't say you're sorry, he answered. I'm sorry, I said. Quit saying you're sorry! Sorry, I said. And realizing what I had said, I said sorry again. He looked at me and shook his head. He hugged me close finally, and wondered aloud what he was going to do with me. I fell in love with him and wrote him some love poems. The next week he visited but did not come to see me. I walked to Wally's room. John was there. When he saw me, he turned to the woman to his right and pulled her onto the floor and climbed on top of her. Wally apologized profusely.

Even now, I waste days wondering what the heck happened. Obviously, it was meant to wound. I have narrowed down the incident to three possible causes. One, I was too romantic: I fell in love and wrote poems, which is a no-no. Two, I played callousness a little too hard and his return to find my virginity gone bothered him more than he let on. Perhaps he was a one-girl guy. Or three, he wanted to rid himself of a nut as quickly as possible.

Do white kids get as many twilight and dawn pep talks as black kids get? My mother used to do this. "This is the way the world is. But you must . . . etc." Why live in a country where a black kid needs a pep talk to go out into the world every day? Good grief!

Bernhard was a monk, a virgin, upper-class Brit. He introduced himself by shouting "Hello, beautiful" to me across the campus center. A black man, a fellow student raped him a few weeks later. He couldn't get over it. He kept getting steadily prejudiced as the year progressed. We ate dinner every night with Eric and Jim. Jim and I were both hopelessly in love with Bernhard. Eric sat among us bemused.

One day, on one of our usual walks, Bernhard sat me down upon a rock. I trembled. I hate it when they sit you down. You know something's coming. "I don't believe," he said to me. "that a white man can fall in love with a black woman. Not in this society. If such a thing happens or seems to happen, it is because the man is obviously working off something against his parents. And that's probably what is happening to me. I think therefore we should no longer see each other because I am feeling very uncomfortable about the way I feel about you." I cried on Eric's shoulder for about a month.

My husband touches me only when he wants to make love or when he is disturbed by the way my dress or eyeshadow hangs on me. He always has to repair me. I know he loves me. He is the kindest of men. I only wish his parents hadn't been so cold in raising their kids. You cry near this family and they think you're odd. I'm usually forgiven for my emotionality. I'm black. Black folks are expected to be more emotional. My sister-in-law, however, is never excused. I warn my husband: "Beware, I might leave you for a 'touchy-feely' kind of guy." He says there aren't any. Not in America. White and black men are not the tactile types.

In my wanderings, I've met all kinds. Men fascinated by my chocolate-brown skin. Men who seemed to have dropped down from Mars and honestly did not seem to realize I was black. Men who held me while their pulse throbbed at the idea of forbidden love. On the whole, it has been a positive set of experiences. I've met men who were less racist toward black men and women than most of the African-Americans I've known. And men who learned all they know about blacks from the *Shaft/Superfly* movies.

When I met Luke, my husband, I knew I was in love. Not lust, not pity, not duty, adoration, or worship. I knew it because Luke had no agenda. (Black women are the absolute victims sometimes of everybody else's agendas. No one wants you to be yourself. Everyone wants you to fit into their plans.) I discovered who I really was. He allowed me to. I was no longer a mirror of anyone else's dynamics. I was no longer burdened by the need to be exactly what the dearly beloved wanted.

A Hair Piece

PAULETTE M. CALDWELL

In 1981, a court determined that the firing of a black woman for wearing her hair in braids at work was not racist or sexist or both. This issue came to public attention again in 1987 when, relying on the 1981 decision, several employers in Washington, D.C., fired black women for the same reason. I tried to comment on this practice relying solely on the language and methodology of legal scholarship, but the structure of legal discourse itself kept eviscerating the power of my own knowledge and experience about the use of interlocking racist and sexist assumptions about black women's physical images to define our economic position in the work force. I turned to my journals to keep me from participating in the trivialization of my own truth.

Initially, while the following journal entries about a black woman's hair and a black woman's place kept me grounded as I negotiated the rift between legal fictions and my own reality, I used them exclusively as solvents for the frequent writing blocks that impeded my "formal" legal writing on the subject of the interactive effects of racism and sexism. I kept the two forms of writing completely separate. Ultimately, however, these journal entries became the core of my legal writing—the principal means by which I attempted to create legal knowledge. They are presented here as they came to me in the first *instance and without the legal analysis that accompanies them elsewhere.*

Rediscovering My Hair

I want to know my hair again, to own it, to delight in it again, to recall my earliest mirrored reflection when there was no beginning and I first knew that the person who laughed at me and cried with me and stuck out her tongue at me was me. I want to know my hair again, the way I knew it before I knew that my hair is me, before I lost the right to me, before I knew that the burden of beauty—or lack of it—for an entire race of people could be tied up with my hair and me.

I want to know my hair again, the way I knew it before I knew Sambo and Dick, Buckwheat and Jane, Prissy and Miz Scarlett. Before I knew that my hair could be wrong—the wrong color, the wrong texture, the wrong amount of curl or straight. Before hot combs and thick grease and smelly-burning lye, all guaranteed to transform me, to silken the coarse, resistent wool that represents me. I want to know once more the time before I denatured, denuded, denigrated, and denied my hair and me, before I knew enough to worry about edges and kitchens and burrows and knots, when I was still a friend of water—the rain's dancing drops of water, a swimming hole's splashing water, a hot, muggy day's misty invisible water, my own salty, sweaty, perspiring water.

When will I cherish my hair again, the way my grandmother cherished it, when fascinated by its beauty, with hands carrying centuries-old secrets of adornment and craftswomanship, she plaited it, twisted it, cornrowed it, finger-curled it, olive-oiled it, on the growing moon cut and shaped it, and wove it like fine strands of gold inlaid with semiprecious stones, coral and ivory, telling with my hair a lost-found story of the people she carried inside her?

Mostly, I want to love my hair the way I loved hers, when as granddaughter among grandsons I stood on a chair in her room—her kitchen-bed-living-dining room—and she let me know her hair, when

I combed and patted it from the crown of her head to the place where her neck folded into her shoulders, caressing steel-gray strands that framed her forehead before falling into the soft, white, cottony temples at the border of her cheekbones.

Cotton. Cotton curled up in soft, fuzzy puffballs around her face. Cotton pulled out and stretched on top of her head into Sunday pompadours. Cotton, like the cotton blooming in August in her tiny cotton field. Cotton, like the cotton that filled the other room in her house—the cotton room—the storehouse for September's harvest, a cradle to shield her pickings from wind and rain, to await baling and ginning and cashing in. Cotton, which along with a cow, a pig and a coop of chickens, allowed her to eke out a husband-dead, children-gone independence in some desolate place, trapped in the bowels of segregation. Here, unheard, unseen, free, she and her beauty and her hair could not be a threat to anyone.

Of Changes and More

1969

A picture of me in the family photograph album, standing in front of the law school, with cap and gown, sad-faced and sullen, displaying none of the joy that should be mine for my achievement. The mortar board sits atop my short-cropped Afro hairstyle, a style that I have adopted since my parents last saw me at Christmas and since I have obtained postgraduate employment that will begin after the bar exam. Since arriving in town for graduation, my mother has spoken of little else: Not only have I disgraced myself by chopping off my long, thick hair, I also intend to aggravate my misdeed through the ludicrous juxtaposition of mortar board and nappy hair. Madame C. J. Walker will surely turn over in her grave. My younger sister has worn an Afro for almost a year, but I would not be expected to stoop so low. I will graduate at the top of my class, receive more honors than I know what to do with, and take a job that will surely bring prestige to my family, my law school, and my race. My hair undoes all of this, recalling for my mother her initial confusion over my decision to study law and now drawing public attention to her obvious failure as a parent for not having impressed upon me the importance of hair as a mechanism for survival. I might as well have had an "illegitimate" child.

Early 1970s

Another picture in the family album. My mother is beaming, smiling across a generation. She is looking down at my nephew, our family's first next-generation child, an out-of-wedlock legitimization of our eternal strength, hope, and survival. My mother is now beautifully Afroed and her smile is filled with pride, love, and understanding.

1985

In a few days I will teach in a four-day workshop for fifty black women. The participants have been chosen primarily because of their status in the corporate world of business and finance. My feelings of performance anxiety seem greatly overshadowed by feelings of happy excitement and expectancy at the prospect of navigating my peers through the murky waters of possibilities and pitfalls for black women in leadership positions. I arrive at the beauty parlor for the grooming of my hair, which, after a year in braids, has grown to my shoulders. Time is short and the hairdresser is late. When she arrives, on impulse, I decide to forgo braids and ask her to apply a chemical straightener to my virgin hair. I return to work a day later and the "significant other" of a male colleague addresses me in that chastising, condescending tone of voice reserved for slaves and women in domestic service: "Every time I see you, you've done something else to your hair!"

Days later I arrive at the workshop site and greet the participants, my hair arranged in a style reminiscent of my former for-profit corporate self. Over the next four days, I am frequently complimented for my competence, unusual insights, and mastery of subject matter, but mostly—especially from those who over the years have watched me alternate between closely-cropped Afros and short, straight bobs —for the beauty of my long, straight hair.

To Choose Myself

Sunday

School is out, my exams are graded, and I have unbraided my hair a few days before my appointment at the beauty parlor to have it braided again. After a year in braids, my hair is healthy again: long and thick and cottony soft. I decide not to french roll it or twist it or pull it into a ponytail or bun or cover it with a scarf. Instead, I comb it out and leave it natural, in a full and big "Angela Davis" afro style. I feel full and big and regal. I walk the three blocks from my apartment to the subway. I see a white male colleague walking in the opposite direction and I wave to him from across the street. He stops, squints his eyes against the glare of the sun and stares, trying to figure out who has greeted him. He recognizes me and starts to cross over to my side of the street. I keep walking, fearing the possibility of his curiosity and needing to be relieved of the strain of explanation.

Monday

My hair is still unbraided, but I blow it out with a hair dryer and pull it back into a ponytail tied at the nape of my neck before I go to the law school. I enter the building and run into four white female colleagues on their way out to a white female lunch. Before I can say hello, one of them blurts out, "It IS weird!" Another drowns out the first: "You look so young, like a teenager!" The third invites me to join them for lunch while the fourth stands silently, observing my hair. I mumble some excuse about lunch and, interject, almost apologetically, that I plan to get my hair braided again, the next day. When I arrive at my office suite and run into the white male I had greeted on Sunday, I realize immediately that he has told the bunch on the way to lunch about our encounter the day before. He mutters something about how different I look today, then asks me whether the day before I had been on my way to a ceremony. He and the others are generally nice colleagues, so I half-smile, but say nothing in response. I feel a lot less full and big and regal.

Tuesday

I walk to the garage under my apartment building, again wearing a big, full "Angela Davis" afro. Another white male colleague passes me by, not recognizing me. I greet him and he smiles broadly saying that he has never seen me look more beautiful. I smile back, continue the chitchat for a moment more and try not to think about whether he is being disingenuous. I slowly get into my car, buckle up, relax, and turn on the radio. It will take me about forty-five minutes to drive uptown to the beauty parlor, park my car, and get something to eat before beginning the long hours of sitting and braiding. I feel good, knowing that the braider will be ecstatic when she sees the results of her healing handiwork. I keep my movements small, easy, and slow, relishing in a rare, short morning of being free.

PART THREE

Meaning and Work

My work kept me alive this past year, my work and the love of women. They are inseparable from each other. In the recognition of the existence of love lies the answer to despair. Work is that recognition given voice and name. **AUDRE LORDE**
January 20, 1980

Consistency. That is what I need to practice on several things. Being consistent with the efforts I make will be what determines the success or failure of what I try to do.

BRENDA FAYE BELL
January 18, 1990

. . . While peering through microfilm in search of Marion Cuthbert and stumbling over many of my sisters and mothers, the likes of Eva D. Bowles, Lucy Slowe, and Juliette Derricotte jump up at me. I only wish that I had twenty arms, fifty pairs of eyes, money and time to reconstruct their stories. [Trying] to tell HAD's story has opened up a window. If only I could fly . . .

PATRICIA BELL-SCOTT
February 15, 1990, morning

I used to write. Before I started talking so much. When I was quietly intense there was power left for focused, forceful writing. When my children were born, having no support systems in place, I suddenly had to become more social, more loquacious.

QUO VADIS GEX-BREAUX
1981–82

Black Woman Artist Becoming

BELL HOOKS

My journal has always been a work space where I think things through, plan, prepare, and dream. Even though I began keeping a journal in girlhood, I saw it even then as a place to record facts and as a place of investigation. All my journals contain the details about what I have been reading and/or studying, how a work affected me. This journal entry, written during my early twenties, like most from that time period, reflects my concern with black female creativity. In those days I was obsessed with the issue of women choosing writing as a career and how that choice would impact on other choices. Re-reading these entries I was amazed that certain assumptions (that I would necessarily have a relationship, or consider being a parent) seemed like such a given then in a way that they do not now.

Reading these thoughts moved me in that I felt in the words such an intensity of thought and reflection, the kind of passion for ideas that I find hard to sustain these days because I am always busy, always writing watching the clock. In those days I took time to contemplate things—to meander all over the place. And it is that serious and sincere mind-set that comes through so clearly in these pieces.

July 30, 1979. Late Saturday night

I sat up reading a biography of Käthe Kollwitz—I am more and more interested in reading about the life stories of women artists. Reading about their lives I learn about their struggles, how they coped with sexist sex-role patterning that makes it difficult for women to motivate ourselves to do art in a serious manner. Somehow it seems cliché given all we know to be true of sexism to wonder why there are not as many women artists visible in the art world as there should be. (I was about to say why there are no "great" women artists—but that term "great," what does it mean?). To me the term "great" means the work of such artists demonstrates profound sensitivity and beauty—and for that reason they have been selected to represent greatest. Ah! but men and only men were doing the selecting.

I feel strongly that one cannot have a family, even a nontraditional one, and be a committed artist without tremendous struggle—a tremendous giving of one's self. I had a discussion with Hannah a couple of weeks ago in which she talked about doing it all, motherhood, work, writing. I believe doing it all, trying to do it all, is a trap women fall into. Why do it all!!!! Then one is running around like a chicken with its head cut off accomplishing things. But what of the quiet moments—the necessary leisure to just experience without structure —Life. If you try to do it all that is gone. Nor do I admire those men, like Rilke, who were able to leave wife, women, children, whenever they felt like it to do art—then return to find them waiting, there to love and give to them. Are we to admire Rilke's commitment to art that was so great he boasts of his inability to attend his daughter's wedding. Well, I say, perhaps he should have been really strong and not had a daughter. A recognition of limits is so much more important than exploiting people. And not just Rilke, not just men, occasionally women do it to. Louise Nevelson also talks of leaving husband, children to pursue Art. I feel as if N. and I have tried in his having a vasectomy to acknowledge our realities as people committed to Art, to writing—to absorbing ourselves in various works. It is not that we would not love children. Certainly, I feel torn. But I am not a romantic.

I know that in life we have to choose if we are not to bring unhappiness to others.

Writing is a lonely process. Writing little poems and stories, however "great" in the anonymity of closed-in rooms, no, that cannot compete with intimacy with humans. It can never be as fulfilling as touching another person, holding them close. But it is a life-affirming energy. Oh me! a necessary energy. I have felt it driving me since I was very young. And the conflict over which world to live in was evident even then. To be outside playing with friends or inside writing and reading. To be clustered with family around the television or upstairs dreaming of words. Perhaps it was the unhappiness of that childhood struggle that has caused me to feel it is better to choose, to accept limits, and live through the pain of choice. And that means choosing to create other forms of human contact and intimacy that become just as significant as the having of one's own children. I believe children bring one into community and connection with others in a way that art does not. You take children to school, meet other parents, especially other women, and share similar concerns. It is a unifying experience. An experience of "togetherness" that is really important to women. It is difficult to know such intimacy when doing art.

Artists approach their work in so many different ways. Some are just driven by the idea of fame, thoughts of money, and greatness. With others the process of making art is a spiritual undertaking, not freely chosen by them, but like a cross taken up, because a higher power called them to art as a vocation. I feel that I am this kind of artist, called to my work by higher powers. And it is so profoundly obvious that there are higher powers in the world than just people, why we alone are very small, very insignificant. It is only that we are present on this earth in such vast numbers that makes us seem important but is that not the very nature of illusions? Even though I accept the call of Art, I know it's harder for women to walk this path and find fulfillment. I want to be fulfilled in life and art. But when I look around me, so many women seem really unhappy with the choices they have made. Sometimes, I do not see any women doing things differently in a way that works, that satisfies, and I need to see this for it to be real.

I know in my heart that it is important for women to see other women doing many things. It gives one a sense of infinite possibilities. Women have not always seen the infinite possibilities, how freeing it is. I feel just now the ability to shake off the depression that for many years has been a burden in my life, weighing me down, and I want to explore every possible path to artistic and personal fulfillment.

Sunday, we went to the Berkeley, to the university museum. I saw a lithograph I liked a great deal. I wish that I knew which would be the better buy—a house or art. I do so love to look at art in the world around me. A few weeks ago, I read an article on the work of Jean Arp. And there was a show of his many pencil and ink drawings. I liked many of them and they were also very inspiring, framed well too. There was one simple outlined sketch of a woman's body that moved me. People were walking around the gallery talking about the fact that the pictures looked so easy (that they could have done them). I know, from my hunger and my endless efforts to produce art that is simple and moving, that it is in fact not easy.

I think that galleries are willing to show work that isn't very good by famous folks. And often this work has no real connection to the more important work. Showing work that is not so good does help us to understand the way an artist develops and matures—where they are coming from. Saw a Miró, de Kooning, Magritte, Bearden—my favorites. I did not like the way the Miró was framed. Framing is so important to the overall impact of a work of art. It can be very revealing the way a piece is framed. I looked up at the museum and saw a painting with a beautiful frame, one that just suited the work. Looking closer I saw that it was done by my artist mentor, Jess. I was so utterly delighted. It was if the feeling of respect and rapport I feel toward him was affirmed by the power of his work in this public space. He impresses me so by his quiet, almost monastic-like, commitment. He is an example to me of the way I would like to be. The picture was another portrait of a woman, Mrs. Sarah Winchester. There was so much junk in the museum posing as art. But isn't that just like life—the false and the real existing side by side. We will never separate the two things. They are infinitely linked.

August 3, 1979

I didn't get much writing done this morning, only a page. It was a very gloomy, dark, damp day. I kept thinking it was a Saturday. It had that Saturday feel. C. came over this morning with her hair grease in the kitchen. And it reminded me of early Saturday mornings back home when Mama would be pressing hair and the smell of the burning hair and hot oil would fill the kitchen. Family, those moments of togetherness, when just doing routine life stuff is fun. I miss so much of the good community feeling that was happening in our house most of the time when we were growing up, the shared cleaning of the house. Well! There are other things I do not miss.

Traded some books and got some interesting stuff—one book on Shaker religion and some writing by nineteenth century white women, Margaret Fuller, Charlotte Perkins Gilman. I made a peach pie, the crust was too soggy. Ironed. I love that feeling—when you are standing up ironing and really doing just that—it gives you such a good down-home feeling of rootedness.

Bought a new art book today. Felt inspired and painted a little. I thought more about the concept of "great" art. Somehow the whole idea of greatness in a capitalist, racist society reeks of competition, of getting to the top by putting down others. I paint a picture. N. says it's already been done by Kandinsky. I remember someone reading my poems for the first time and saying, oh, you've been reading Robert Creely. I had no idea then who Creeley was. But what they were saying to me was that I am not unique, not original. We are so done in by that whole concept of originality. I know that part of the reason I was unable to develop my artistic talent for a long time either as a visual artist or a writer was that I had this deep seated feeling (bred into me by years in academic institutions) that if I am not original, if I am not doing something that has never been done before—then I am not really an artist, only an imitator. I do not agree with this but neither do I agree with the other extreme which argues that everyone is an artist or a poet (the good old myth of democracy strikes again). No! There must be some middle ground between what we consider "good" art and the idea of originality. What if one studies Miró and uses a similar style, because one has similar feelings that are expressed in the same way, and perhaps one comes up with something better; something not so good; or something that just vaguely resembles. Judging the value of artistic expression seems so arbitrary.

I believe in the necessity of standards, but at the same time I feel that the concept of originality has led people to see art as "original" that may simply be only the changing of a form. It is like the ceramic suitcase we saw at the Berkeley museum. It looked exactly like a real-life suitcase, old leather, well carried. So what is that, art or merely part of this quest for the unique sign—the bizarre, that something to capture attention. Or Arp's cutout hole that looks like a doughnut. There is in fact value to be found in forms that are consistent, that may indeed be constant in our imagination, through generations. And it does seem that a real problem of consumer capitalist life is that everything—love, family—everything becomes obsolete, goes out of style very fast.

Swift changes make me sad. It hurts me when people are divorcing and changing partners as though merely changing forms means that things are different, or will be different. I, myself, am a devoted lover of the constant. I love the tree that always remains in front of the house for hundreds of years, until it meets a natural death or is destroyed by haphazard fortune. When I look out at this tree I think this is an image of constancy. It is not that the image gives me a sense of security. It gives a sense that amid the insecurity there is an order that stands firm—that is constant. And it is the whole idea of that, of constancy in the midst of change that I find reassuring.

August 7, 1979
Late nights, reluctant days. Have not made it in here to the typewriter. I have been thinking and talking again about the issue of why there are not many committed women artists who achieve their full potential. Having spent much of the summer reading the life stories of male

artists it appears that one characteristic of their life experiences that is different from biographies of women (and it is so hard to even find the recorded life stories of black women artists) is that they, these men, irrespective of race or class, approach life with a total lack of restraint. It seems that so many female children, from the very onset of our lives, are being taught the subtle art of restraint, limits, how to exist comfortably in small spaces, how to accept confinement, so much so that it becomes a habit of living. Not at all conducive to creative exploration.

Some women like to suggest that it is because men have had wives to care for their daily practical needs that women have been unable to totally commit themselves to art. While I think this helps most men, I do not think it is the decisive factor (let's face it, there are a lot of male artists that aren't into women who make it). I believe there are crucial factors that make it easier for men to realize artistic potential, to fulfill themselves through work; only I have not discovered them all yet. But I am looking. One awareness that comes from my own life experience is that I seem to have a much harder time validating my creative work than males I know—that is, to self-validate. I tend to seek some approval from outside myself. When that approval is not forthcoming I am not so motivated. And yes, to really sustain creative work one must be inwardly motivated. The inner impulse that compells one to create is totally necessary. I have met so many women who have talent but are not motivated. They create, but in a half-assed way. On the other hand I think many of us look at how men create, achieve, and do not like what we see.

Women pay attention to how men live and work. And women pay particular attention to how men who are dedicated artists live. And we rarely like what we see. We do not like the fact that their individual creative work is often deemed more important to them than all else in life—family, children, wife, lover/s, friends, whatever—maybe even more important than their health. Women look at that, and while we admire the steadfast dedication, we get suspicious. We feel the coldness of those "creative" hearts, their indifference to others, and we are afraid to be like them. In fact, even when we overcome our fears we don't want to be like them because they seem to be experiencing life in fragments. They seem to compartmentalize everything in ways that are dangerous. And yet many of us, women, have not found a way to keep alive responsible, loving relationships with others and work in a dedicated manner.

It seems to me that there exists a higher, more life-affirming work order than the one men have established as the norm. I see it as the holistic work order. Using that as the model, one would struggle to attain the discipline and energy necessary to be wholly alive both in art and in other daily experiences. I think that men who give all and everything to art have been pushed to an extreme just as limiting and possibly unsatisfying as women who sacrifice all for home and family or material desires. I think some of that feeling of lack, of an enormous void, that art with all its greatness and wonder could not fulfill has never been acknowledged by most male artists. This recognition comes through in the writings of Van Gogh. Of all the male artists I have read about recently, I think he is one of the most sincere. He does not try to pretend that painting pictures is analogous to women having children. But I do not think that women's ability to have children is better or more fortunate (as Van Gogh suggests—that smacks too much of patronizing sentiment) but simply that the two experiences are not the same. And the lack he felt was surely caused by the terrible one-dimensional nature of his life, the door opening only to one room—the one window in the room, looking out to the same old scenery. At least Van Gogh had the courage to admit that art was not enough, that he wanted and needed something more.

Surely there must be another way. There must be a way that men can create art without exploiting women (who bring them other dimensions of life served on silver platters when they take a break from their "real" work). Women who serve in the roles of mothers, sisters, wives, daughters, or friends. Such men act as though everything that exists apart from art is mere entertainment. Look at Picasso, or Romare Bearden. And there must be a way for women to create Art without having to be cheap imitations of alienated, emotionally retarded men. I suppose that is what we women fear, being so estranged and alienated from Life. I reread Tillie Olsen's *Silences* in which she attempts (makes what I think is a rather feeble attempt) to understand why it is that white women or black people don't write. Her analysis disturbed me because she wants to blame it all on no money and lack of leisure time. But I've seen too many talented women and black men who do not do art even though all the right conditions exist in terms of economic and material comforts. And I think what she leaves unexplored is the question of self-esteem and self-confidence—that feeling that one has something to offer that is worthwhile, that will be acknowledged and affirmed. Since so many men (especially white men) are taught from childhood on that anything they do is potentially important, valuable, they may not consistently ask themselves questions about worth the way women, and many black men do. Like Midas, some men feel that whatever they touch will become gold. And even if it's really dirt, or shit, they see it as important and are able to make other folks see it as important. I know we women artists on the fringe, and especially us black women artists, judge ourselves very harshly sometimes and fear the harsh judgments of others. We want to create only the best. And this longing for excellence torments, sometimes it prevents us from producing anything at all, as nothing we do seems good enough. Oh well, silence and sleep, have to do more typing on the *Ain't I a Woman* manuscript tomorrow.

The House That
Jill Built

RITA DOVE

My first personal writings took the time-honored form of the diary—one of those pink-and-silver, personal, five-year volumes, complete with lock and tiny golden key. I squeezed as much as I could in the fifth of a page allotted per day, mostly commentary on my classmates and complaints about the injustices perpetrated by those bastions of benevolent authority, my parents. The cramped framework of each day's slot inspired me to trenchant—even cryptic—notations, so that today I can barely decipher some of the more important observations. Further complicating this decoding is the fact that, halfway through the second year, I invented a hieroglyphic alphabet in which to write my top-secret memoirs—until I find the key to this alphabet (somewhere among the crumbling cardboard cartons in my parents' attic), those significant pubescent memories are revealed through a glass, darkly.

There is no doubt in my mind that the format of that first diary informed my adult preference for writing within the lucid cage of poetry. And although I no longer keep a dedicated diary or even a journal, my notebooks are fat with interior monologues and musings;

snatches of poetry are interspersed with personal contemplations, newspaper clippings and glued-in wine labels, vocabulary lists and quotations, making these collections genuine "day books," which function as repositories for all that fascinates, appalls, and consoles me as a human being.

Tamarra hunts me down to invite me to lunch. "I'd like to compare our creative processes," she begins. No preamble. Tamarra is a photographer teaching in the School of Art. She also reads voraciously and has required Annie Dillard's *Living by Fiction* in her graduate seminar because she believes art students can learn something about their creative activity by studying other genres. She suggests that we bring our graduate workshops together and see what happens.

Despite my crammed schedule, I agree to an extra evening meeting. This woman's cut-the-crap-let's-get-down-to-the-bones approach appeals to me; it reminds me, here in Arizona, of the East Coast and the edge there that makes intellectual inquiry so urgent. We discuss creativity over soybean burgers and power milkshakes. I had never realized how much serendipity is involved with photography, how the perfect image may please the eye but somehow disappears when it enters the lens; or how the portrait photographer learns to be journalist and counselor, coaxing subjects to reveal their secrets, keeping them at ease while the tripod is set up and rolls of film are changed. All that business in the darkroom seems so much like my process of revision; I wish I could turn on a red light when I'm at work in my study.

I'm sure our classes are getting something from the exchange, but it's patently clear to me that this extra meeting is also a way for us to become better acquainted by watching each other work. The deal is: if we respect each other professionally, perhaps we'll take a stab at becoming friends.

This is my first relationship with a woman that is based on the rules commonly associated with men. Brought together by our jobs, we pool resources, then ideas; later we drag our husbands to each other's houses for dinner, and while the men sit about discussing Reaganomics and pool chemicals, Tamarra and I chew over everything from Jungian symbols in religion to the morality of an artist toward her subject to violent mother-child dreams.

It's a new semester. Tamarra has horned into an impossible agenda, this time with an irresistible long-term project. We agree to meet weekly to explore the connections between image and word. The "Photo Collaborative Facility" at the university is interested in producing a letterpress book of my poems with Tamarra's images, transferred to print by collotype, a nineteenth-century photographic process.

I'm in the middle of a dry period—not a writer's block, just a dearth of creative activity. I've just sent back the first set of proofs for my next book of poems and am awaiting the second set; no wonder I can't write. Maybe this project will give me a push in a new direction . . .

We're determined to make this collaboration unusual, not another look-at-the-pretty-pictures-ignore-the-text-and-put-on-the-coffee-table book. We want to collaborate from the bottom up; we want to make a book grounded on the idea of working together, woman and woman. But how to begin? "We'll just see what happens," Tamarra replies, scribbling a date for next week in her red organizer.

Before Tamarra arrives I am frantically leafing through old notebooks, looking for a clue to—what? I don't know, anything, a thread that links the disparity in the poems of several books, some motif that will leap from the page like a red line of reasoning and make all this eternal fumbling clear. I reread my books—a depressing exercise I recommend to nobody. Why are so many women in my poems standing in rooms or at the threshold to rooms? Why are they so wistful? Why aren't they *doing* anything? Do I live only in my mind? And in the poem "Upon Reading Hölderlin on the Patio with the Aid of a Dictionary" . . . why, at the moment of revelation, do I "step out of my body"? Am I afraid my body will hold me down? And yet I don't feel stapled to the earth; that is, I don't consider gravity consciously, I don't think of it as a grounding.

Tamarra brings two cameras and a plastic bag stuffed with film because, step one, I have agreed to serve as the model in order to better understand a photographer's "field work," as well as experience what it is like to study oneself as a visual object. We are both too tired to look for a common subject; we don't want to go anywhere. We sit down with glasses of iced tea on the patio. "Why not *here*?" Tamarra suggests. I look at our ragtag yard. The scrap-lumber fence, nailed up by the previous owner, is a soft weathered gray; I like the gaps and knotholes but my husband periodically swears and closes them up, furiously nailing more scrap lumber over the slits. The fence is a patchwork of human enterprise.

"Why not?" I nod. As a city girl who can sprint twenty gates through O'Hare but who'd collapse at the mere mention of hiking South Mountain, this suits me just fine. The backyard is as much nature as I can stand. In fact, last summer I spent the first week back from Europe waking up at 5 A.M., wired up with no place to go; so I'd take a chaise longue out to the side yard to "commune with nature," but, between the bees and the distant drone of the cheese factory five blocks away, I never lasted more than thirty minutes.

We troop into the side yard and Tamarra shoots a roll of warm-up poses which I call "Ruminating Author Gazes Off into the Distance." The yard's a mess, with Aviva's sun-bleached tricycle shoved against a tree and a burst water hose snaking through overgrown weeds. Tamarra exclaims over textures and the interplay of light and shadow, but I'm acutely self-conscious—what if these shots actually appear somewhere? Then I hear a rustle of paper, a squeal coming around the corner of the house, and I stiffen instinctively, not daring to look at Aviva rushing into the photo session with her crayon masterpieces.

"That was terrific!" Tamarra says later. We've switched to beer. "Just as Aviva came around the corner your body got tense, but your eyes were still trying to hold the horizon. And that tricycle and the holes in the fence . . . perfect!"

I was afraid she'd say something like that.

Tamarra brings the contact sheets. God, the lawn mower was showing! I'm mortified. But even on the contact print I can see that the composition is interesting, the stiffness in my pose weirdly appropriate to the shabby domesticity.

She's also brought along several quilts. I don't own a quilt; my grandmother was the last member of our family to make them and the last quilt, faded and worn through, is in my mother's cedar closet. I can't wait to lie on these and suggest spreading them under the serrated shadows of the dwarf palm tree.

"I've got an idea you won't like," Tamarra says, spreading the quilt between the palm and plate-glass window. "I'd like to photograph you both—you and Aviva—nude. You know, a kind of a variation on the Madonna and Child stuff."

Oh, dear, here we go. I think of Vanessa Williams and the Mormons in the neighboring town who watch the university for "signs of immorality." I remember my father forbidding us to read *National Geographic*—not because there were photographs of naked women, but because the only naked women were dark-skinned; evidently Third World nudity did not offend Western sensibilities.

"All right—but only if nothing shows."

Nude in the backyard in the middle of the day! What a luxury! The only time I'd been nude outdoors (not counting beaches in Yugoslavia and northern Germany, where it's common) was one summer night when I sprang out of bed to hang up the laundry I'd forgotten. It was delicious, standing under the paloverde tree with nothing between my skin and the stars but the desert air. I dallied until footsteps from the alley sent me scurrying back inside.

Tamarra offers Aviva a quarter if she'll stay still, and like an exemplary capitalist she curls into the most provocative infant positions. Where'd she learn to do that? I find myself relaxing in spite of Tamarra's chatter (which is meant to relax me). When was the last time I spent hours doing nothing? During breast-feeding maybe, when there was a legitimate excuse for lying down to float for a while . . .

That night I study the contact sheets. The lawn mower *did* look kinda good where it stood. In fact, if I considered the scene objectively, the disorder of the yard had a beauty of its own. A beautiful lawn mower? What an outrageous idea! But why not? In a notebook I scribble:

> From the beautiful lawn mower
> float curls of evaporated gasoline;
> the hinged ax of the butterfly pauses.

On second thought, I transfer the lines to a clean sheet of notebook paper, about five lines down: they belong to the middle of a poem; somehow I know this. Then I slip the piece of paper into a green plastic folder and put the folder back in the drawer.

For years I thought the only "proper" way to write was to start a poem and plug away at it until it was done—sort of like finishing all the food on your plate at dinner. I worried my poems like a dog does a bone. Then, one afternoon about seven years ago, I was wandering through a stationery store in West Berlin. (Like many writers on the eternal search for the Perfect Writing Implement, I haunt stationery stores.) I discovered an array of plastic folders, closed on two sides, that came in clear red and purple and yellow and blue. I bought the entire rainbow. And suddenly everything changed. If a poem I was working on eluded completion, I'd slip the pages into one of the colored folders. Instead of producing whole poems I began to collect fragments and let them grow in the dark. This way I could work on several poems at once; some, of course, were doomed to remain fragments, and some would complete themselves within a month or ten weeks or two years. Now when I sit down to write, I first spread out the folders, choose the color that suits my "mood," and leaf through it until something strikes me. I'll work on that fragment until I get stuck, and then I'll go on to another poem in that folder, or switch colors. After weeks of fiddling I often complete two or three poems on the same day.

I like to compare this process to the housewife who can prepare a four-course dinner on two burners while changing the baby's diaper, smearing a peanut-butter sandwich for her five-year-old, and setting the table. Or it is like the hostess who balances the shyness of one guest with the drunkenness of another while passing the canapés. After all, the skill of juggling has been required of women for centuries; women were raised to please others, to put their demands on the back burner instead of wrestling their desires to the ground.

After a longer hesitation, I pull out the red folder (the one I secretly call *The Hot Line*) and leaf through the contents: angry poems, war poems, fragments petering off in despair or choking on bile. But nothing already written in this folder touches the niggling patch of anxiety that has been with me since . . . well, since the afternoon. Something about the way Aviva had stretched out, comfortable in her nakedness, while I hunched over her, fighting the memory of my first *National Geographic*: the shame I felt at witnessing this full-color delectation of "the exotic," the rage as I understood how erotic fascination could replace any liberal call for empathy and acceptance of the other.

Altogether too hot to handle. I put the folder back in the drawer, but even then I knew I would have to bring it out again—although it would take half a year before the photograph was made that spawned "Genetic Expedition," a poem Tamarra praises for getting down to the "nitty-gritty."

All winter Tamarra and I work like maniacs. I finish the poem with the lawn mower and call it "The Other Side of the House," Tamarra pulls two achingly beautiful prints from the Madonna on the Quilt series. For those photos I write "Pastoral," a poem on breast-feeding. Tamarra comes by when I'm not home so that she can convince Aviva to be photographed in a swimsuit holding a dead grasshopper in her palm. She makes another appointment to photograph the yard "naked," without people—the empty hammock, the broken rocking horse. I see the contact sheets and write a poem about dolls instead, which sends Tamarra out to the yard to fling several of Aviva's dolls in various positions of abandon on the (still unmown) grass. I write the rocking horse poem. And so on, into the spring, squeezed between workshops and job-search committees.

All spring semester the graduates of the Gynocritics class stop by for critiques of new poems. Many of them are floundering, hurt by the lack of response their work receives in other workshops. In general their new poems are not as polished as their former work, thus susceptible to the standard artillery of peer critique—economy of words, objectivity, specificity of image—and yet on the whole these new poems are more interesting, more connected. How to tell them this without making them combative? "My body needs air," one student writes, and it is so perfect, this line, that it alone is worth a semester's agony.

West Berlin, September

My dear Tamarra,
Is there life after a Pulitzer? Well, yes, there is—a glittery, breathtaking-in-flashes life; but the inner state is fraught with dread, anxiety, and a terrifying emptiness. Even lassitude. (Because you're an Easterner, I know when I complain like this that you won't take it as an international emergency.) I suppose I was asked the question "Are you afraid that getting the Pulitzer (at such a young age!) will affect the way you write from now on?" a few too many times. It is damn hard to face the blank page (or even one that's been scribbled on), especially when people expect you to. If it hadn't been for your insistence, dear lady, the Aviva series would have never been completed, I would have written no poems worth publishing since that bloody prize, and then where would I be now? I thank you. And I miss you.

But sabbaticals were made in heaven. Now we're in Berlin for three weeks. We've installed Aviva in a wonderfully chaotic *Kinderladen*. (At first she thought we were going to trade her in at the "Kid's Store"; we explained that "Kinderladen" stood for day-care center.) We drop her off at ten every morning, then walk to a friend's architect's office, where we work in two unoccupied rooms overlooking Kurfürstendamm. With free time until 3 P.M. and nothing to distract us, we're forced to write. (Why is what one longs to do such a torture when one "has to" do it?) After writing like crazy for the first three days, I hit a snag and all the self-doubts crept back—no, swooped in—and I spent a sour afternoon storming up and down Kurfürstendamm, blazing into boutiques and trying on clothes I had no intention of buying. Then that evening, Fred in his infinite wisdom began joking about Rilke and the Sonnets to Orpheus, suggesting that I write Sonnets to Diana. "Not to Diana, but to Demeter," I replied, and this morning I dashed down the beginnings to five sonnets (would you have believed that I'd ever write *sonnets*!?), and they're about missing periods and trying to lose weight and all that nitty-gritty stuff. So it goes—

Diary entry:

What happens when a writer doesn't want to write anymore? When the progression of fingers across the keyboard is like an old dry horse hitched to the millstone, blinders and yoke lashed, the only path between day and nightfall one's own scoured rut of circling footsteps? This is of no use to anyone, if anything is of use, if utility is to be more than what one suspects it is—the plank across the mudhole.

The sonnets are stalled. I've become self-conscious; after all, how far can a Greek goddess lead a Black poet? It's an old stumbling block: I'll be lost in the luxurious foliage of Western civilization when a passage from *Lady Chatterley's Lover* will bring me up short—"never a woman who'd really 'come' naturally with a man: except black women, and somehow, well, we're white men: and they're a bit like mud"—with the brutal reminder that the culture I was feeding on had no interest in nourishing me.

The only useful method I've found to combat this is to insist upon inclusion; in other words, to rewrite the tradition. If, as a woman, I can connect with the Demeter-Kore myth but still feel something is missing, it's my task to find the missing link or, failing that, to invent it. I scour the bookstores in West Berlin until I find her, the other Demeter. Her name is Isis, Queen of Egypt.

BACK HOME in Arizona—the telephone ringing, ringing, everybody wants a reading and I feel like a fraud. Why? Because I haven't written enough, not six months' worth at any rate. (And what is six months' worth of poetry?) Besides, I still have half of a sabbatical left and this is the half the writing is supposed to "happen" in.

But there's our daughter's fifth birthday to plan: She wants a Siamese cat on the one hand and a "princess dress" on the other. I recognize the influence of Disney videos (in this case, *The Lady and the Tramp* and *Cinderella*) but say nothing. Instead, I spend an afternoon in the fabric shop, choosing the sturdiest pink lace for the skirt and white pique for the bodice; then I stop by the public library for a book on how to sew lace.

"You're out of your mind," my husband says late that evening, watching me on hands and knees, scissoring along the pattern pieces spread over the living-room floor. "What are you wasting your time for? You should be writing."

"This is fun," I answer, checking the carpet for stray straight pins. "Besides, I always make her a new dress for her birthday."

"But lace? Come on, Rita; she's turning five. Thirty minutes in that concoction and it'll be in shreds."

"So what? At least she's had the dress she wanted. And she won't have to stand around like a porcelain doll, afraid to sit down because the organdy petticoat will prick her legs." I make a mental note to cover all the exposed seams with bias tape.

He shrugs, turns back to *PC Magazine*. "Do what you want; it's your sabbatical."

"Unfair," I call out. "You have your video equipment, I have sewing." I want to remind him of the long poem I've been working on with sewing as the central metaphor and cite this dress as fieldwork, but decide it might be a tactical error to bring up writing again.

On the night before the birthday the dress is finished. As Aviva tries it on, we approach the pet question. Pets and travel don't mix; doesn't she like visiting Oma in Germany every summer? (Oh, but haven't I held a lifelong grudge against parents who refused to harbor even a single grasshopper after the guinea pig my brother and I caught in the garage died a terrible and obvious death of dehydration? Don't my brother and I argue to this day over whose turn it was to feed him?) After careful consideration, our daughter gives up the idea of a dog or cat and agrees to a turtle and some goldfish. Secretly, we decide on the turtle, with goldfish to come if she proves responsible. Off to the pet store we go the next morning, two intellectuals who don't know that you can't buy turtles in January, even in Arizona. "They're hibernating," the pet shop owner explains, smiling gently at our ignorance. "Come back in March."

So it'll be goldfish. I've never liked goldfish because they turn belly-up-black when they die and are flushed down the toilet. An actress doing a guest appearance at the Freie Volksbuchne in West Berlin once told me how her goldfish froze in his bowl when she had left the windows open in the middle of winter; then her boyfriend came over and slowly warmed the bowl over the electric burner until the fish swam again. I jotted down the episode in one of my notebooks and was surprised when it emerged two years later in a poem called "Dusting," in which a housewife reminiscing about her courting years remembers coming "home / from a dance, the front door / blown open and the parlor / in snow," and that instinctively "she rushed / the bowl to the stove, watched / as the locket of ice / dissolved and he / swam free." That poem slipped out like the fish, freeing an entire book of poems.

The first time I remember writing in the headlong fashion bespeaking "inspiration," that pure electric streak, was in third or fourth grade. In school we had spelling lessons—those horrible lists of words to memorize week after week, and the boring exercises geared to teach us how to use each word correctly. I would finish the exercises as quickly as possible; then I'd look around for something to occupy myself with until my classmates finished. So I would use that week's work list to write a little story. And every week I'd write another story, and they began to fit together, and before long I couldn't wait for spelling lessons so that I could find out where the words would lead me. Through language an entire world opened up that I hadn't predetermined.

By the end of February the goldfish have become another piece of the furniture. I feel sorry for them; we pay them such scant attention. They remind me of the urgings circling inside me, urgings occasionally nosing the surface, hungry and mute. During the course of a day we throw a few flakes onto the quivering membrane and hope they will filter down: notebooks clogged with scattered lines and grocery lists, notebooks thrown away in fury when the child finds them and, delightedly imitating Mommy, scribbles them full. Poems squeezed into a bright afternoon when she goes to the home of a classmate, silent thanks to that other mother. And of course, the reciprocal gesture, inviting one of her playmates home, deciding that this madcap visit is the perfect time for writing business letters, since letters can be easily and often interrupted. (They can also turn into computer salad.) Or ironing while making phone calls, so that chores won't cut into writing time, and then having to ask husband or child to massage out the neck-kinks later.

Many of these stratagems are most convenient; but what's insidious in this pattern is the guilt that emerges whenever I need to take a block of prime time for myself: Sit the child in front of two hours of video-taped *Sesame Street*s so that a poem can be written? Guilt. Accept my husband's offer to stay at home while he takes our daughter to Kiwanis Park? Guilt. Hire a baby-sitter so I can write in my office at the university (only on weekends; otherwise students will knock to say: "How lucky to catch you here!")—in other words, farm my baby out? Guilt.

Goldfish, I've heard, will grow to fill the space they are put in. My study is compact, a converted child's bedroom, and the window looks out on the fenced-in yard but at chest level, so that when I sit down at the desk all I can see is the upper lip of the fence and the neighbors' palm tree. I chafe against this impediment even while realizing that most older ranch houses have windows like this. I want a second story, so that I can look down on the neighborhood—not in arrogance, but so that I have a clear and composed view. Of course, I'm lucky to have a room for myself, where no one disturbs the (dis)order of my desk.

For all the years of my self-reflective life, I have hankered for space molded to my liking, searching for rooms to personalize. Even part of a room: a dining-room tabletop polished to a dark sheen upon which to place my writing pad at 6 A.M. before Mom comes downstairs to fix Dad's breakfast, a cheap metal desk painted turquoise to look less sterile. When I was ten, a few months before my first period, I built an entire house in my mind, daydreaming through muggy summer afternoons, arms cocked behind my head on the chenille bedspread. It was a small house, one room fashioned of adobe block I would make myself, hacking clay from our backyard, mixing in water and straw, packing the goop in wooden forms and praying for drought so that they could dry evenly. This dream house would stand in the backyard, away from the house with its clinging odors but close enough to run back . . . just in case. It would be whitewashed inside and out, with no chairs—just a ledge along three walls, spread with thick red rugs and set with white candles, and burning myrrh, and an Aeolian harp singing in the doorway.

That final bastion of childhood lasted just one summer, but I have re-created that room wherever I have resided, Ireland, Oberlin, Berlin, Paris; whether in the bare little side room in Alabama which flooded mornings with filtered light from the pines or the white walls of the upstairs living room at Madison Village, one of a thousand Styrofoam apartment complexes in Arizona. Or the arched alcove in Jerusalem with a view across the Kidron Valley to the gold facade of Mount Zion; or my mellow tangerine-and-cream study in "Old Tempe," in our house made of concrete block.

After about six years in this study I find myself hankering for more space. I am sick of looking at this yard. I remember my resentment of a month back, confined in a motel room without the option of going for a walk after dark, deprived of the luxury of choosing a restaurant and eating alone. Can it be that even as one grows to fit the space one lives in, one cannot grow unless there's space to grow?

FROM THE red notebook:

> Dana has moved into her first house and is painting it white. Only the floors are darker, in deference to practicality; the carpet is a trim

dove gray, the shadow of white. I don't tell Dana about my first dream house. But I wonder—how many women have the dream of both light *and* containment?

March 24

Tamarra and I have a meeting with the printer at 9 A.M. I love the world of the printshop—there is a calm and order, an *adagio* sense of time that permits the appreciation, the *heft*, of each detail—the positioning of a comma, the measured appraisal of every letter and space, the sheer physical investment of setting a page of type. Isn't this how every writer imagines writing, setting down each letter with deliberate care, setting it to last, tamping it in?

The photographs, softened through the collotype process, look as if they had grown into the paper. And my poems are so elegant, so confidently genteel in their beds of Rives Heavyweight Buff, that I am abashed. Did I write these? And the paper so thick, the pages so large!

The director of Pyracantha Press lays out several sample packets of binding materials with exotic names and hair's-breadth variations in color and texture. Then endpapers. Then discussion of price. He suggests a working figure.

"Nobody will buy it for that price!" Tamarra blurts. "We aren't worth . . ." She stops, suddenly aware of the import of what we're both thinking.

"This isn't just another book," he replies. "Tamarra, how much would you charge for a single one of these images? Rita, how much time did you put into each word, each line? There are seven images and seven poems. And they've been set by hand and handprinted on fine paper and the bindings glued by hand and sewn by hand. How long have you worked on this book? How long have we worked on its conception, and now, the book?" Then, very gently: "This book is worth more than you can ever ask for it."

I'M WAITING for the goldfish to die. But they keep on living and growing, not monstrous at all but burgeoning. Aviva continues to ignore them. My husband cleans out the bowl periodically and I find myself sitting by them at odd moments, lost to everything but their silent, open-mouthed appeals. What are they saying? I know I should be writing; but I keep on listening.

Sometimes a Poem is Twenty Years of Memory

CARROLL PARROTT BLUE

Love has a melody and a rhythm for me.
For I am love's song to sing.
I am great and wise.
I purge myself of ill feeling.
I drink deeply of my own well.
I learn to love myself.
For love has a melody and a rhythm for me.
I am love's song to sing.

—VALERIE HARMS AND RHODESSA JONES

I started keeping a diary in elementary school, close to forty years ago. Today, it is called a journal. Sporadically over time, I keep at it. Yet, I don't review it with the regularity that some books advise because I squirm when I read my emotional perceptions of faded events. In spite of the fact that I don't "journal the right way," I find I am getting better over the years. That is, through my writing, I separate my emotions out of events that occur with more objectivity. Inside my journal,

I am my own guide. I am empowered to know that sometimes I can heal myself just by writing to myself about myself as I go through the world. My journal keeps me going to my core; to the heart of my vision, to the beat of my wisdom.

Every so often I face a recurring question: why am I an artist? "Sometimes a Poem Is Twenty Years of Memory" is one of many of my written answers to that question. It is an example of how I use journal writing to relive life's questions and rewrite personal answers. Our stories, our feelings connect us. They are the invisible arms whose silent embrace unite us.

Due to my work, I have had to resign myself to the fact that I move around frequently. Because of this, on many occasions, I feel isolated because I am new—new in a town, new on a job—miles away from friends. Many of the African-American women I meet are like me, very much alone, cut off, underpaid, overworked, often with no public or private confirmation of our worth and value.

During rough times like these, I use my journal to create an especially safe world for myself. Here, on paper, I make my dreams come true. I draw pictures, write poems, press flowers to dry between the leaves, collect postcards of famous Blacks, store cherished letters, and mesh together inspirational sayings like the makeshift poem from the writings of the two women in the epigraph above. I hoard favorite photographs; I shelter old prayers. And I write what lies inside my heart. From this deep well lined with my tattered papers springs the water that quells my empty thirst.

Winter 1967

It's a very cold and gray day at an old deserted train station in Houston, Texas. As I walk down the tracks, in my mind's ear I hear the sounds of a bustling, crowded station twenty years before. How I loved the excitement of my relatives' good-byes as they went to California with the brown paper bags grease-stained from fried chicken and cookies. There was the white, dewy steam with the loud whistle as the train chugged away. My sounds ring in the hollow space as my camera and I dance around this empty, forlorn museum. After work the next night, I print a photograph of a baggage cart in a corner by a huge wooden door. The station's stillness pops out as the developer darkens the silver. I watch my first real photograph appear before me. This picture tells me yes. Yes, I can use the camera to show what I see and what I feel.

January 1970

The rain turns into a storm. I run through the fierce wetness with a large portfolio of my photographs to meet the photography department chair. I've been told that this is the best school to go to and I want my work to make a good impression. I wait in a dank and darkly lit hallway for this man for forty-five minutes. Then I go to the department office and ask the secretary to call him at his home. He vaguely apologizes for forgetting and agrees to meet me in twenty minutes. He arrives thirty minutes later, flips quickly through my hard-won photographs, sighs deeply at the end. He turns at me, quick, blunt and demanding: "Why do you photograph only Black people?" Later, he shows me his prize student's work. It is a group of five separate black-and-white photographs of a couple making love in different positions under a tree. The grass is hand-painted a brilliant green. "See, how important," he says. "It's conceptual."

August 1972

I see the first *Black Photographer's Annual*. Every night I read it over and over again. In the following two volumes, they accept two of my photographs. On my next vacation to New York City, the editors introduce me to Roy DeCarava. Edward Steichen has called this man one of the world's ten best photographers. I am overjoyed. He looks at my work and tells me to go out and photograph a smile.

October 1974

Robert Nakamura shows me *Wataridori: Birds of Passage*, his first film. It is about his father's return from Manzanar, the Japanese detention camp, at the end of World War II. Bob and I met as still photographers. As I look at his beautiful film, I realize that cinema is a way to tell the story of the multicultural experience in America. We sit in silence a long time after the film is over. I am not uncomfortable with the quiet. Very gently, Bob tells me that it is time that I learn film. I am afraid. Financially and emotionally, I feel it is too expensive.

November 1976

I am thirty-three years old, the oldest student in my first film production class. Some young kid who is around twenty and who has made films for eight years is talking about the segue in his music track. "Segue," I think "What the hell is a segue?" I am too ashamed to admit my ignorance. I grit my teeth. I make my first film knowing absolutely nothing. One day, while we shoot a sunrise, from nowhere a bird appears, soaring into the frame as the sunlight flares into its wingspread. In the screening room, I view this spark of magic. It is the first time that film speaks to me directly. It invites me into its world. Technique becomes secondary. I learn that if the story is compelling and the meaning honest, the film just may be encouraged to deliver its magic.

Winter 1979

Barbara McCullough arranges a public screening for the UCLA Black women filmmakers. It is the first time a general public has seen my film, *Varnette's World*. The film shows a young Black woman in a beautiful light and the audience reflects that love back onto the film. They laugh. They clap. I feel what happens when chemistry occurs between an audience and a film. Barbara makes sure we all are paid. She treats us with tremendous respect and I thank her.

January 1981

My Aunt Lillie Bell dies. I see my family at her funeral for the first time since the national airing on PBS of *Varnette's World*. I am now working on the film *On Golden Pond*. This film is the cover story of both *Time* and *Newsweek* magazines. Over the ham, grits and eggs, biscuits and homemade preserves, my cousin from Houston asks me what I am doing. I show her the magazines and tell her I'm working on this film. Sharply, my other cousin from Oakland interrupts . . . "And just what do you DO for a living?" I try to explain independent filmmaking, free-lance work and I talk about being a production assistant in the industry. When I stop talking, the silence weighs long and heavy. Finally, my uncle looks straight up at me, tells me that my cousin Cheryl makes $50,000 a year as a CPA. Following his significantly placed pause, he adds, "And that's GOOD money." Unspoken agreement goes round the table, a silent pact that leaves me feeling devastated and isolated. My relatives. My blood kin who do not understand nor respect what I name as my value. Old and familiar, the pain and the sadness flood over me. This is the battle I expect I may never win. Cultural expression means nothing to my folks unless it is inexplicably tied to financial success.

April 1982

Edith and Brad invite me to photograph the birth of their first child, Aisha. Once the birth starts it goes fast and with power. Edith sings a song she wrote for her daughter as she pushes her out through her legs. The song is about the dawn breaking through the darkness into a new day. When Edith and Brad look at Aisha together for the first time, I photograph my first smile.

July 1985

I am invited to meet Euzhan Palcy at Daphne Muse's in Oakland. I look with admiration at this beautiful, strong young Black woman filmmaker who could well be my daughter. Is it her confidence that creates her beauty? She tells us Robert Redford cried upon seeing *Sugar Cane Alley* at Sundance. Invisible to this group, I turn and in my mind's eye, I see Frances Williams standing behind us. Frances, who met with Eisenstein while touring Russia in the 1930s; the first Black woman to attend USC film school in 1943, the year of my birth. She was a strong force in finishing *Salt of the Earth* in 1952. She now appears on CBS's *Frank's Place* and television commercials to make a living. When Frances sees any of us, her eyes sparkle, jumping out of her old and crippled body. She greets all of us equally, with her "Hello there, my little babies." I meet the courageous eyes of Euzhan and realize now that Frances greets herself in meeting all our eyes. Our heritage makes us a real family.

April 1986

One Saturday afternoon, I browse in a bookstore with nothing particular in mind. A large book, *Viewfinders: Black Women Photographers*, captures my eye. I sit down on one of those squat round stools to read it. Half an hour later, I turn to the last pages to see a list of Black women photographers from 1860 to 1980. One hundred twenty years and one hundred eighteen Black women. I come to my name. Disbelieving, I retrace the list of names with my fingers. Here. Here I am, one of the pioneers. Part of a history. I close my eyes and remember. The slights, the hardships, the rejections. The bits of hope when my art would shine, quick-like to be smashed by long, dry periods of no work and me thinking it's got to be because my work is no good. That day, holding that book, my heart filled up. I sobbed so hard that people turned to watch. So hard that the sales clerk ran over and asked me what was wrong. What was wrong. I was alone and scared in a new town with a new job, constantly broke and remembering too much of the past and worse of all, I was real discouraged. That was close to what was wrong. But here someone had remembered my work and had validated its worth. So I got up. I dried my eyes, sucked back the snot, and wrote a check for the book that I knew would not be covered for ten days, refused a bag, and clutched that book close to my heart all the way home.

January 1987

I grope through the flicking darkness for a seat because I want to hear Valerie Smith lecture on the Black Female Independent Filmmaker at the Whitney Museum. As I sit, Monona Wali's film, *Grey Area*, unfolds before me. Later, Valerie tells us that ten Black women film-makers are represented in this exhibit. Publically, I protest. "But Mon-ona is East Indian," I say. Valerie acknowledges the difficulty of my question. But she also says that Monona says that politically she is Black and Valerie accepts her definition. One Black sister in the front of the audience turns to face me directly and strongly defends Monona's right to call herself Black, adding how important it is for us as Black people to not be so rigid in our definition of what Black really means. An older man behind me loudly agrees with her, saying that it is politically and humanely correct to include all people of op-pression in our analysis. I want to reply with the passion rising inside my breast, but eloquence escapes me and the climate of the audience overwhelms me. And most important, I agree with them. They are right. But, my films were not accepted for this exhibit and this rejection frightens me. To be recognized at the Whitney is important. It means coverage in the *New York Times*, the *Village Voice* and all those jour-nals and magazines that are important to people who sit on juries that hand out money to filmmakers. Recognition at the Whitney would mean that I exist. Many times recognition is translated into money and I am working on two documentaries—a portrait of Ralph Bunche and the history of the Black Woman in America since the seventeenth century—and I need money to see these ideas become films. I am frightened and they are right. Everyone who is "the other"; everyone who is a projection of the shadow side, the puzzle side of humanity is Black. Everyone's birthright is to express her uniqueness. Every lib-erated voice can be a power tearing down the dominance of the white male social structure on our planet.

Relentless and continuous, the tentative and fragile quality of this tightrope walk called my life as a creative Black woman fills me with a fear and a hunger and an anger at the loss of any crumb that escapes my brutally desperate grasp.

Light dims and flickers before my eyes. My mind flashes that my soul possesses an inner capacity to stop my suffering and become a whole and happy person. Vaguely, I realize the soft play of black-and-white light signals a film starting. In the dark, I focus onto a grainy image of an old Black woman moving about in a chalk-white background. Her story begins. I settle back to watch. With my nostrils, I use my breath to feel me inside and out. Just as slowly, I realize I've entered my twentieth year as an artist.

At Yaddo

BARBARA SMITH

The following excerpts were written in the journal I kept during September, October, and November of 1984 while I was at Yaddo, an artists' colony in Saratoga Springs, New York. Yaddo is a former estate with four hundred acres of land, a huge nineteenth-century mansion, and numerous other buildings.

Material in brackets was added for the purposes of publication. The names of fellow Yaddo artists have also been changed. No other editing of the excerpts was done.

9-15-84, 1:30 P.M.

'm sitting at the table in my study. I was thinking when I was eating and watching the rain drop off the eaves of the porch through the square leaded-glass windows, with the pine grove across the path, that this looked like a scene from one of the old movies we used to watch with Aunt LaRue on Saturdays. A rainy Saturday afternoon in Cleveland, watching a movie about people who were struggling with something [while] living in an English mansion. That house with the Steinway baby grand in a corner of the living room is not *the* mansion here, but to my eyes it would qualify. I would imagine there are at least eight bedrooms. There are at least three down here. Maybe when Judith comes we'll go exploring, although I see that it's against the rules to have her come in before 4:00 . . .

9-17-84, 8:11 P.M.

. . . I went to check out the rose garden [at lunchtime] and found it all appalling. The huge marble fountain in front of the mansion, the garden on a non-human forbidding scale. I didn't even try to look at it, just high-tailed it back to the side of the road, always thinking that something might be gaining up on me. At first I thought of our house where we grew up, how Aunt LaRue slept in a tiny room with Mommy Matt on weekends when she brought her home from the nursing home.[1] That the two of them were in there together when Aunt LaRue had the stroke and died. What would they think of this place? It would be on some levels incomprehensible just as it is to me.

9-20-84, 11:17 A.M.

. . . Clearly I haven't made it to Saratoga yet. Instead I went into my study to try to dig out some other writing, stuff about the murders,[2] a story I began but never finished in 1979 that I'd like to finish now. I got caught, found the envelope with the manuscripts I'd submitted with my application here, was pleased to see my disarmament article and read through it, the Zora article, and the *Home Girls* introduction. I'd told Judith that I needed to find a writer who could inspire me, and the best person to do that is myself. I'm always amazed at how much unfinished work I have. False starts? True starts . . .

10-6-84 9:58 A.M.

I'm afraid I'll run out of this little notebook pretty soon. I got a decent night's sleep. Probably still have enough of a cold to need it, although I've managed to have insomnia [even] when I'm ill.

I've stopped thinking as much about certain subjects. Last night I thought about Pat, what happened to her, her being raped—twice. I got paranoid about what I said in my letter [to her] about wondering which parts [of her short story] were made up, hoping she didn't think

I'd forgotten about what happened to her. It's like race in some ways, trying to be so careful all the time.

I was reading some stuff that Dorothy gave me last night. Violence is such a given in their lives, in our lives. Somebody tried to rape Jan just a few months ago [while she was running around Prospect Park]. Beat her up. A Black man. I was thinking how they almost never find grown men naked or attacked, little boys, yes, who they can use like women, but not men . . .

10-7-84, 10:31 A.M.

I slept a lot last night. My right shoulder is killing me. I think the Arthritis Formula Ben-Gay that I got helps. I woke up about 7:00 and read for a little less than hour, *Ironweed*. It's fast reading so I'll get it over with . . .

10-8-84, 2:29 P.M.

. . . I'm trying to get through *Many Voices, One Chant* . . .[3] I read a couple of Langston Hughes stories late last night. Damned good. Craft is exceedingly important. He had it. Both stories were about Black women domestics and very sympathetic. *Ironweed* makes me sick . . .

10-10-84, 11:08 P.M.

What it means to be queer is that when you're watching "Dynasty" on the huge color t.v. at the corner of the bar and Diahann Carroll comes on you say, "I just love her." And the straight white woman you're with says, referring to Billy Dee, "I just love him." You check your response.

At dinner tonight, just four of us, David, Linda, and Betsey, we were talking about comedians we liked. I said that I thought Richard Pryor was still funny after his accident (disagreeing with Betsey), but that he's so sexist he makes you want to die and David looked at me as if I'd just gotten off a space ship from Mars. I mean really stared. Perhaps because he'd never thought of it before.

I gave him the issue of *Radical America* tonight about the Mel King campaign that I started reading again this morning, the most heavily

underlined article being the one about Lesbians and gay men's partic-
ipation in the campaign (which was fascinating). He knew about Mel.
I realize it's a step perhaps in coming out to David. I was going to
give him *Sister Outsider* on Sunday [when we went to the museum in
Albany], but decided not to.[4] It's so f_____ing complicated.

When Betsey and I were driving back tonight she was saying how
David can [really] get into the kinds of dreadful conversations we
usually have at dinner and she said something like he has his "white
side." I disagreed totally. She was quite apologetic. I defended him
and did once before to her, not about race, but countered her saying
he was nervous, or uptight, by saying I thought he was great. The
question is would either one of them defend me if they knew explicitly
that I was a Lesbian?

Betsey also asked to see things I'd written. I told her that I'd decided
not to do that here, because of what happened at Millay with that
b_____ M.N. I felt good that she asked and before she leaves week
after next I'll let her see something.

10-11-84, 8:50 A.M.

. . . I then began to think about the conversation at dinner last night
which Linda initiated about how long we'd had certain friends. Everybody except for me had friends going back at least to high school.
One reason that's not true for me is the fact that Aunt LaRue died.
But the other factor I realized is coming out and homophobia. How
many of us have lost straight friends after we came out? I thought
about Shay and Ellie, my "best" friends from college who did not
respond when I wrote to them almost five years ago to tell them about
Conditions: Five, to tell them I was a Lesbian.

I think I thought about something else after that, but it escapes me.
Oh yes. When I looked out my bathroom windows at the red tree it
was really foggy and the words "The morn in russet mantle clad . . ."
came into my mind. Shakespeare from Hamlet. I thought about these
fools who rave on and on about white culture, white authors and how
I don't participate. And how they'd perhaps be surprised that I've

taken whole semester seminars in Shakespeare, Milton, Melville, etc., gotten A's in all of them and don't give a f_____. Sometimes I think I'd like to get a story out of this experience, indeed every night after dinner I think that after witnessing another of their white cultural festivals . . .

10-12-84, 8:32 P.M. *In the Air Again*

So I look out the window and see a round reddish light in the sky. I put on my glasses to see if it is the moon. It is. Coppery, golden, nearly full. Almost like a new penny. But instead of looking up at it I'm looking across at it. Can see the face so distinctly. The same moon I see high up between the pine trees when I leave the dining room at night at Yaddo. It's silvery there. One thing I'm realizing is that although I don't have a lot of "finished products" to show for these first four weeks, the thing I do have to show is the habit of writing. The almost reflex of it.

Notes

[1] In order to fully understand the dynamics described in the excerpts I feel it is important to know the racial identity and sexual preference of the individuals named:

Aunt LaRue—My aunt who raised me after my mother died in 1956.

Judith—A friend who lived near Yaddo. White, Lesbian.

Mommy Matt—My grandmother.

Pat—A friend. White, Southern, Lesbian, working class.

Dorothy—A friend. White, Southern, Lesbian, working class.

Jan—A friend. White, Lesbian.

Betsey—An artist at Yaddo. White, straight.

David—A Black artist who I became friends with at Yaddo. Straight.

Linda—A writer at Yaddo. White, straight.

[2] In entry 9-20-84 "the murders" refer to the murders of twelve Black women during a four-month period in Boston in 1979.

[3] I was working on a review of *Many Voices, One Chant: Black Feminist Perspectives*, an excellent special issue of the British journal *Feminist Review* about Third World feminism in Great Britain.

[4] *Sister Outsider* is a collection of essays by Black Lesbian feminist Audre Lorde. (The Crossing Press, Trumansburg, NY, 1984).

PART FOUR

Living Love

I have always missed my mother all my life. All my life I have looked for her face, her love, her strength, her beauty on every American street. She was never there, But I have always carried her in my heart.

SONIA SANCHEZ
September 6, 1988

Dear Diary,
I went to Cathy W.'s Halloween party. Scott P. picked me to chew the licorce with him. You put one end in the boy's mouth and the other in the girl's and you chew it up until you get to the end then you kiss. (Scott is white, I am Negro). . . . I think Scott really likes me and I like him.

Yours sincerely,

SHELLY (MICHELE L. SIMMS-BURTON)
October 25, 1968, age ten

Yetta wd say, "a woman's got to bathe you can't do like a man and run in and out the shower let a little water roll down yo' legs you gotta put that thing in some still water and soak and get some of the crust off those elbows looks like you been walking round on 'em." Now, I'm telling L. same, but gently. "Girl, take the time to love yourself."

HERMINE PINSON
January 1, 1992

Once, in one of the all-male process groups that I was allowed to observe at the new jail, a gentleman with sorrow in his face said, "I just need to hear someone sincerely say to me that I'm special, that I'm loved, and that I can make something of myself." The room was silent for a while. Then I raised my hand and said that I could sincerely tell him those things. Then he said, "Thank you, Thank you."

RISË COLLINS
September 1992

Not Letting Go
of My Anchor

I finished writing "Not Letting Go of My Anchor" on August 26, 1991. It was a healing piece to write. It was also a painful piece to write. I have thought often since writing it that I should tell my mother and father about the article and that it is going to be published. So far I haven't.

My mother called me the other day to say my dad is back in the hospital. He is getting a toe on his left foot amputated. He's already lost half his right foot. This pains me, especially because it's so hard for me to know the right thing to do. For years I have tried to prepare for the time when my mother and father would pass. When Mom and I talked last week, it was the first time we've enjoyed talking to each other in years. I may actually go home for a visit in April.

I love my family more than ever. My mother says my older brother has also left the Jehovah's Witnesses and is making a pilgrimage south to discover his roots. I hope that some day we can connect with each other again.

Whether we do or not, though, it cannot change what has gone

between us in the past. I will always love my parents and my brother.
Love is all.

I remember the day my parents disowned me. It was in July 1983, the summer before I started law school. I was living in Tucson, just finishing up my senior year at the University of Arizona.

My parents and brother believed, with the support of Scripture, that those who strayed outside of the flock, those who lost the camaraderie of their brothers and sisters in the faith, should be isolated, lonely, lost, and yearning for acceptance in the fold again. But from what my family saw of my life, I was not at all isolated. I had friends who loved and cared for me. And I did not consider myself one of those "lost sheep." I had no longing to be a Jehovah's Witness again; on the contrary, I found my parents' religion stifling, a claustrophobic prison that so dimmed the light of my passion, consciousness, and reason that I wanted to exorcise every trace of its narrow beliefs. I used to wish I could concentrate every vestige, every minute particle of my old faith, roll it into a ball, then skillfully cut it out of my body; only then would I be free.

I looked on my parents' religion as the primary source of my angst, loneliness, and misery; I wanted no part of it. After I left the church. I was able to savor the tastes and textures of life—the sweetness of wonderful sexual experience, the joy of getting a college education—but I also knew the bitter taste of loss, the loss I felt as my parents consciously, and too often smugly, removed themselves from my life.

On that day in July, when my father's letter arrived, he let me know I was no longer a welcome member of the family. I was in a pre-law program at the University of Arizona, living in a dorm room on campus. The letter was scrawled in my father's hard-to-decipher hand, on four pages torn from a spiral notebook. I've kept the letter for nine years, but I've only read it once, on that hot day.

The letter's message was clear: I had betrayed both the almighty God and my family by my decision to leave the faith. I would not be allowed to go home or even phone my parents, unless it was an "emergency." My father's tone was bitter, vindictive even. And I sat on the bed, holding the letter in my trembling hands, wondering how my father, my dear Black father, could say such things to his only daughter. After that initial shock came a numbing fear. What would I do if I were to get into trouble, I wondered? What if I needed to borrow money or just get advice? I knew after reading my father's letter that I had better not stumble, because if I stumbled, I might fall, and if I fell, there would be no one to help me up. Fear had me in its grip; I was terrified, not only of how to manage my upcoming move to San Francisco without my family's help, but also about how to survive the remainder of the trials I knew were awaiting me. I was young, afraid, and too ashamed to share my plight with anyone. I found my parents' actions so shocking I felt personally stigmatized by them. How could I possibly tell anyone that I'd been cut off by my own parents?

I found out several days later that my fears of stumbling and falling were justified. The stress brought on by my father's announcement, coupled with worry about the profound changes on my horizon—a move to the West Coast, which I had to arrange and finance almost completely on my own, and entry into law school—was severe. One afternoon I collapsed and had to be dragged, my knees so weak and useless I could hardly crawl, to the emergency room at University Hospital. It was a virus, the doctors said, a particularly virulent strain that left me limp from vomiting, diarrhea, and fever; sitting up in the wheelchair was nearly impossible. The doctor in charge took one look at me and said, "Get her an IV fast, or she'll go into shock." The next statement out of the doctor's mouth, though, seemed to be of more immediate concern to him. "You do have health insurance, don't you?"

I shook my head.

"Where are your parents?" he asked.

"In Phoenix."

He instructed me to give him their phone number, which I did. One of my worried friends ran off to place the call, a collect call to my family's house in Phoenix. My mother and father, my brother and his wife, all lived together in the same house, a large brick bi-level on the northwest side of town. Tim, his wife, and their two children lived upstairs, while my mother and father lived in the smaller downstairs area. Kathy, my sister-in-law, a woman who seemed to delight in keeping me out of her house, answered the phone. "Will you accept a collect call from Viki Radden?"

"No."

My humiliation and pain knew no bounds when my friend returned, his face perplexed, and announced, for the crowd of doctors and nurses and my friends to hear, that my family wouldn't accept my collect call. My already grieving heart writhed as I thought, "They meant it. They really meant it." The doctor searched my face for a clue, some understanding of this mystery, but there was no time for questions. An orderly wheeled me to a table and within five minutes I was given the two things which would be my companions for the next eight hours: a bed pan and an IV. The tears rolling down my cheeks were as cold as the IV that dripped, dripped, into the vein of my left hand.

That was the worst night of my life.

And, like the Pharaoh, my heart hardened against my mother and father, my brother and his wife. After the blood from the wounds they inflicted began to congeal and form deep, jagged scars, I nurtured a bitterness so profound I gnashed my teeth in a tirade of incrimination against everyone I blamed for my misery: my mother and father, my brother, all Jehovah's Witnesses everywhere, Christianity, the whole of organized religion. The mere mention of the word "God" turned me into a raving Medusa.

The Beginning . . .

When did it all begin? How did my family become Jehovah's Witnesses? It began, as it does with millions of families around the world, with a knock on the door. I remember the woman who came to our house. Her name was Betty Smith. She was a redhead, a kind, well-dressed woman with a gentle, sincere manner which touched a place deep in my mother's heart. I was young, only a six-year-old child, but I still remember Mrs. Smith coming over once a week to study the

Bible with my mother. Even I felt a warmth from her that was distinctly missing from mass at our local Catholic church. Perhaps the racism at our town's church deeply disturbed my mother; she never talked about it. She made an effort to keep the unpleasantness of racism from us kids, especially me, since I was the youngest, and as a girl I don't remember any overt racism in the church. I went to my First Communion in a white dress staff with starched ruffles and shiny white patent leather shoes, just like the other girls. My brother and I went to Catholic schools as well. While I don't remember any racist acts at church, I do remember them at school. As I child I had to learn to fight.

When my mother contrasted what was happening to her children at Catholic school with the benevolence that Mrs. Smith and her religion offered, that no doubt helped sway her. Jehovah's Witnesses, rather than condoning prejudice, believe that everyone is equal in God's eye. They believe that all races should live harmoniously together, that there will be a war, Armageddon, in which the righteous wrath of God will kill all his enemies and make peace reign forever on earth. My mother was already devoutly religious; she needed nothing to convince her of the benefit of a religious life. Most of her life had been spent searching for a more meaningful relationship with God and a better life for her children. Then came Mrs. Smith in her smart tailored suits, quoting Bible passages from Creation to the Apocalypse, without stopping for air. Before I knew what was happening, I was at my first "meeting"—we didn't call it "church"—at the Kingdom Hall of Jehovah's Witnesses. I remember feeling disappointed when we walked in, wearing our Sunday best. The Kingdom Hall looked more like someone's house than a church: gone were the golden idols, the larger-than-life crucifixes. There were no ornaments, none of the showy pomp and circumstance I'd grown to love as a Catholic girl.

The Witnesses are conservative; they live deliberately and quietly; modesty defines everything they do. They drink but frown on getting drunk; smoking is not allowed; and drugs are strictly taboo. My mother and father, after attending meetings for several months, began to feel they were part of a caring family that stretched around the globe. It wasn't long before they were baptized, and after that, the religion began to completely permeate our lives.

Being a Jehovah's Witness does not involve a mere nominal commitment. Services are held three times each week: Tuesday evening "Book Study," Thursday night "Kingdom Ministry," from 7:30 to 9:30, and finally on Sunday, the public talk and study of the *Watchtower* magazine, another two hours. We all had to do door-to-door preaching as well, which we did faithfully every Saturday and Sunday morning. As is usually the case, we children had no say about our parents' newfound faith. I was too young to understand the complexities of life; how at that age was I to decide if I "believed in" my new religion? All I knew was that when it came time to go to meetings, I had better be dressed, with Bible in hand, waiting at the door.

There were some benefits that even my brother and I recognized, following our parents' conversion; the first of which was that we stopped going to Catholic school. We had friends our own age in our local congregation, and my brother and I, with our family gift of gab, actually took some pleasure in going door-to-door. We astonished our white neighbors with our maturity and well-spokenness. These benefits outweighed, at least when I was very young, the things we had to give up. I celebrated my last Christmas and birthday when I was seven, but our family life was warm enough that for the most part I didn't feel too deprived. My parents made sure we got everything we needed, and most of the things we wanted, too.

In many ways, my childhood after the conversion was a happy one. Jehovah's Witnesses frown on ostentatious displays of any kind—wealth, talent, or beauty. One phrase which they loved, words I heard for years was, "Don't think more of yourself than is necessary." Still, though, there was nothing, no dogma, no doctrine, that could convince me I came from less than extraordinary stock.

I wasn't conceited, just unshakably convinced of my self-worth. From the time I was only a few years old I remember my father and mother telling me, "Viki, you're smart. You can do anything you want to do." I took them at their word because I was, at the same time, in absolute awe of my parents. My father seemed godlike. "My dad is six-feet-two and he weighs two hundred twenty pounds," I'd brag to the kids at school. "He can beat up your dad." Not only was my father the biggest, handsomest, strongest, kindest man on earth, he could also heal the sick.

One Saturday afternoon when I was eight, playing in the front yard, I saw a boy about my age riding his bicycle. Soon, he lost his balance, tumbled from the bike and crashed heavily onto the hot pavement directly in front of our house. He began to howl in pain. "Daddy, Daddy!" I shouted to my father, who immediately came running to me.

"Where does it hurt?" he asked the frantic boy, trying to calm him. My father, a medical technologist, saw the boy's arm was broken, and without a worry about malpractice, said to me. "Go get my bag." I returned with his black bag and watched him take charge, set the break, apply a splint and soothe the boy enough to get his parents' name and phone number. The distraught father soon appeared to pick up his son. I beamed with pride as the man, obviously shocked to see a black man holding his son in his arms, thanked my father profusely, then sped off toward the hospital. Never will I forget that experience, which cemented in my mind the certainty that my father soared far above the ranks of the ordinary mortal. He could heal the sick. In fact, I believed both my parents were able to perform miracles.

My mother was a gardener who transformed our backyard into a showplace of wonder, with a round, three-tiered strawberry patch, as pretty as a debutante's wedding cake. I loved the garden as much as she; together we spent hours pulling weeds, burying compost, picking the choicest rhubarb for a pie. There was also her sewing, knitting, and crocheting. I watched openmouthed as Mom first drew the plan for, then embroidered a huge map of the United States that still graces the wall in my parents' house. What awed me more and made my mother a constant object of my bragging, was her gift with words. She was a high school teacher with a solid reputation for teaching slow learners to read. When the Denver public school system had a child who'd been judged "unteachable," they called my mother. She took a thirteen-year-old Black girl, who the school system had labeled as retarded, and taught her to read. When we were about to take off on our six-week summer holiday, my mother told the girl's parents she shouldn't be away from her lessons that long. So, we all left the following week: my mother, brother, the now happily literate Cecile, and me, on a trip from Englewood, Colorado, to Long Island. My mother was not just Roslyn Radden, English teacher, to me she was Superwoman, a woman who did it all. And she was beautiful, with her smooth milk-chocolate skin, perfect smile and long, slender fingers, graceful as a swan.

My mother graduated from Tuskegee at the age of fifteen. She spoke French and German, and was a skilled linguist whose command of the English language left me envious. Throughout my childhood, when I thought of "what I wanted to be when I grew up," I realized that what I wanted to be was someone who could win a war of words with my mother. Her brilliance inspired and awed me; it was from her that I got my love of the English language. My mother taught me to read when I was three; words were a teething ring, my security blanket, the compass of my imagination that guided me on flights of fantasy. I used to sit cross-legged in the basement, in front of the shelves upon shelves of books there—art collections, full-color plates of Picasso and Degas, works by W.E.B. DuBois, Langston Hughes and Lillian Hellman, Faulkner and Fitzgerald, an atlas with gold-embossed letters on its cover.

I still remember the day I got my first library card: the excitement I felt when I asked my mother if I could check out all the books I wanted. When she said yes, that was it for me. I strutted from the Englewood, Colorado, public library, my arms overflowing with books. I was one of those children who had to at times be encouraged to go out and play: I was so caught up in reading. I looked forward to my Saturday visits to the library as only a child could. My parents beamed with pride at my excitement, particularly since my brother was also an early, enthusiastic reader.

After we converted to our new religion, however, things began to change, gradually, as the years passed. A creeping sense of shame began to overtake me; this feeling never left me until I left the church.

The shame arose from my inability to completely accept all the tenets of my parents' faith, shame I felt among my classmates when I couldn't take part, couldn't do the things they did. I was embarrassed to have to explain to them, "I'm a Jehovah's Witness. We're not allowed to . . ." In the fifth grade, our class put on a Christmas play in which I could not participate. I felt humiliated having to sit in the rows of empty chairs in the theater while my friends were on stage, practicing their lines and singing Christmas carols. Not being able to celebrate my birthday caused me much more distress, since I knew it was my own special day. I wanted recognition, gifts, and the feeling that people were acknowledging my own unique qualities. We didn't celebrate birthdays at home; there were no gifts, no cake, no birthday cards; but at school it was different. I always made sure to tell enough of my friends, so I always got some type of birthday celebration at school.

As I grew older, my shame became more acute. One significant belief of Jehovah's Witnesses is the necessity of having one's close friends come only from the ranks of believers. It was accepted that we had to go to school and work with non-Witnesses, but after this obligatory association, there was to be as little contact as possible, since association with nonbelievers could be catastrophic to our own faith. If there was one thing that eventually drove me from the religion, it was this segregation from "the world." In junior high school, friends became even more important. When they invited me to go out, I'd make up excuses, rather than tell them the truth. "I've got homework to do," I'd tell them, or "My mother says I'm grounded." Never did I tell my junior and senior high school friends the truth, that I was a Jehovah's Witness who wasn't allowed to be friends with anyone who wasn't. I was too ashamed.

My shame was all the more painful to me since I was a vibrant and sensitive child. My brother and I were among the brightest children in our entire school, and the fact that we were the only Black kids in our school, made us a puzzle to some classmates and a threat to others. My brother and I were both popular and well liked; we received many invitations to our classmates' houses, all of which we had to turn down.

There was an incident, during the summer of my fourteenth year, that became a catalyst of my final disillusionment. A family from Texas moved into the house next door to us, a family with three children. Their oldest child was a daughter, who, it turned out, was born in the very same German hospital where I was born. The girl and I became inseparable, particularly during the summer that her engineer father was away on business. Since my friend was not a Witness when we met, my religion dictated that I must convert her if I wished to keep our friendship. I set out to do just that; there was no obstacle I was prepared to let stand in the way of our friendship. Her mother saw no harm in her coming to our religious meetings; she was pleased her daughter had found such a good friend, and that we were both happy. Her father, however, upon his return, put an end to her going to meetings with me. He didn't want his daughter turning into a Jehovah's Witness, and that put an end to our friendship, since I was not allowed to associate with her anymore. My sadness overwhelmed me. I began to wonder, at fourteen, how God, who I had always thought of as so loving, could possibly be pleased about my loneliness. I needed friends, companions I could talk to, people who understood me. Unfortunately, I only grew more distant from my friends at the Kingdom Hall.

When I had to break up with my next best friend, a young Witness girl whose clothes, makeup, and "womanishness" my mother found "too worldly," that was it: the die was cast. I began walking a path of loneliness and disillusionment that would eventually lead me away from the church.

As Jehovah's Witnesses, my brother and I were still encouraged to do well at school, but not with the same vigor as before. Higher education was shunted aside in favor of missionary work. When I finished high school, with such a good record that I graduated six months early, my parents encouraged me, not to go to college, but to become a "pioneer," a missionary who spends one hundred hours each month preaching door-to-door. I knew I had no choice but to do what they said: at seventeen I was a full-time missionary, selling the *Watchtower*, cleaning rich white people's homes for spending money. But oh, how my heart rebelled! I spent at least half of my one hundred hours in my car, cruising the streets of suburban Denver, looking at men, driving up to Boulder to be alone in the Rocky Mountains. I was biding my time, trying to find myself, searching for a way out.

The prospect of the emotional and mental wasteland that lay ahead terrified me, and I couldn't help wondering why I had been singled out, why I had to live a life for which I had so little tolerance. I used to sit for hours in my room, listening to haunting music, nursing my pain, daydreaming of what I imagined to be a beautiful life—a man to love me passionately, good times with my friends, nice clothes, travel to other countries, having friends who truly understood me. I was thrown into fits of brooding and depression; my religion was making it impossible for me to realize any of the dreams I had locked in my heart, those things I already knew were going to be essential to my survival.

I knew no way out of my dilemma. I felt completely alone in the world, unable to leave my tiny island and venture out into open seas. By the time I was seventeen, I was also in the full bloom of sexuality, and not an hour passed when I was not deep in fantasy, via Nancy Friday's sexual fantasy books, Erica Jong's *Fear of Flying*, the latest issue of *Cosmopolitan*, or the constant sight of men—muscled, handsome men who I saw everyday in my travels around town. I spent my sixteenth and seventeenth years on sexual alert, and my parents' "I don't know what's wrong with it Viki, but God says only married people are allowed to have sex," did nothing to cool my ardor.

Finally, I made my break from the church. I was nineteen, with no job skills, no higher education, no money, and no friends. I was petrified at first, but at least there was some hope for the future. I sought help from an employment agency, and for a fee of $375, found a job as a file clerk at the Continental Insurance Company on Central Avenue in Phoenix. My salary was nowhere near what a clothes fiend and makeup hound needed, but I had at least begun to feel free. I had the car my father bought me when I was sixteen: a blood-red 1966 Pontiac Tempest, and soon I made friends at work. What still evaded me, though, was the feeling that I would be able somehow to make a good life for myself. I hated the whole idea of insurance, and I knew that it would be all too easy for me to get stuck there, locked in a dead-end job. One day my brother came to my little apartment and told me he'd heard of a government-sponsored college and job-training program that was starting, where I'd be able to get an A.A. degree and job training, without having to pay.

Within months I went from bored insurance clerk to fledgling college student. I was sipping the nectar of a newly discovered world: literature, from exotic countries and times, to classes in photography and psychology. I knew from the first semester that I had found rare jewels, and the chance to save my life. I had been blessed; I had found my way out of the morass. But at the same time, I had also set in motion a series of events that put me in direct opposition to the wishes of my family, and there, an untenable conflict arose.

The years I spent in college were rich, and full of experiences. I worked on the student crew at the local Public Broadcasting Service affiliate, KUAT-TV, whose offices are on the University of Arizona campus. I did a semester-long internship at the Arizona state legislature in Phoenix, during which time I couldn't help noticing feelings of resentment from my parents. Predictably, their feelings about my successes—my 3.9 GPA, my summer backpacking trip to Europe— were ambivalent. On one hand, I was a living testament, proof that the sacrifices they had made in my behalf had not gone in vain. I was hope personified, the embodiment of that hope all Black parents cling to so fervently—that their children will live the entire span of their lives without having to face the indignities they themselves faced. My father rejoiced that I would never know the horror he faced as a boy when the Ku Klux Klan stormed across his family's South Carolina farm on horseback, their torches casting an eery light on the terror: slaughtered, bloody cows, dismembered hogs and fowl, yelping hounds, the screams of his younger sister, the winter crop of corn and tomatoes gone, trampled by stampeding horses. With my acceptance at a top law school came an almost certain guarantee of comfort, of moderate fortune, the freedom to choose my own course. This must have pleased my parents. On the other hand, however, my successes, indeed the mere fact that I had been allowed to attain them, was a slap in my parents' face, a cold, sharp slap whose sting left them shaking their heads, questioning beliefs which they had thought until that time infallible.

Yes, even before 1983, when my father's letter that "officially" disowned me arrived, my family had given me signals that I was going to be cut off. The year I noticed the most profound change in my parents' and brother's behavior was 1982, when I worked as a legislative aide in Phoenix.

My brother and I had always been close, but when I began to have successes in life of which he was envious, such as going to law school—he had always wanted to be a lawyer, but our religion frowned on higher education—he began to be cruel and sarcastic. As I grew more confident, and my knowledge increased, the bars of my prison loosened even further. My newfound confidence, though, disturbed my family; to them I was a sinner who had yet to be punished by God. From all they could tell, I clearly had Providence signed on to my team. Since it appeared God wasn't going to punish me for my wrongdoing, they set out to punish me themselves. I don't think it was a planned conspiracy, but in the span of just a few months, my parents ceased to be my allies and set themselves in direct opposition to me.

A sobering incident happened one day just after I finished my semester at the legislature. I was about to leave for a summer backpacking trip, alone, in Europe. In many ways my trip to Europe was symbolic, since I was born in Germany. Ever since I could remember, my parents stressed the importance of my returning to Germany to see the place where I was born, the town where I spent the first three years of my life. The fact that I was going alone, with a mission, and little spending money, made my trip more a pilgrimage than a college student's summer frolic.

I found it nearly impossible while working at the legislature to save enough money for a holiday with just the bare necessities—a room in a youth hostel or a spot on the beach, a hot meal from time to time if I was frugal. My plane ticket I'd charged, but I still needed $270 for a Eurail pass. The relationship with my parents had deteriorated to the point where I no longer cared to ask them if I could borrow money. I didn't want to be obligated, yet sometimes we're left with few choices. I reluctantly called my brother several weeks before my departure and asked if I could borrow $300, which I promised to pay back at the end of the summer, when my financial aid would come through. Ignoring my misgivings about asking favors of my family, I decided to ask Tim because once, when he was desperate for money, I loaned him $600, which took him years to repay. Our mother finally had to intervene to get him to repay me. I thought he owed me, so I asked. But he was adamant. He had the money, but wouldn't lend it to me because a trip to Europe was not a necessity, but a "frivolity." "I haven't been to Europe," he reminded me. He admonished me to postpone my trip until I could afford the trip comfortably. I reminded him of the loan I had made him, but he was firm; he would rather that I forfeit my ticket and the entire trip, he said, than lend me the money. After I hung up the phone, I had a realization, which, though painful at the time, was a help to me in the future, one of those lessons I have never forgotten. I realized then that my brother was jealous of me, and that my parents were too. I went to Europe feeling like a vagabond; I was alone, there was no one back home with whom I could share my struggles and enlightenments. I envied those travelers I met who talked of worried mothers and fathers who sent little gifts of money, candy, and books to American Express offices as they traveled from country to country. I became truly adept at the art of feeling sorry for myself. I also became bitterly set against even the mere idea of organized religion.

When I was leaving Corfu, on my way to Athens, I met a Black woman named Debbie, a senior at Georgetown who was also law school bound. She was a zealous, fervent Christian. In the room of our budget hotel in downtown Athens, we stayed up late into the night, arguing about religion. It was a stressful conversation that left me with a migraine, in deep emotional pain. I was too young and bitter not to believe that religion, rather than being a boon to society, was a malevolent curse.

I didn't know it then, but I was on a journey of revelation that would take me from the healthy love I felt for my parents as a young child, to a disdain for them and everything they represented. A disdain so strong I simply dropped out of sight for two years, cutting myself off from any contact with them or anyone else in my family. I was also unaware that within a year of my trip to Europe, my parents would disown me outright, make the break formal and final. Most important, though, I didn't know that the journey would take me full circle, and that I would come to know a purer, higher love for my parents than I had ever thought possible.

When I returned from Europe, I had changed. It was in Europe that I began to believe I had a guardian angel sitting on my shoulder, guiding my steps, making me able to walk through fire untouched, like the three Hebrews. Unbelievable things happened to me on my journey: I'd seen the place I was born; the very room where my mother gave birth to me, I went to the concentration camp at Dachau, had an affair with a handsomely dark Greek railway worker in Athens, and had my own studio apartment on the ninth floor of a Paris apartment building that overlooked the Eiffel Tower. When I returned to Arizona, I was a different person. I was also broke. Absolutely broke.

I went home to ask my family for a loan of $200 until school started. They reluctantly gave it to me, and my father confided in me that Tim had been complaining about my visits home. Tim said my visits were fundamentally against church doctrine, since the Bible says to "Cut the unbeliever from your midst." My father and I were so close emotionally that I could tell my brother's attitude troubled him deeply, yet he felt in the end there was nothing he could do. To make matters worse, Tim and my mother nearly always shared the same views. My visits home made my mother uncomfortable, I could tell, and though she didn't ask me not to come back, I felt so awkward in her presence that I no longer wanted to.

My mother and I have always had a somewhat strained relationship. We nearly drove each other mad when I was a teenager. My mother, I learn as I get older, is rifled with insecurities about her own self-worth, her achievements and accomplishments. These insecurities began to trouble her all the more when I began to walk like a shadow behind her, studying the same things she studied: reading, writing, gardening, knitting—these are the things that I love, the things my mother loves. The presence of a grown-up, about-to-become-a-lawyer-and-published-writer was too much for her. It seemed to saw away at the pedestal she imagined she was standing on, and she grew cold toward me. When I was applying for the legislative program, I asked her if I could borrow a suit to wear to the interview. She met me and gave me the suit. "It's good to see you mom," I said as she handed the navy skirt and jacket to me. "Don't I get a hug?" I asked, when she seemed to turn away from my advance. "I don't know if I should hug you." she replied, in a way that left me in a rare state—complete loss for words. With my mother, things only got worse. The same was true with my brother. He told my father that I was not to play with his children, because I was a "bad influence" on them. In fact, he said, I should not be allowed to come into the house at all since I had been "disfellowshipped," removed from the church. The idea, he told my father, was to punish the unbeliever, not welcome them home as if they'd never transgressed.

The year passed by uneventfully, for the most part, and when I was preparing to move to San Francisco, the day came. The official day when my father told me I was no longer considered worthy of having the privilege of being part of a family.

When I arrived at law school, I found that each student had to fill out a card which let the school know whether we wanted our addresses and phone numbers told to people who called the school looking for us. Of course, I checked the box that said no. When I signed that card I bound the University of California to tell no one how to get in touch with me. I embarked on a plan which I thought fitting punishment for my parents, as well as sound protection from further hurt for me. I vowed to lose touch with my family, to never contact them again and never let them know where I was. I knew that in order to see the plan through effectively, I would have to lose touch not only with my immediate family, but with my extended family are well: my aunts and uncles, the cousins I'd been close to all my life. I weighed the sacrifice and the benefits and decided to carry my plan through. I couldn't risk one of my other relatives telling my parents where I was. And since I'd just moved, it was easy to lose touch. For two years I wrote to no one.

I savored the sweet taste of my revenge and I also vowed not to help care for my parents in their old age. It was heady, this plot of revenge, this feeling that I would make them regret how badly they'd treated me, but the anger didn't set well—like a heavy fried meal on a too hot day in August. Nevertheless, I refused to give up my angry bitterness. I persisted with vengeance until . . .

One night during summer vacation I had a dream—certainly not the first time I'd had upsetting, prophetic dreams—that my father was trying to get in touch with me. This feeling plagued me for two weeks, until I returned home. When I walked in the door, there was a message from my roommate: "Viki, your father has been trying to reach you. He's been calling the law school and getting angry because they won't give out your number. The school called and asked me to tell you he's been calling. Maybe you should think of giving him a call." My premonition confirmed, I finally decided to go ahead and call my father —I wondered if it might not be some emergency. It wasn't. Dad said he was worried about me and had been trying to reach me for weeks; he'd even threatened the school that he'd sue them for not telling him where his own daughter was. I appreciated his position, but the inequity of the situation did not escape me.

"Dad," I said, "if I'm not supposed to get in touch with you unless it's an emergency, shouldn't that work both ways? That's only fair. If I can't just pick up the phone and call you, you shouldn't be able to just pick up your phone and call me, either."

My father became petulant. "Now don't you tell me I don't have the right to call my own daughter. I brought you into this world, young lady. You better not forget that."

In the end I capitulated. I agreed to always let him know where I was. I wanted to scream at him, flail my arms like a madwoman and ask him how he could have treated me so badly. Before he hung up, he told me he loved me, and I wanted to tell him I did too, but I choked on the words. "I know, dad," I said. Then I went in my room and cried.

For three years after that night, I neither saw nor heard from my parents, but I did make sure they could always find me if they needed to. During those years I became more convinced of my ability to take care of myself without my parents, but I still wallowed in the hurt and anger I'd felt all along. It all came spewing out, in a vile and bitter stream, on the Pennsylvania turnpike on a hot night in August 1988.

I was about to move to Japan, and to fortify myself for the move, I made a "Homegirl Journey," filling my eyes and soul with Black people. I went first to the West Indies, then flew to Philadelphia to meet my mother's family for a reunion at my uncle's house in Cape May. I drove my uncle's car that night to the Cape. In the back seat were my mother and two of her sisters. My uncle sat beside me. I hadn't seen my mother in five years. I was glad to see she was healthy, but I seethed as she sat blithely chatting in the back seat. One of her sisters asked her if my brother Tim was coming to the reunion.

"He can't afford it this year. You know he lost a lot of money in that stock market crash. He might send his two kids though," my mother said.

The mention of these two children, my nephews, with whom my brother had forbidden me to play, started the roller coaster catapulting out of control.

"Hmmm," I said, noticing that my heart had begun to pound more quickly, "Tim's kids might come? Really?"

"Uh-huh," my mother answered rather crisply. She was just as on edge as I was, perhaps even more, since she was with her brothers and sisters. "They might fly out at the end of the week."

"And we'll be in New Jersey, won't we? Across state lines."

"What?"

"Well, if we're in New Jersey, that means the kids won't be in Arizona anymore."

"So? What does that have to do with anything?" Her voice rose an octave as I readied my first verbal assault. After two years of law school and a master's degree, I no longer worried about not being able to triumph over her in a war of words.

"Well," I said, "I just wonder if that edict your son made—you remember, when he said he didn't want me to play with his precious sons because I was a bad influence on them—I just wonder if that edict would still hold, if the kids aren't in Arizona. I mean, now that we're in New Jersey, maybe I'll actually be allowed to touch them."

For a moment, a pregnant silence filled the car. I was charged, doing 85. And climbing. "Slow down, girl," my uncle advised.

"I don't like your attitude, Viki Ruth," my mother warned.

"You don't like my attitude! Well let me tell you what I don't like. I don't like you. How dare you sit up in this car and tell me anything, you phony hypocrite! You call yourself a Christian, the same woman who won't let her own daughter into the house."

My temples were pounding. I was up to 90. Uncle Walton grabbed my arm with a firm grip. "Slow down now. You're going too fast."

I let up on the accelerator but shifted my mouth into overdrive. "You make me sick," I told her, turning to snatch a quick glance at my mother's horror-struck face. "You're a lousy mother. I owe you nothing. I owe you less than nothing. It's just a good thing your son's rich, because I'm not lifting a finger to help you when you're old. You don't deserve a thing from me."

My mother didn't reply. Neither did anyone else. After my tirade I felt momentarily justified. Then I began to feel horrible. Horrible for speaking so disrespectfully to my mother, for humiliating her in front of her sisters and brother. And for putting my aunts and uncle in the middle of my family's quarrel.

Things only got worse: the beach house was not the peaceful, quiet place I'd remembered as a child. The air was thick with tension. My mother, always in earshot, complained loudly to her family about me. "Viki might be going to Japan, but she has no morals. You know she sleeps around with men—I don't know when she's ever going to get married. What kind of daughter is she when she moves across the country and doesn't even let her father and me know where she is?"

After only a few days, my mother vowed to leave if I didn't. I decided to go. One of my aunts took me aside as I was leaving. Of everyone in the family, she had been the most kind to me, the most understanding of my position in the world, as a daughter with no mother and father.

She held tight to my arm. "Let it go, Viki," she said gently. "Just let it go. There's nothing you can do about it. You know that, don't you? There's nothing you can do. You just have to face it: your parents are gone. And unless there's a miracle, they're not ever going to come back. It can't ever be the way it was."

I knew she was right. I nodded.

"Don't you know how much it hurts me too? She's my younger sister. It breaks my heart to see you two this way. And there's something else you have to understand." She drew closer to me. "Your mother is jealous of you—you must realize that. It makes her feel insecure just looking at you. You've done so many things that she hasn't. You've had more education. You've traveled more. You have freedom to do things she couldn't even imagine doing when she was your age. Look, I know how you must feel, how much it hurts you. It hurts me too. The other night in the car, I know how you felt, but you know it just doesn't do anyone any good when you talk to your mother like that."

I started to cry. "I know!" I was almost shouting at my aunt. "But I don't have a mother and father anymore!"

"Yes you do. Don't say that. You know they both still love you. It's just that they don't know what else to do. They think they're doing the right thing, what God wants them to do. She handed me a tissue from her bag and went on. "You know I don't like that religion any more than you do. It's just brainwashing. That's all it is; just plain brainwashing. But it's all your mother has. She's old. If you take her religion away from her she wouldn't have anything."

I knew she was right. What would young Black women do without our aunts, those strong women who, no matter what, are always on our side? I owe a debt to my aunt I can never repay; that day, thanks to her, was the beginning of healing, of reconciliation, of forgiveness.

The End . . .

So how did I arrive where I am today, August 26, 1991, with my love for my parents intact, deeper, in fact than ever before? The same way we all get to that high ground of enlightenment: through the slow, painful passage of time. Thankfully, that time has been tempered by blessings. Truly I have been blessed. I am thankful most of all that I have lightened my load. No more carrying the heavy weight of resentment; my shoulders no longer sag under an oppressive burden of anger. How did I do it? In short, I forgave my parents for two reasons: one, because I finally learned to stop taking their rejection of me personally; I knew they had not set out to harm me. They were doing what they believe God wanted them to do, but more than that. I forgave them because I knew that if I didn't let go of the anger, I would lose everything else, including my deep love for my family. That love bubbles like hot lava in the core of my being; if I let go of that love, I have to let go of everything, including all the memories. What a sobering thought: a Black woman, living out her life, unable to allow herself to cling to childhood memories, or to remember the comfort of her mother and father's love. That loss, which would have followed me into eternity, was too big a price to pay.

I was living in Japan, isolated, the only Black woman for miles. How desperately I needed the love I felt for my mother and father! And my memories—my father's southern fried corn, the vacations we took together as a family, my mother's wedding-cake strawberry patch and her beds of blue irises—I dared not let go of my memories! Memories were all I had.

The most sobering thought, though, what finally prompted me to let go of all the anger, every last particle, what prompted me to sit down one day, after six years of silence, and write to my mother and father, telling them that nothing, in time past or distant future, could cool my love for them, was this: my parents are in their seventies. I did not want them to die with our relationship in anything less than a state of grace. My dearest mother and father, I wrote, no matter what has happened in the past, nothing can deny our kinship of blood. I am and will always be your daughter. I told them how deeply I love them, and how thankful I am for the sacrifices they made so I could be who I am today. I told them there is nothing in the world more precious, more sustaining, more life-giving than my memories of them. My memories of my mother and father are my balm in Gilead.

We all know, although certainly we need to be reminded from time to time, how complex and fragile the family relationship is, how tenuous, especially for Black families in America. Here we are so vilified, so under attack that very few of us are blessed enough to have the unconditional love of our families. And on this battleground, we must be thankful if our families are even functionally healthy. If we are blessed enough to have a wonderful relationship with our families, then let us be thankful. And if our relationship with them is less than ideal, let us still be thankful. We must be thankful that our mothers are alive, that our fathers are not fatally ill with the myriad of diseases that plague Black men. If our brothers have not been gunned down in the streets, that is cause for elation. In these post-Reagan-but-still-Bush years, we must be thankful if we have families at all. The number of Black children in foster care, the crack babies, all bear witness to this necessity.

As much as possible, we must learn to be gentle with our family members, loving and loyal. Loyalty is essential. We must be loyal to our families and to each other as Black people.

When we encourage our children: "Strive to be the best," we can not put any limitations on that striving. We must love our children unconditionally, not only if they pour themselves into the mold their parents cast. If we dream of our daughters becoming doctors, of our sons being electrical engineers, we must still love them when they decide they want to sell shoes and do landscape gardening. If we want our children to be Baptists, but they aspire to be Buddhists, we must still rejoice that we have been blessed with sons and daughters at all.

In my own situation, there's one irony which has not escaped me: I have become the person my parents used to dream I would be. I have begun to achieve some of the success they hoped I would, yet I cannot go home. My parents and I are on speaking terms, barely. There is simply no getting around the fact that my relationship with them will most likely never be good. It's not that too much has already happened between us; rather it's that too many obstacles still remain. My mother can't seem to help preaching to me whenever we talk on the phone; she criticizes me frequently and openly; I feel uncomfortable. I can't help wondering if she will ever accept the decision I made and respect me for having had the courage to make it. I hope she will. But I'm not waiting. I plan to live overseas again. I know that I may never see my parents alive again. After all these years of estrangement, there's one thing I still don't understand: Why me? Why did I have to lose my family? I still ponder, hoping for clarity, for understanding.

I realize, however, that I may never know why. Sometimes we humans simply are not granted that luxury. I may never know why I grew up in a religion that would later be the cause of the dissolution of my family. My knowing or not knowing, though, changes nothing, negates no facts, nullifies no emotions. Nothing can diminish my relationship with my family; the kinship of blood with my family remains. The fact that I no longer have my family makes them all the more precious to me. Thankfully, I have finally begun to consider myself a blessed woman, because I can announce to the world, "I have a mother and father who love me."

Not Letting Go . . .

I am the reincarnation of my parents' former selves. Who they were, and who they are, will never die in me. I am thankful, most of all, that I have been able to transcend my feelings of anger and betrayal. I have had to let go of everything except the love, which is what I cling to now.

My love for my family is my anchor, my compass, my wings. I can't let go.

Breaking the Ties That Bind Me

ANN LYNN

My journal is my lifeline to my feelings and thoughts. It lets me write those things that ramble through my mind during the day and cause my heart to pound furiously without fear of reprisal or judgment. When I write, my mind is often far ahead of my pen and I have to make a conscious effort to slow the free-flowing thoughts to allow an intelligent sentence to filter through. My journal is my reflection of myself like a mirror. I see the flaws that I wish to change and the beauty that I acknowledge. It has helped me to grow and become someone I like while still working on other parts of me.

The odyssey of reviewing my writings is often funny, often painful. I see the insanity during periods of my life and the glory of overcoming obstacles that I once believed insurmountable.

What is interesting is that my focus used to always be on "him." What he did, did not do, did not want to do or was not. How I was hurt, angry, pissed off, happy or sad based upon his behavior. He dominated not only my conversations, but my private thoughts—he rented a lot of space in my head. He invaded my being and I was at a loss to prevent it. When I read what I wrote about "him," I realized the object of my obsession had to change from changing him to changing me.

> *As long as the ties that bind us together are stronger than those that would tear us apart, all will be well.*

This is the preamble of the twelve traditions of a twelve-step group I attend. I am recovering from a drug and alcohol addiction. A friend of mine said that we are all recovering from something. My main focus right now is recovering from a relationship. It seems that I am always recovering from a man. I am fortunate enough to have had a network of sisters in my life to help me through the pain of ending it and begin to come to terms with who I am. I need to state at the outset that this is really not about a man or degrading African-American males. This is about me.

I recently read a book by Pearl Cleage entitled *Mad at Miles: A Blackwoman's Guide to the Truth.* It is a must-read book and I have shared it with my friends as it was shared with me. Although it is a slim paperback, it is full of me. I see me in every word of every page. In this book, Ms. Cleage describes the qualities of a good brother. I read it yesterday and realized how off the mark I was. However, a year ago, I thought, this time, I had found a "good, righteous brother," as Ms. Cleage states. Turns out, I ignored the early-detection warning signs of a bad relationship. Instead of Mr. "Good, Righteous" brother, I met Mr. "Rock Bottom." The only difference between this relationship and countless other bad ones in my lifetime was my ability to end it quicker. However, I was not able to do so before the painful episodes of infidelity, emotional abuse, lying, stealing, and cheating had occurred. I was also unable to leave until I had left some of my self-esteem behind. To beat it all, I had left it with Mr. "Rock Bottom."

I met him at a twelve-step group meeting. That raised my antennae, but I put them back down. I came to the meeting to not only learn how to stop using drugs and alcohol, but to find out what it was about me that I had to work on. Why did I not love me enough to stop abusing my mind and body with chemicals? After listening to the discussions, I realized that it was also the primary reason most people were at the meetings. We were selfish, self-seeking, and dishonest in most aspects of our lives. In one word, I was sick. I came because I wanted to get better. Not well. Just better. But if he was there also, what did it say about his character? I listened to the voice in my heart, that was pounding and fluttering at the sight of him and told my head, "shut up." This was different. He was different. I continue to wonder what makes my heart allow my head to black out and take a vacation when I need the rational part of me most.

We met. We made love. We moved in together. All within six months of meeting. This was the man I knew I would marry and have children with. I was willing to give up my career as a lawyer and wait on him hand and foot. Never mind that he did not have a college degree, permanent employment, a car, a stable place to live, ambition, or any other of the tangible or intangible qualities I wanted in a man, a partner, or a husband. Never mind that one of the suggestions in the twelve-step program is to stay away from a relationship for a year. The reason behind the suggestion is to allow you time to get to know who you really are before trying to find out who someone else might be. All of that did not matter. I was in love.

True happiness was short lived. We argued over his constantly changing channels with the remote control while we were watching television together. We argued over changing the radio station in my car—the station I always listened to. We argued over my faults also. We just plain argued. Initially, we tried to resolve our arguments, regardless of the subject, by expressing our feelings without blame. This is what I learned from daily twelve-step meetings and visits to my therapist. It worked for a little while. This type of mediation of our conflicts soon disintegrated into pointing our fingers at each other, blaming the other for all our problems and eventually cursing and screaming at the top of our lungs. We continued to live together. The bottom line was—I loved him.

Prior to this relationship, I had developed a close network of sisters in my life who I could be real with. We would go to lunch and talk for hours with our masks down. No pretenses. We could just be who we were without fear of judgment or being chastised or whispered about when the lunch was over. We were soulmates. I treasured our relationship like a jewel. But, sometimes in the midst of our conversations about our black men, I swore to God that certain behavior was intolerable in a relationship. I did not believe being unfaithful was proper. Call it infidelity, sneaking around, messing around or whatever name you want. I called it just plain downright, low-down cheating. As time progressed in my relationship with Mr. "Rock Bottom," I tolerated that behavior also. My heart said I loved him. He had just made a mistake. He said he was sorry and that it would never happen again. He brought me flowers, fruit baskets when I dieted, and cards. He was romantic. We would make love and make up. I believed him. I needed to. I had to. Until it happened again. And again.

I withdrew from my network. I was ashamed and embarrassed. I could not face them and not be honest. I feared the very thing our gatherings did not include—being judged. I was addicted to this man. He was my new drug. The thought of letting go of the relationship was more painful than staying with him. I did not want to be alone. I was willing to take part of him and tolerate the bad part that I did get rather than know that I was worthy to have all of somebody.

I had no self-esteem. I did not love myself enough to stop the abuse. The boundary lines of what I would accept were moved further back each time he crossed the lines. I now realize that my issues of self-worth and co-dependency go back to my childhood. They are deep rooted like a stubborn dandelion. But at the time I was crying for days over what this man had done to me. I did not see that it was what I *allowed* this man to do to me. I only wanted to be what I had to be to keep him home and happy. I felt I was the reason he needed other women in his life. I was inadequate.

Finally, after the puffiness in my eyes went down, I told my friends the whole story. Not just the parts that made me look good. In fact, there were not any parts that made me look good. And, I received love, guidance, strength, and hope from these women. I received affirmation that I was worthy of more in my life. I was an attractive, professional, African-American woman who had a lot to offer any man lucky enough to want to be with me. We laughed, cried and hugged. I left our luncheon with a better perspective on me and my relationship. I was not whole. I was healing. I also knew that these women were very important in my life. They were like a family to me. We gave unconditional love and accepted each other for who and what we were—women struggling to make peace with ourselves in so many ways.

I did not run home and pack his bags. I did not throw his belongings out the window as the wife did in Spike Lee's *Jungle Fever*. I did think about doing it. Instead, the transition was gradual. I had to learn how to like me for me—faults and all. I finally understood that I could not change his behavior. I had to focus on what I could change about myself. His behavior did not equate with my being somehow less than anyone else. I worked on a closer relationship with my God to fill the void within me that made me so needy. It is an evolving process for me.

It has been painful to close the door on him even though the relationship was not healthy for me. It has also not been easy trying to break the ties with him that bound and tore me apart. With a lot of support, I have been able to start looking within instead of outside of me to find a fix for whatever ails me. I am starting to believe that I am worthy. At thirty-two, I am learning to enjoy being with me and not require somebody, anybody lying next to me at night. I still want to share my life with someone. But, I also understand that unless I address the issues I have with my self-esteem, co-dependency, and spirituality, I will continue to attract Mr. "Rock Bottom" as my ideal mate. I want to love and be loved. Until that time, I am learning to love myself. I look in the mirror and repeat affirmations to strengthen the inner me.

I still attend twelve-step meetings, but I have my antennae and radar working overtime. I try to associate with the women in the meetings. I try to strengthen those ties that are good for me. I keep talking about what goes on in my life. I am working hard. I know I will never be finished. I am grateful to know that I can always do something each day to make me a better person. I do not have to wait on "Prince Charming" to rescue me before I get busy living. Yes, as my friend says, I am still recovering from something.

Setting Relationship Limits

YIN QUILTER

For the past two years (I can't believe it's been that long!) I have been struggling with the issues I set out in this piece. At the beginning of the fiasco, I would never have thought I could go through it and come out on the other side being anything close to sane. But I have. And it's getting better all the time. I'm not yet at the end, but things have progressed so much further than anything I could envision in the depths of my despair.

Some of my most healing moments have come from the insights gained in writing this piece. It was like having someone take a jumble of fabric scraps lying on a table in a mess and make a wonderfully warm and beautiful quilt. I had all the pieces in my head, but had not brought them together. Going through the exercise was wonderfully healing.

Even though it was about my own relationship, I gained a new perspective that was there all the time waiting for me to put it together. I have grown even more since then. In fact, I am convinced that a part of why this all happened was to make me move to the healthier *place I am now. It never would have happened without such a cataclysmic event. In that somewhat strange sense, I am grateful for it.*

How much can a relationship take and still survive and be healthy? I've had to ask myself that question a lot lately. I am a lesbian in a long-term relationship with a partner who is finally coming to grips with survivor issues arising from childhood sexual, physical, and emotional abuse. Almost simultaneously, my partner began seeing someone outside our relationship. I was brought up to be a "strong black woman." Having these things all come together for me to deal with has been most trying, to say the very least. I would feel immensely better if I thought that my slogging through this morass and sharing it could help others.

My parents had four daughters before having the son my dad longed for. Because they knew of the vulnerability of females in our society, particularly African-American females, right along with our pabulum we were given strong doses of what we should and should not take as women, and what we needed to do in order to protect ourselves. It was pretty much the stuff of which "strong black women" are made.

Among the many things I learned was that I must get an education, no matter what I decided to do with it, so I would never be placed in the position of having to take something I didn't want to take off of a man. As rural African-Americans who had recently moved to the city, my parents realized the advantage this would give their offspring. Another lesson was to take no prisoners when it came to being hit by men. My parents had witnessed enough of what happens when societal frustrations run high among African-Americans, and how easy it is to strike out at those closest to you. My mother taught, and my low-keyed father endorsed, making the first strike the last. My parents believed that the surest way to encourage physical abuse is to let the man get away with it the first time. The antidote, if it ever happened, was to strike back the first time with whatever heavy object was at hand (and think about consequences later), or, lacking that, my mother advised grabbing his balls and holding on for dear life. While

I have never had to deal with being mistreated by a man, the lessons of courage and self-confidence included in my parents' lectures have come in handy. The day before my mother suddenly died when I was twenty, she said to me when my boyfriend decided to leave our house rather than stay for a big family dinner, "Don't ever be a rug for any man." I never forgot it.

I learned my lessons well. I had mad crushes and heart-stopping relationships with more than my share of males. Though the lessons I was taught by my parents were as much a part of my relationships with men as kissing, they did not stand in the way of my forming healthy and close relationships with them. This includes, marrying one who, though we are divorced, remains one of my closest friends to this day. As it turned out, it was an African-American female who truly won my heart after all. I had no way of knowing that this relationship would be the most intense and satisfying of my life, yet one in which virtually all of the well-learned lessons from my parents would be very nearly totally useless.

I have been in a relationship with the same woman, my only one, for nearly thirteen years. That is no small feat when society holds up no mirrors with which to view yourself and your relationship in a positive light. It's the sort of thing you don't miss until it's not there. As an African-American woman, I was fairly used to not seeing reflections of myself fully mirrored in society. But as someone who had been in relationships with men all my life until falling in love with a woman (something I did not even know was possible until it happened to me), I took little things for granted. For example, hearing about your love in songs, seeing it in movies, on TV, in books, magazines, and billboards, or even seeing couples hold hands, share an anniversary with family and friends, display family pictures on the desk at work, etc. When that is all suddenly taken away (I had experienced having this available with my husband), you view things differently. You realize how much society supported you in a relationship. When that support is taken away, the task of maintaining a relationship, in isolation, is much more difficult.

When all of our challenges are considered, raising three daughters together, our demanding professional roles, and the problems related to childhood sexual, physical, and emotional abuse which my partner suffered under, the thirteen years becomes even more admirable. Though we have been together and for the most part happy for those thirteen years, as is commonly the case with abuse survivors, we have had intimacy problems for probably twelve of those years. We have now at least progressed to the point where my partner is undergoing professional therapy. It took virtually all the years of our relationship to get her to that point. As it turned out, that was only the beginning of the battle. I thought that getting my partner into therapy was hard, but it is far more taxing to be in a relationship with someone who is dealing with those issues. The therapy sessions are draining, the issues that come out are incredibly complex, and relationship consistency and security during this time are only words that you feel exist in the dictionary.

Unfortunately, at the same time my partner entered therapy, she also entered into an intimate relationship with another woman. For reasons neither my partner nor I can figure, this woman touched something in my partner that helps her with the issues she is facing. To say that I was hurt by this is, of course, a ridiculous understatement. My pain was intensified by the fact that my partner's relationship with the other woman seemed to have the very intimacy my partner and I lacked, but so desperately yearned for all these years.

From the outset my partner was clear that the other woman was not someone with whom she wanted to be in a lifetime relationship. From the beginning my partner has seen the person only as someone who facilitates her getting where she wants to be for us.

Now if you don't think that calls upon me to want to use the lessons of my parents, you haven't listened very well. My upbringing would tell me that I'm being used. Why have the cow when you can get the milk for free? Why bother leaving our comfortable home and family when she can have this other relationship on the side and still have me? Why leave, for the virtual unknown, someone who loves you to death, takes care of the kids, make sure the bills get paid each month, and is a sure and steady rock to depend upon? Especially when you can have the other woman and all this too?

My first instinct was to look to the lessons I had learned about what to do when I was mistreated by someone. The ones that would tell me not to even bother to give this crap a second thought before throwing my partner's stuff out the door. That would say I'm crazy and a fool for letting someone do this to me. The lesson that would make me think I wasn't being as strong as I should be because if I were strong enough, I would leave anyone who hurt me this much and this way.

But the lessons I learned from my parents just didn't work here. The dynamics simply aren't the same, the politics aren't the same, our cultural positions as two women rather than a man and a woman are not the same; and, because of it, my responses are inappropriate if they are the same.

It has been my experience that when you're in a relationship with a woman there are higher highs and lower lows. The intensity and depth of feeling is unmatched by anything I have ever come close to in a relationship with a man. On the other hand, the frustrations can also be great because, among other things, when two women are in a relationship together, everything is up for grabs. There are no predetermined, preset roles to be filled. Unlike male/female relationships, there is no such thing as "you're a woman, so you do this," or "you're a man, so you do that." It's simply, you are two people, what do you wish to do? (it's a drag when it comes to who puts out the trash, checks for a noise in the middle of the night, or washes the car . . .). Without the roles that we all take on without even thinking much about it, we're on our own. As restrictive and confining as those roles can be in male/female relationships (and Lord knows I have done my share of railing out against them) they at least provide a modicum of predictability (though that too can be a problem). As a lesbian couple, we have no such predictability. Nothing to rest on. It's all up to us. It's like the therapist said when we went in for couples counseling, "You two are on your own. You are the ones who have to make the rules. They can be whatever you want them to be." While the wonderfully freeing release this provides can be exhilarating, it's a lot of work getting to that point.

If a man was "running around on me," I'd cut him loose faster than I could say the word "hound." I would be perceived as a fool (and certainly not in keeping with the dictates of a strong black woman) if I did anything less. There is a presumption, rightfully or wrongfully, that a male having an extramarital affair is using both women, and no one wants to be used. There is also the factor of men being acculturated to seek power and freedom by having as many women as is feasible so that their perception as strong masculine figures is enhanced. While it may not be absolutely uniformly accepted, it is certainly a strong part of traditional acculturation as African-American females and males, respectively.

That same acculturation is not present with two women. We just don't come from the same political place. This is not to say that there are not some women for whom this is true. But by and large, women are simply not acculturated the same way and do not have the same presumptions at work. There is not one of us that we can point to, culturally, as having or wishing to have the upper hand, or more power or freedom. There is no presumption that one of us wants to have multiple "conquests" in order to live up to some societally induced notion that doing so makes us more of a woman. Rather, with two women, we are equals on an even playing field with few rules.

For me, this means that I have to look at what is actually going on in my partner's relationship with someone else, and not simply deal with the preconceived notions as I might if it were a male/female relationship. This is difficult to do since those preconceived notions are all I've had to deal with because prior to this I was in male/female relationships with the accompanying baggage of power, femininity, masculinity, etc.

When I look at our present relationship in its reality, I have no reason to doubt that things are as my partner says they are. That is, that the other woman (the relationship between them ceased to be sexual after a short while) helps her to deal with her survivor issues. Further, that when all is said and done, what my partner wants is for us to be together, healthy, and whole.

My lessons taught me that I should feel used, cheated, and foolish. In using the lessons, when my partner would tell me her side, I couldn't hear it because it didn't fit with what I'd always grown up with, what we see in movies, what we hear in songs, etc. She was cheating on me, pure and simple. That's what fit with the worldview I'd always seen. There *was* no way to justify it. Who in the world ever heard of having an affair that ends up helping you get yourself together?! I certainly hadn't.

But I kept coming back to the fact that my situation just didn't fit into this view. It didn't make sense. It didn't feel that way to me. It didn't *look* like it felt that way to my partner. I'd look into the big, beautiful crystal-brown eyes that I had loved for so long, now the pained and saddened eyes of the woman I'd loved more than anyone else in the world for thirteen years, the one with whom I'd spent some of my most intimate moments, and I just couldn't make myself feel she was lying to me about this. *Despite* what it *looked* like, I could look at her and *know* that despite what things *seemed* to be, she was hurting *immensely* at what this was putting us through. We had struggled together for so long and so painfully with her survivor issues. We were so hopeful when she finally decided to go for the help we'd sought for so long, but that she was so fearful of obtaining. I absolutely could not *abide* the thought that our relationship would become another in the long list of all too painful casualties in her life caused by survivor issues, simply because I refused to deal with what was really going on rather than what my rules told me was going on.

I had to think about whether I was going to deal with my relationship in terms of society and how things *appeared* or in terms of my partner and me and how it felt to us—regardless of how it looked or seemed to *others*. I knew what to do with the rules my parents gave me, but they never told me I might have to deal with a woman and an abuse survivor, and that the rules might be different then.

I decided I had little to lose by giving the relationship a chance and dealing with us as this was to us, not society. Thirteen years isn't so easily discarded. I don't mind discarding it if I *have* to, but I am willing to go the extra mile to be sure it is what needs to be done so that I don't spend the rest of my life second-guessing the decision. I don't want to discard the relationship because I made that decision based upon someone else's rules. I had already broken society's rules by choosing to be with a woman; since I had gone this far, I had little to lose by hanging in there and waiting to see what happened with our relationship after she dealt with her survivor issues—even though the way she dealt with them seemed highly unorthodox. I realized too that being an African-American in a European-American-dominated society also prepared me for going against the grain. We do it every day of our lives, just by our very existence.

So what did it mean for us? It meant that I was willing to change my limits. We realized that the issue of overriding importance to us was being together the way we had always dreamed of being if she was healthy and whole. I had to rethink the fact that how she became whole wasn't being accomplished as either of us envisioned it would be, but my concern cannot be with how it happens as much as whether it in fact *happens*.

That made me have to rethink my limits. I haven't reached them yet—though I sure have *stretched* them farther than I ever thought they could go. I don't know when or if I will reach my limit, but when I do, I will know. I also know that I cannot have my limits artificially set for me. I couldn't let them be set for me by the lessons my parents taught me for another situation or by my friends' reactions to my situation. Limits are set by personal values and beliefs, not by specific acts taken out of the context of the relationship. If your partner runs around on you, that's the limit. If your partner buys an expensive gift for another, that's the limit. It's not that simple. Rather, it's looking at the totality of what has gone on between you and your partner and judging it against who they really are, what you want and how you think the offending act fits into it.

All of these issues keep the bigger picture in focus. Keeping the bigger picture in focus is difficult to do, but absolutely necessary. For us, the bigger picture is staying together and realizing our potential as a couple. We know that in order to get there from here, there will be many irritations along the way. I have to constantly remind myself that the big picture is that we want to be together and not let those smaller things defeat us.

It would be so much easier if I could use the lessons I was taught, summarily apply them and be done with it. They were good lessons, and I used them an awful lot—still do—and have passed them on to my own daughters. But I had to learn that a part of learning lessons is learning when they do not apply. Having to deal with what I've dealt with in the context of survivor issues has given them a completely different dynamic and dimension. It will not violate being a "strong black woman" to do what I have done.

I am still finding out how much a relationship can take and still survive. Some days are better than others, and there has been unbearable pain, but things get better. Since I don't want us to become another incest and abuse carnage statistic, I am willing to test the limits. Our nearly-thirteen year history has a depth that cannot be replaced. If going through this can continue that history and make it even better, it will be worth it. It will also make us feel that the monsters of incest and other childhood abuses can be defeated and hopefully that will give courage to others.

Golden Boy

QUO VADIS GEX·BREAUX

"Golden Boy" speaks to the heartache that often accompanies single parenting. The entry was written when we were living in the married students' dorm on Tulane University's campus. My portable washing machine, because of the scarcity of space, was stored in my bedroom in the efficiency apartment. I was adjusting to the life of an older returning student who was also a single parent. The university didn't know what to do with me and I was certainly trying to figure out what to do with myself and this other life that had been entrusted to my care.

I was so inspired by the wonder of my young child learning what existence is coupled with the nature of our constituting the "family unit" that I had to talk about it. With my level of introversion, that discussion was saved for my journal. This all came as a day's-end reflection on simple occurrences.

1979

Your jack-in-the-box with no Jack sits on the washing machine in my bedroom where you left it reluctantly before going to bed. You wanted to play with it. To bring that metal box with sponge blocks stuffed into it to bed with you. Some children like teddy bears. You have a lion that you call your baby and put to sleep when you remember to rescue him from the floor or the bottom of your toy box.

You come home with nursery rhymes sung in tune to little people's rhythm and say the pledge of allegiance with at least five lovely, mispronounced words. I wonder why I didn't remember that children were taught that.

You're a golden boy with long legs. Defiant. Wondering about your father without exactly asking. A neighbor tells me her daughter has been looking out for you. She asked a man on the elevator if he would be your daddy. Said you were a nice boy and needed a daddy. Wouldn't he like to be yours? You tell my friend he must be like a daddy as you ask him about his son, his boy. Inside I still hurt a little, wishing that of all the things I can give you, I could make that one.

You're into asserting your wholeness, your differentness, your existence. You tell me the cold water I give you makes your newly bit tongue feel better and I try not to be the alarmist mother, ready to run to the doctor for any and everything.

When we read you say every book has come from the city public library and I wonder why no one else is as charmed by you as I am, imagining that somehow that air about you could buy you anything. But I am your mother and you are only three.

Three Daughters

DAWN D. BENNETT-ALEXANDER

My mother died suddenly when I was twenty years old. Seven years later when I was pregnant with the first of my two birth-daughters I had so many questions that only a mother could answer. I felt a deep sense of loss. Especially since "being a mother" was always special between my mother and me. From the time I could talk I had always wanted to be a mother. Ma got a kick out of asking me in front of company, "What do you want to do when you grow up, Dawnie?" and I'd say, "Be a muvva." And here I was doing it, and she wasn't around. And all my questions went unanswered.

I decided that I did not want my daughters to go through this. If I died suddenly, I wanted them to have a way of finding out things about themselves that only I could tell them. So I wrote. In addition to my own journals which I have kept since about age eleven, I keep journals on each of my daughters. I write only when time permits and content myself with the thought that anything is better than nothing at all.

My daughters are now fourteen, twelve, and five and I still keep the journals. From about age six the older two have kept their own. The youngest does it as a kindergarten project. All are well attuned to the importance of journal keeping. We joke that one day we will publish the first mother-daughter journals.

As you'll see, things changed over the years. I started out writing in the third person and eventually moved to the first, feeling it to be more personal. And some entries are more descriptive than others. There are other changes, such as my divorce years ago, though my ex and I still remain close friends.

Looking back on it, it was worth the effort to write. Even though I only had a very few minutes to devote at times, those otherwise-forgotten insights are now there forever. The girls get a tremendous kick out of hearing entries about themselves from my journals. They are wonderfully revealing and one of the dearest gifts I could ever give them—the gift of their own personal history.

Jenniffer

10/7/78

Our first daughter, Jenniffer Dawn Bennett Alexander, was born on May 18, 1978. Honey (Willie) was with me through it all except the time it took him to register me into the hospital. We married on his birthday (9/1) in 1976, just after he finished law school and the year after I finished. He saw Jen when she first started to come out. He held my hand and kept telling me to push when it was time—just like in our Lamaze classes. When I first saw Jen's head, I couldn't believe it. I was having her by natural childbirth, so I had no medication for pain. I couldn't believe that I was finally going to see this little creature that had been kicking me and being in me and that I had grown to love for all those months. Then came her whole head. I was ecstatic. Dr. Sewell turned it from one side to the other and back again. Then the rest of her came out. Unbelievable! I just cried and cried and cried with joy and exhaustion and exuberation. It was here! The baby was here! And it was a girl! Jen was born on the first beautiful day of spring that we'd had all season. When I saw the weather, I knew it was a good sign.

The pregnancy had been a good one, even though in my fourth month we'd moved, on the day before Christmas Eve, to our new home which wasn't finished being renovated yet. No heat, except the three fireplaces, so we always had a fire going. The house was covered from top to bottom with dust from the construction. Honey has been wonderful through all of this. He worked very hard to have things ready for Jen. He suffered through all my cravings with me. For cherry Jell-O—which I hadn't had in absolute years, but suddenly couldn't get enough of—for BLTs smothered with hot sauce and loads of pickles, and for hot, spicy, Italian cold-cut sandwiches. And I only gained fifteen pounds the whole time with Jen!

Anne

Monday 10/22/79

First off, let's establish one thing from the very beginning so we'll all know—I think you're wonderful, Baby. You sure are. Your daddy thinks so too. So who are we? We're your parents—you don't know about that kinda stuff yet, but you'll learn. We'll teach you the ropes real good.

As for this literary endeavor, as you'll learn soon enough, your mama has a philosophy about most things. Especially about kids and how they should be treated and stuff. Part of my philosophy is that you only get to go around once (presumably), though my mother— your grandmother, who died eight years ago of a heart attack—believed in reincarnation. Maybe I do too since I see her in almost every flower I see, among other things. Anyway, so since we only go around once, you've got to get while the getting is good. I'm sure you'd like nothing better than to sit by a nice crackling fire at the age of thirty and read about what it was like when you were a day old, then five months, etc. Especially since time has a way of eroding the memories that seem so vivid while they're happening. Plus, this way you have a contemporaneous account of what you were like, and I'll bet it will come in handy when you have kids of your own. You sort of want to know what you were like, so here we are.

You are a sweetie. You are now about three months old in utero. You are expected to arrive on April 24. You have one sister, Jenniffer, who is now seventeen months old. She is an absolute doll and a hard act to follow, but we promise to love you no matter what drumbeat you march to. Your daddy, Willie (whom I call Honey—at *all* times), is an attorney and if the bar results come out well, I will be one too. We call you our bar baby because we planned to and did get pregnant right after I took the July 1979 bar exam. In fact, you may have been conceived on the night of the first of a two-day exam. I get pregnant very quickly. It only took one try for Jen and I'll bet the same is true for you. Actually I speak of you as one, but the doctor tells me you may be two.

At three months, just as with Jen, I have started to show somewhat. I had to buy maternity clothes at three months with Jen. You've not been hard on me so far. My first pregnancy was an absolute breeze. I love being pregnant, except that my usually blemish-free, smooth complexion breaks out—especially on my back and forehead. I also get stretch marks (which really aren't so bad since they're nearly my same color—it could definitely be worse) and I keep a nasty taste in my mouth and can't stand to chew gum, which I usually do every day of my life. I pee an awful lot because you babies love to sit on my bladder. But other than that, no problems. I don't get morning sickness and all that like some folks. But you do make me feel tired a lot. I almost absolutely must have a nap each day, though generally, unpregnant, I *never* nap during the day. Your father and I live here in the house that we renovated while we were pregnant with Jen. Right now we have a first-year law student living with us.

Tuesday 4/15/80

Well, Friday we finally got the full report on you. That's when you were born. I guess you'd like to know all about it, huh? Well, for starters, even though the doctor said you'd be born on 4/24, I always said it would be before, and the date I said was 4/11 and 4/11 it was. I knew it just the way I knew Jen would come exactly on her expected date of 5/18. I just knew. You are Anne Alexis Bennett Alexander. You are named Anne after my mother. You and Jen both are named Bennett as part of your middle name because my Dad is big on boys carrying on the family name, but he had four girls (and finally a boy), so I told him I'd fix him, I'd let my kids carry on the family name whether they were girls or boys. And I did.

I worked up until Thursday. I went to visit my dad in the hospital the day you were born. Naturally he had a fit when I told him I was in labor and he insisted I go home promptly. But my contractions weren't close enough together yet. Linda came home soon after we arrived and was *vastly* relieved that we hadn't had you without her. I had you by natural childbirth. Linda photographed the whole thing, but your dad blew it when he developed the film in the wrong solution, so there are no pictures. You came out after only two or three pushes. I was so glad to see you. You cried on your own and didn't have to be spanked. The doctor told me you were a girl and plopped you down on my tummy—cord and all. I just laughed and laughed and marveled at you and felt your smooth, wet, slicky little back and butt. You were squirming all around, of course. Then Honey held you, and finally the nurse took you to clean you up. I was so glad you were here and a girl and healthy. Linda was completely taken out by the whole thing. She'd *never* experienced anything even *close* to a live delivery and she was *very* excited and taken by it all.

Alexandra

Mon. 9/14/87

Four weeks, one day—Now really isn't a good time to write about you because I feel so tired and my poor feet hurt (surgery). But I've meant to do it for so long, till I can't wait a bit longer. You are so wonderful and we are *so* very glad to have you. The girls are crazy about you and spend every free second fluttering around you. Poohksie wants to hold you all the time. And I love your little cheeks off. The day you were born was a Sunday and we were all at home relaxing. When we got the call (we'd been waiting for four months) we all jumped up and down and screamed and screamed with joy because you were finally born and you were a girl. It *killed* us to not be able to see you till the next day (under the HRS rules). We went to see you as *soon* as we could the next day, and fell in love.

You were born on the rarest of rare events—the Harmonic Convergence. It's supposed to be when peace is to reign and all good forces come together or some such nonsense. It happened the day you were born (Sunday, August 16) and you had the most peaceful face. People looked at you and just felt peaceful. It happens (the Harmonic Convergence) only once every sixty-six years or so, and all the planets are supposed to be in alignment or something. It was in all the papers and magazines.

All we know of your biological mom is that she is nineteen, white, dark-haired, a college student, plays the piano, is adopted and living at home with her mom, who was divorced from her husband. She has an adopted brother. We know even less of your biological father. Only that he is black and the relationship was *very* brief. Your biological mom did a very selfless act in giving you up and for that we will be eternally grateful. We love you as if you were our own, and it doesn't get any better than that.

Right this minute you've awakened after an hour and are crying. It's only because you're so sleepy. Jen and Anne hate for you to cry. You're at the stage, after four weeks of constantly being held, because we can't get enough of you, where you're used to being held. I won't say "spoiled" because it's not your fault. But it will take some restraint on our part. You were up for so little time till we held you the whole time you were awake, so now you're used to it. Sort of. Yesterday when we took you to church for the first time, you sat there in your seat just as pleased as punch. Not a peep. Drifted in and out of sleep and didn't make a sound.

We also know that your birth mother delivered you by cesarean birth. She never saw you and she left the hospital the same day you did (Tuesday 8/18)—two days after you were born. Usually cesarean-delivery moms stay for a week. We're told (by the adoption attorney) that she just wanted to get on with her life and try to forget what happened. She gets sort of sad when she talks to the attorney, but she's firm in her decision to give you up. She doesn't know anything about us—didn't want to.

Pooh is so happy to have you, till her toes are curled. You look just like you belong to her and that's probably one reason the girls took to you so. Your little pink cheeks and big brown eyes remind them of Pooh, so when they see you, they can pretend it's baby Pooh. They love you for yourself too, of course. But they love Pooh so, till you were automatically "in" with them. Then when you *looked* like her, it was even better.

PART FIVE

Naming Violation and Betrayal

Dear Diary,
I think one of these days mom and dad are going to get divorced.
To me if two parents get divorced they shouldn't get the children.
If they were going to get divorced why did they get married? *I won't go to anyone if they get divorced.* Your someone,

SHELLY (MICHELE L. SIMMS-BURTON)
November 3, 1968, age ten

I'd rather be a tree, even a willow
At least then I could stand life's wind pulling and pushing
Trees grow a new layer of skin, bark is hard, not mine

HERMINE PINSON
May 19, 1982

That damn JW is supporting Clarence Thomas. Typical. Even
some Black men of privilege want it all—money, power, and the
right to shit on women. **PATRICIA BELL-SCOTT**
October 10, 1991

After hearing the verdict on the Rodney King vs. the California
Police case . . . I made a point of hugging black men, even those I
didn't know, of speaking to them in the street, of smiling,
nodding, and waving to them more than usual. And because a part
of me was grieving—I wore black for two days.

RISË COLLINS
April 1992

Reflections of
Breaking Glass

SAPPHIRE

. . . why does everything come back
to the lies of childhood
the first betrayal of trust
my uncle's finger in my
pants . . .

So went a segment of a nine-page "stream of consciousness" poem I was writing in my journal at five o'clock in the morning, December 14, 1988. I didn't think much of it at the time. Later that same day at work, teaching in a JPTA program for high school dropouts, I was standing at the blackboard and when I looked out from the front of the room instead of Black and Latin faces, peeling paint, and a dirty room with windows that looked out onto urban devastation I saw a park with picnic benches, green grass, and trees. I excused myself from the class, went to my boss's office, called my own phone number and left a "message" for myself on my answering machine:

> . . . I just remember it was out in the open, there were trees . . . It was there that it happened. Just my uncle sticking, um you know, sticking his finger in my clothing, uh yeah . . . I can see his face clearly now—mean, he was a mean man . . .

When I got home that evening I played back the "message" and recorded it verbatim in my journal. December 14, 1988, was the beginning of a long journey backward and forward simultaneously. My journal became the means, vehicle, by which I traveled to the past. By May of 1989 I realize my father is part of the story. In June of 1989 I write:

> I feel blessed to be alive. I am a survivor. And a survivor's job is to tell—tell her story for the generations to come, in hope that we will have generations to come . . .

In the spring of 1992 I see a call for submissions to a collection of Black women's journal writing. Instantly I know I will submit something and what it will be.

I can barely see over the dashboard. Daddy and I are riding in the car through a pretty land like cartoons with giant rabbits, pink flowers, and green hills all around. Riding with Daddy is fun. I laugh to be riding with Daddy. But I'm scared. Sometimes Daddy changes to a nervous, mean man with a tight face. He gives me a white tablet and red, sweet, sticky stuff in a paper cup to drink. Tastes good. We go to a house. It is empty. Daddy takes me up the stairs. The sunlight is shiny and bright on the pretty wood floors. Green curtains float like dreams in the window. When I look over at Daddy he's leaning in the doorway, his pants are unzipped and he has put whipped cream on his thing. He calls me to him then grabs my head and pushes his thing in my mouth. I choke and pull away.

Daddy leaves. When he comes back he has zipped up his pants but his face looks nervous. He pulls me into the middle of the room, presses me down on the floor and pulls my underpants off. He unzips his pants and takes out his thing. He pushes his floppy thing between my legs. What is he trying to do? His smell climbs up my nose, his whiskers feel like needles. His thing is hard now. He pushes his thing, *pushes* his thing and my pelvis cracks in half when his thing goes in my body. I can't breathe. I hear Daddy say, "Your mama says it's all right. Be a good girl now." My head rolls to the side and falls off into the black. My eyes close and I float up to the ceiling and from far away I see a child's bones come loose and float away in a river of blood as a big man plunges into a little girl. The man humps up like a dog, shivers and shakes like an earthquake. Then he pulls himself out of the little girl, gets up off the floor very fast and runs away.

I float down from the ceiling back into my body and open my eyes. My legs feel like broken glass. The green curtains seem like flags at half-mast and the sun seems old. Where's Daddy? What happened? My body burns like a knife has been stuck in me. A cool breeze from the window rushes over me and I feel the wetness around my hips. Scared I have peed on myself I put my left hand in the puddle spreading from under my hips. It is cold. I raise my hand to my face, it is covered with blood. I put my hand down and look at the light disappearing on the hard, wood floor.

Love in the Time of AIDS

AMA R. SARAN

This story emerged from my sad 1991 summer sojourn in the pediatric AIDS ward of a large urban hospital. My sister-friend Pat, a pediatrician, has been my gentle guide. I am conducting collaborative ethnographic research for my dissertation, "My Sisters, Their Palms, Their Psalms: African-American Women's Magic and Religion in the Time of AIDS." I wish I could report there are too few people to research—I can't . . .

Day One . . . July 2, 1991, Marshall Memorial Pediatric Ward

We whisper-walk into this cool Jell-O-green room of little things: tiny brown bed, miniature gray wheelchair parked at the skinny chrome pole trailing see-through tubes anchoring the sharp, shiny needles hooked into the vermicelli veins.

5:00 P.M. Dinner's served. The lean little hand plucks two limp string beans off the pink plastic tray with red-nailed, fine-as-cat-hair fingers. Caramel ladyfingers that wave and sway turning beans into

ballet while she frowns down on chopped pork chop, the chilly
mashed potato mound and the beans in green fatigues.

Her cloudy eyes clarify the meaning of this disease draped as it is
in humongous pieces of her short little life.

> Wee high-tech weaponry stuns and silences me.
> But only for the moment it takes to know it's not enough
> to fight this flood of leaking life.
> This child's life that the shush-shush machine sings to sleep
> amid the tangle of tubes caressing her to calm.

She talks. Looking toward doctor-friend Pat but inviting me in through
secret swipes of long, still-lush lashes, Imani speaks. Words stroll from
her self-possessed parched mouth:

> My family misses me. I had a birthday.
> I want two presents. You missed my birthday.
> Bring me two presents. Blocks and clay.
> I'm not eating this. Not the bread, not
> the beans. Not the mashed potatoes. Chop-
> chop meat; I'll eat that.

Pat tells me before we enter Imani's private room:

> Her mama Jackie is Jehovah's Witness; was Jehovah's Witness.
> Imani born too soon and too small at two and one-half pounds
> has been transfused over and over again for all the bad
> things that come along with getting here before
> your mama's ready for you.

Pat says:

> As her primary physician I have had her
> institutionalized in a hospice-like setting
> that generally houses babies. Imani is here

in the hospital doing battle with diarrhea.

Again.

Jackie, Imani's young, pretty mama lives too far out to visit too often.
And she has other children.

A son who is gifted.

He recently took a knife to her.

He is ten.

She has a son who is severely retarded.

He is five.

Imani, only daughter, is eight on this birthday.

Day Two . . . Wednesday, July 3, 1991, 12 Noon
We visit Imani this very next day bearing presents. Two presents. Pat
instructs me to wipe and wash the dirt of the street off me as we enter.
"You can do more harm to her than she can to you."

Pat leaves.

Imani and I open the deliciously ribbed, satiny rows of modeling
clay of new (not-when-I-was-a-child) colors—cool and silky to our
touch. We make a duck. She pounds out perfect duck lips. Corrects
my upside-down slicing of clay with the white plastic knife left from
a lunch untasted.

The clay moves her. She speaks. This time I have words too. Pat
walks in to doctor her a bit. Peering into, pulling on her blood crusted
ears. Her lips, lacy ledges of papery skin I ache to pull. I don't know
the rules for touching—not yet.

Imani tells me:

> I love the name Natasha. That's what I'll name
> my daughter when I grow up and have a little girl.

I lose my way in her words. Her long-life talk writes itself across the
ceiling tiles, sucks the air out the Jell-O-green room of this twenty-
nine-pound eight-year-old of needle-thin face and frame. This young
sister I cannot recruit to Spelman.

Day Three . . . Monday, July 8, 1991

Imani's father, her daddy, is here. Young, capped, sneakered, and t-shirted. Imani grins; so-o-o happy. "Right Daddy!" They pound and pull and pleasure their clay into an exquisitely fashioned sofa of three cushions, a coffee table, and vase in which Daddy sticks a sprig of baby's breath. I watch and fling out bits of talk. "Would you like more clay?" "Any color," she answers. Imani laughs, giggles, lays back grandly on the fat, plump white pillows with deep pleasure all the while using the "Daddy" name as often as she can smuggle it into their small talk. Daddy—he is shy. He is friendly. They play, they touch, they tease. I leave. Wash my hands again. Pick up my many bags drooping under her little brown bed. Blow a kiss and walk out.

Day Four . . . September 25, 1991

Pat calls:

> Imani's back in the hospital. I don't know if she'll
> live through this one. Her mama has a new boyfriend.
> He's got a job in North Carolina. She wants to join
> him. She knows all about what we can't do for Imani.
> This is her chance to go.

I call Sonja, my Brooklyn Jamaican sister-friend doll-maker. I order two of her babies. One for Imani. One for me. Imani gets the one whose long, swishy dress is edged in lace and pearls. The one holding her soft brown hands to her mouth and slyly laughing.

Sister-friend Sonja soothes in Jamaican word-song:

> I'll make her baby and deliver it to her myself.
> I'll take the bus 'cross town and get it there.

Hanging up the phone I huddle under my cabbage-rose covers crying. Ten again; hurting . . . forty-three and grown knowing what's coming.

Day Five . . . Early November 1991

Pat calls me at home in Atlanta. It's on my recorder when I return from work. The message to call her is at work when I return from home. I do not return sister-friend's call. Run scared for weeks from news I already know.

I worry . . .

> Did the doll go with her?
> Were there real flowers?
> A pretty Kate Greenway dress with smocking?
> A full couch; the casket open all the way
> for black patent-leather shoes to shine and show?
> Did they use ChapStick for her lips?
> Q-Tips for her ears?
> Vaseline for her face knees and elbows?
> Did they grease those little brown legs?

> Crawling into the corners of things never believed in I conjure
> my comforts . . .

> Will there be more clay to play with?
> Golden slippers that fit?
> Wings to wear?
> Something more exciting than milk and honey?
> Can she grow up now?
> Finally have a daughter
> Name her Natasha . . .

Writing, Screaming, and Healing

R. H. DOUGLAS

During my years in therapy I came to realize the importance of the Diary. My therapist did say "the Diary kept you sane." How sane I never did know until I saw how desperately I clutched that notebook and how it had become a part of me—an extension—like an extra arm or a second heart in which I absorbed all of life's pain, disappointment, and emotional scrambling.

Through the Diary I viewed my childhood with eyes averted and feelings detached. Through the Diary I became acquainted with another woman whose voice I feared yet revered, since she spoke all those truths I shunned. Timid, she was not. And, I in my timidity admired her and dreamed of one day being like her, having her voice, her boldness, her ability to dream.

Slowly, that day did come and, again, through the Diary I was able to see the merging of the woman who lived only in the Diary with myself, the woman who lived outside its pages. Our voices have become one. Still questioning, still sifting, still searching, but accepting. Accepting the pain, disappointments, embarrassments, rejection, abandonment, abuse (sexual and emotional). Accepting this life that has *been given me. This life that strengthened me as a Woman, as a Writer. That taught me to love myself, while embracing the past as mine. My past. A past that could never belong to anyone else. A past that has paved the way, even without my knowing it, for my future. Now, here I am, using that past to focus on the future.*

The Diary allowed me to see for myself, within myself, parts of me I would not otherwise want to see, been able to see. The Diary has helped me let go of those things that no longer nourish, no longer encourage growth. The Diary has helped me to say, to hell with it all, this is my life. Abandoned and abused child, emotionally battered woman, overworked mother, unfulfilled artist—it is my life anyway, and through the pages of the Diary, I continue to scrutinize, sift it through, and remove the weeds from my flower garden. Most important, to share the beautiful blooms I am able to pick, bunch together, and display for others to see and examine the complex beauty of Divine handiwork. I have survived. And the Diaries testify to that phenomenon.

May 27, 1976

Aﬆfter session with my therapist, Jim Maguire, I feel relaxed. But I cannot remember flow of conversation. Cannot remember remarks at my admission of past experience. I know I talked a lot. Feel empty inside. Wonder if he's bored and it's just a job. Does he work for money or work for work and caring's sake. Maybe he is saying: What a confused bitch! But, he does not look as if he would use such language. He asked if I felt embarrassed or happy because I was smiling. I thought I only smiled when I am happy, but when the question was asked I was smiling because I was embarrassed. Big, stupid grin too. He also said writing in the Diary is like locking thoughts away. Bad thoughts. I write most often when I am in a depressed mood. No gaiety in my writing. It blends with my sad, sorrowful self. I told him that I never look back at my childhood and also my writing. He apologized for its being so painful for me to talk about Mammy and drinking and sex. I shed a bucketful of tears on this subject. Is it for the same reason/reasons I do not remember my childhood nor do I read what I have written? What I recall of childhood does not resemble me now. I recall the boys hitting me with stones and slapping me and running me from school straight home, chasing me with big sticks because I would not talk to them or become friendly with them. They did not understand my shyness and my fear of them. And with a mother who was so free and easy, they could not understand why I was so stuck up and not willing to "do it" with each and every one of them.

I recall the first time I saw the lovers in their act covered by a big white sheet. They were on the floor of the galvanized house in which we lived in the South—after my mother (this stranger, this beautiful looking woman) had come and taken us away from the lady my father left us with. The roof and siding of the house was galvanized and when the sun beat down it was steaming hot. It was steaming hot this day and our mother and her girlfriend and their two men friends, despite our presence out in the yard and with the doors ajar, were doing it. I knew my mother was on the bed and her friend on the floor next to the bed. I could hear their muffled noises and see the bodies of the men moving up and down under the white sheet. I never forgot that vision of the sheet-clad bodies and the embarrassment of knowing what they were doing.

I recall meeting Mr. Clark, Mammy's boyfriend, in order to get money to play mass at carnival. I did not like him. Thought him fat and a dirty old man. But I had to have the money. He liked to put his penis in my mouth. At that age I did not understand what I was doing or what pleasure he got from such a stupid nasty act. I did not know the reason for these actions. It was what he wanted me to do and I did it. I remember also another of my mother's men friends letting me do the same for money. Money attracted me because we were so poor before we went to live with my great-grandparents on the cocoa estate and had all of nature at our disposal and then money did not matter. But before that we would walk to school, could not afford to ride the bus like other children, took no lunch or my mother would hustle up something and bring to us at lunchtime and then we walked home afternoons after school. Long, long, long joyous hours in the afternoon—since we did not have to hustle like in the morning—we would roam for hours along the train tracks and eating our fill of sugarcane, burned and ready for the mill or rooting it up from the field; guavas, doncs, mangoes, whatever fruits we did find along the way. We arrived home with our bellies filled and sometimes could not eat the stewed tomatoes and rice or spinach and rice or whatever and rice she could dish up for us. Anyway, this time when the man friend put his penis in my mouth, he gave me one dollar because he had the pleasure of having his orgasm in my mouth—gagging and humiliated and believing I would die, I went on to school spitting all the way. But I had the dollar to buy whatever I wanted for myself and my brother. Never to this day could I forget the hot, shocking, gushing fluid—awful, tongue-tying, ghastly tasting liquid which shot up into my mouth and nearly choked me with its unexpected arrival.

1976

I remember the first day I saw signs of my period. I was curious and afraid wondering as to what could cause the bleeding and the intense pain. I remember I played mostly alone that day. Did not pitch marbles or go by the seaside. Stayed under the cocoa estate walking around, prodding the dry leaves with a stick in my hand and wondering about the pain in my belly. I lay in the hammock under the cocoa trees waiting for Mammy to tell her what was happening to me. I was very young. Still running around in knickers. She showed me what to do, but in dead silence. I cannot remember hearing words of my having to be cautious because I was now a young lady. When I got pregnant I was not aware how such a thing was possible and how it happened. I never connected having a baby with having my period and with sex without protection. With sex, period—excuse the pun, Dear Diary. I was completely innocent, foolish, and ignorant of the facts. Even when I became pregnant I was not aware of it for months. Until she said that I was, and if I wanted to go and meet my father in America I couldn't have any baby. I did not know what she was talking about.

Baby? Me? I was like a blank page that life was writing upon, experience after experience, after experience.

1976

My great-grandmother thought I was very rude because I stared her straight in the eyes when she punished me. She would become angry and say, "What are you looking at . . . Why are you looking at me like that," in patois. She seldom spoke English, and even though I spoke no patois, I understood quite clearly what she was saying. We all did. And some of my cousins spoke patois. Wish I had learned the language. When we looked at her boldface, as she would say, she would hurriedly reach out to strike us. You were afraid to look anywhere in her direction for her eyes were crossed and she maybe could not tell whether or not you were looking at her or away from her. She would confuse me, for when I thought I was not looking her in the eye, she would say that I was and would be angry with me. It was forbidden to stare. Is this what she was taught by her white masters, through her mother and her mother's mother before her. I was taught to be meek and submissive. I was not taught to be strong, but I wanted to be strong like my great-grandfather. I loved his strength. That's the meaning of my dream. I have accepted his strength and his knowledge and his wisdom and gave my great-grandmother back her weaknesses. Although she was a mighty strong woman herself, she weakened me like she weakened her daughter and her granddaughter, my mother. Her husband was strong and gallant. Always cheerful and smiling, always proud and aware. She was always sneaking around, always grumbling, always fighting, always suspicious, always negative about everything. Very fucking negative. Could you imagine not being able to stare or even to raise your eyes at someone because of fear at the order not to do so, and made to believe that doing so was rude and fresh-up. Not to say what's on your mind. Not to speak up or talk back. How could you look at them to say I love you then. I was so afraid of her. Her darkness, her weirdness. Her one swollen foot because of a severe case of elephantiasis and her crossed eyes. Cockeyeye Sandrene we and all the villagers called her. With just a stare of her crossed eyes she would silence me for hours. I would only walk and be silent within myself. Afraid to do anything. Afraid to sing, afraid to dance, afraid to play with other children, especially if they were boys. Afraid to whistle because it was considered to be of the devil and an evil thing. Afraid to be free in spirit and in body. She controlled you like a military officer. And was not backward when it came down to punishing us. She would fight with my male cousins like men. Hold them and cuff them and kick them with her one good foot or her big foot—amazing how she lifted and swung it. She would do whatever her cruel mind desired. She would throw things at you, anything—from rocks to water to pails of urine, to the tobacco-soaked saliva which was readily gathered in her mouth. That was her major way of getting to you when you were too far away from her reach and she could not grab hold of you with her hands and choke you near to death. She would rake the spit from the pit of her dark soul and throw back her head, then aim, coming up swearing and spitting at you three times. It must always be three times "thwah, thwah, thwah" she would say—whatever that meant, but it was used to emphasize the curse she was muttering in patois as she spat at you in between the muttering, three times. And could her spit fly. The saliva and the curse would come flying at you full force. At times it was so unexpected that you were not aware of it, so you might be caught in the shower of saliva. Seldom would I cross her that way. Girls were treated as things to be protected from the lustful eyes of men and from themselves desiring men. We had to be well behaved, so we were overly suspected. We all were punished with the same severity. Anything that they laid their hands on would land on our backs, our heads . . . ropes, plaited switches, stones, hands, feet, words. Everything close at hand or prepared. Like the tree branches that hung nearby or the green switches that we were sent to cut from the tree since they had more sting. She walked around in her yards and yards of dresses, petticoats, bloomers and it seemed as if she wore dresses on top of dresses, full and flowing to the ground. In this hot weather. I would often wonder what was between her legs and try to peek at her when she dressed and was tying up the drawstring of her petticoats and bloomers. Her legs were long and brown and were strong, not the legs of an old woman.

She wore real heavy black boots, man-shoes. And heavy silver bracelets which would make so much noise as she moved about. And did she move about. At times I would sneak a look at her when she would go to the sea to bathe, which was not too often—at least not as often as we children did, which was every day. When she did, she bathed in full clothing, bloomers, and petticoat, gray or blue and long to the ankles. The wet material would stick to her skin. The once or twice I caught her tying up her bloomers and saw the black hairs, I was surprised. I never saw her totally naked and often wondered what she looked like naked. When we saw her in the morning she was fully clothed, and when she went to bed at night she was fully clothed. She was always modestly overdressed but nothing in her personality and mannerism was modest. She would curse you in her patois tongue and fight and stone and run you around the yard with big sticks and pails of urine or cold water to cool down your heat, she would say to me. I remember when I came home from school one evening and saw her with false teeth which could not fit into her mouth properly and she would have to take them out to talk and they would fall out when she tried to eat with it. Guess her gums had gotten so used to being without teeth they fought even the false teeth. I hated to see it and see the saliva dribbling from her mouth as she took it out and said what she had to then placed them back again. I could not eat from her from that day on . . . and would try to eat as much fruits as possible or go to my grandmother's pot instead.

1977

As I write about it in the diary and talk to Maguire about it, I now feel that I have dealt with the fear of her, my great-grandmother; I have gotten rid of the numb feeling in my legs; overcome the fear of looking someone in the eyes. I see now that there is nothing to fear by looking someone in the eyes, but rather a whole lot to be learned. Eyes tell the story of the soul. Is that why I was forbidden to look her in the eyes? So I would not know her story?

October 31, 1991
"Happy Birthday Mother" Happy Birthday from your oldest daughter." How I wish you were alive so I could bring you flowers and shower you with gifts and kisses as is befitting a mother as you were to me. Open and warm with your own sensuous charm, which I hated as I grew older and the men flocked and you gave yourself without much of a wink. But how much I wish I could kiss you and hold you close to me as I never did in life. Mother, Mother, Mother. You never demanded my love, you never requested it either. You never demanded my respect. You lived your life, burying your unspoken hurt, pleasing the woman in you, knowing of my objections and embarrassment and yet knowing that accept it I must for, on the other hand, you never rejected or deserted me even when you were wrapped up in the pleasures and delights of living your drunken, whorish life.

It is ironic, that today, on your birthday, I feel at peace in my heart and know that I have made peace with you, that you have forgiven me, and now we move in love, mother and daughter. It is the first birthday that I have acknowledged with love in my heart, with gladness, with wanting to share in your birthday joy—amid the rum and the men and the women and the noise of merrymaking that could continue for days. But now, I don't care and you're not here.

How old would you be today? Imagine, I don't even know your age—fifty-seven, fifty-eight, fifty-nine, sixty? Not yet sixty-five I am sure. Living fast and dying young. Forgive me Mother. There are no flowers for your grave but in my heart there is the largest bouquet of all. Love. Thank you Mummy. Thank you Mummy. Thank you Mummy for loving me even when I rejected you. Even when you knew I hated you. I love you.

Saturday. November 16, 1991

On my way to Trinidad. At the airport in Puerto Rico. Heard these men talking and joking around, loud and boisterous as only West Indian don'-give-ah-damn macho men could talk. "Ah can't wait to get home and open up dat bottle ah rum, man—just change meh shirt and go straight to dat fete, boy. . . ." They heckled each other unmercifully and began talking about areas of Trinidad which I was familiar with. L'Anse Mitant, Point Cumana, Carenage. . . . I asked if they knew Micey.

Their eyes opened up wide . . . One said, "Boy, dat was ah nice 'oman. Sweet, sweet, sweet too bad. Dat 'oman could cook . . ." And he kissed his puckered fingers to demonstrate how sweet she was and how sweet she could cook. The others joined in, "Dat woman would welcome anybody with open arms and give dem she las' plate of food. . . ." (Open arms and open legs I thought and smiled.) Another added, "And she could drink she rum . . . like any man. What ah nice, sweet 'oman." What that—"nice, sweet woman"—meant was that she had a wonderful, cheerful, always happy-go-lucky personality, laughing always, making everyone around her happy, except her children, whose heads were always bowed in shame. She was a good limer and rum drinker. It meant she was totally liberated and free to herself and her desires. What "a nice woman" meant was a woman without any, any inhibitions about her sexuality, a woman with warmth and a human touch and kindness which surpassed any moral indecency she exhibited. They talked about her in such glowing terms. Calling her Miss Micey, these grown men—and I recall that young, old, male, female, all called her Miss Micey, fondly, affectionately, even when she was in her most drunken and vulgar state. I mentioned to the men that "rum killed her eventually." They were annoyed at me for saying that and insisted, "No, when you' time come, you have to go, you have no control over dat. She time come and that's dat . . ." I listened to them and I marveled how much they believed in this woman and genuinely loved her and saw her as the ideal 'oman. Ideal liming and drinking partner, I thought . . . but was quite proud at that moment to say "that's my mother" without feeling the shame and embarrassment and the pain. Looking at their surprised faces as they recognized the resemblance and began to recall the times they came to the house when I was small . . . the older men, especially . . . wanting to know if I remembered them and some of them looking quite sheepish and embarrassed as they looked at me. And I wondered which one seemed likely to be the one she had gone to bed with—all of them, I smiled. She really was some 'oman. Miss Micey.

March 5, 1992

I want to scream to my father—hey, look at me. I am a woman now and deserve some of your attention. You neglected the child—left her still looking out that window for your return—still looking out at life—still looking out on an empty, hot, deserted road, upon which you never traveled back to her, upon which you never set foot again. You walked away forever. Did you know it was forever when you left that first time. When you walked with your pride, arrogance, and ambition. Did it fill your chest to know that finally you were on your way to freedom. You had gotten rid of the mother, even though your argument now is that she left, but it was because of you, her fear of you, her uncertainty of you, her need of you—to be accepted for who she was and not compared against another whom you had chosen under the facade of friendship and forced this friendship upon her so you could have your cake and eat it too. So how did you feel, Father dear, as you walked away? Did you feel the burden of painful guilt or the relief of freedom? No baggage, extra baggage—for I am sure to you, when she left us with you, we were nothing but extra baggage which you could not travel with. Where in the world will a man alone with two small children go? Isn't it best what I am doing? Leaving them behind with this woman who seemed kind, and nice and caring. Isn't it best I go to prepare a way for them. But did you? Years later, maybe forced by that other woman—our mother's best friend who by this time had become your wife. After you walked down that road, you never looked back to see us—to see me—staring out that window at your back as you walked proud and free away from my heart and taking all my love with you. That hot, tropical day—or was it night?—under the cover of darkness you sneaked away while we were asleep. And that is why the morning brought with it this new search for you, this staring out the window for you, this pain and realization that you had left us, left me, and I did not know when you would return. You had left me so many times before—so very many times— with anyone who would care for us after she left. But those times, you always returned, sometimes after weeks, once after years; but now, it seemed different. It felt different. This time it felt like forever. This time it felt like abandonment.

Wednesday. March 23, 1992

My husband in calling my father's home has helped to loosen the barriers that were holding up the already forceful dam. She, his wife, my stepmother, told him that I should try to get over this hurt and pain and that everyone makes mistakes when they are young and that he, my father, should not be told what was happening to me. My husband should not discuss with my father that his daughter is having an emotionally rough time and that I should learn to deal with my own problems; and that I am not the only one who was brought up without a father, and my mother is not the only woman to bring children up alone and then she went on to tell my husband about the things my mother did to hurt my father—taking away his manhood, she said—so he suffered enough and should not suffer anymore. Hear who's talking . . . ! I said when my husband told this to me, hesitantly, for he did not want to add to the feeling of rejection that had slowly brought on this depression and the emotional outburst. Why? Why should we, his children, go on suffering by holding all of this in, not letting go.

It's too late. Note: too late . . . to know a daddy. I may yearn to know about this man, this father. But a daddy he will never be, for I am no longer a little girl—from the day I came here and saw the man. I came as a woman, premature, yes, but a woman nevertheless—with all womanly experiences—and although I tried to play the little-girl role, Daddy's little-girl role, I remained always in my heart a woman and experienced him always as a man. Girlhood for me ended so early, so very early that I cannot recall the details of it. I can only remember the hazed pain, the abuse, the overwork, the having to grow up quickly to take care of my brother and sisters and my mother when she was drunk and all her drunken friends. Growing up was fast and abrupt. One day I was out under the mango trees collecting and eating my fill of mangoes and walking on the beaches by the bay and the next day I was standing behind the one-burner pitch-oil stove or fanning the coal pot or three-stone fireside, struggling to cook a meal for my brother and sisters because our mother did not come home from her drunken spree. Like my brother said last week when I saw him, "You know what it is to have a mother disappear for a week and have no food to eat." Although I don't remember going hungry for so many days, because we had our fill of fruits and our great-grandparents who provided until their death. But it is possible that she did leave us for days and we did go hungry, but I have a tendency to block out patches of my life. My brother on the other hand, who was so very silent all through out childhood and even now, buried all that had happened— it lies deep down in the pit or his memory and he will not forget, not forgive our mother and blames her totally and excuses his father.

Saturday. March 28, 1992

Went to the therapist for the first time again in four years. Needed to talk about my father I thought, but also to my surprise spoke about my husband and leaving my leisurely, comfortable, well-established, successful life in Trinidad because he wanted to emigrate. The burden I feel of having two small children again after bringing up a well-adjusted, independent now eighteen-year-old; and a husband who is loving, helpful, but leans heavily upon me, still needing his mother, emotionally; a timid career as an emerging writer; and a heavy, deeply rooted fear that if I allow myself to truly explore what I feel I will find out that I really hate my father and regret that I got married and have two young, very young, children again to raise. I have to get in touch with my feelings the therapist says. But I know that! How? First, letting myself feel. Allowing myself the pleasure of feeling rage, hurt, pain, revenge, regret, hate—feel it all! Directed at whoever and not feel guilty. There is so much to write about.

Friday night

Well, the big event happened. So uneventful. Did not break down. Did not rant and rave. Did not tell him he was a fuck and a bastard. We had a good meeting. We sat in the sunny boardroom with bay windows looking out at the sky and talked. Of course he wanted to dominate the conversation, telling me his story, or part of it—a little more than he ever told me before. Wanting to know why of all his children I questioned so much of the past. But I knew if I did not speak and tell him how hurt I was and how disappointed I felt that he left us with a strange woman who treated us like orphans, I would still feel bad and burdened by it all. So I told him. He responded that they were not strangers but the woman's husband was his best friend just as my friend Carol is my best friend and he sent her money always to take care of us, which her husband abused and used to travel around the Caribbean. He knew we were suffering, he said, but he could do nothing about it, being in England; so he asked his mother to come and do whatever she thought right. She got our mother to come and take us and that is where the saga with her began. She took us, yes. Apparently she did not leave us with him when she left him. The court granted him custody of us since he proved she was not a fit mother. But that could be one of his righteous stories to erase the blame, guilt, and shame from his eyes.

He still proclaims that she always was a "bright girl" meaning that she was hot, sexually alert, and active and sensually explosive. Of course he went on about how much he loved her and married her even though he knew of her "ways." And the total embarrassment she was to him when the landlady forced him to move because she would bring men home when he was at work and how the neighbors and his friends called him "cunumunuu" (foolish/stupid) because he would not leave her. I said, but she became a Seventh Day Adventist because of you: she must have loved you. He said she became an Adventist because of some man who was coming to the house to give her Bible lessons and with whom she was sexually involved. He told me some of the old horror stories about her and some new ones. All in which he portrays her as a beautiful whore whom he loved despite it all; and himself as a martyr—devoted husband who was being taken advantage off. I said in my mind, "bullshit," for I knew he was telling me what he forced himself to believe and it was only sprinkled with truth and not the whole truth. He had removed all the guilt from him and placed it on her. But, I said to him, there must have been a reason for her to act like that. My uncle and aunt told me that you were the cause of it all. Of course he denied it all, saying that they did not know the entire story since he was too embarrassed to let them know what she was doing. But I know he was lying for my uncle, his brother, called me to his death bed two days before he died and my aunt told me her story only last year and both versions collaborated. And from the grief in my aunt's voice and the tears in her eyes as she spoke of my mother and what she was and what she had become "drinking all that rum and living like that. . . . When I remember Everline. . . . My heart does break. . . ." That is the truth. I kept my cool and listened to him. He believes that it is a family curse, that the manner of life my great-grandmother and grandmother and mother lived was not natural; and he prays every day for God to spare his girl children that sort of life.

When I think back on my life and the many experiences I have had with drugs and men, I could see his point of its being a curse on the women of the family . . . But my aunt and her daughter (my mother's sister and niece) escaped the rum and the men but succumbed to insanity. They went mad out of their head. What a choice these women had. Funny that I did not have a bucketful of tears and did not expect to be so dry-eyed after either. We hugged and kissed as usual, deliberately turning my cheeks for him and not my lips as he expected me to. I could see he expected it and must have wondered why I gave him my cheeks. I could never understand why as my father he should want to kiss me on my lips, never.

I did not hate or despise him. I knew when he was blowing up the truth and when he was boosting his ego. I knew that I could not change him and did not want to. He is who he is—professor, actor, writer, director/producer, British/West Indian gentleman, with an enormous ego he smothers in humility.

The most revealing thing to me is to find out that I do not hate him as I believed I did. I can love him or leave him. I can go on and write the book without guilt because I know where I am at. I also asked him about his present wife being my mother's best friend. He looked at me with that snicker of a smile and began to deny it. I stared him down and told him that my mother did tell my sisters that she was and that she betrayed her friendship by going back to him and telling him everything they had discussed in confidence. He was surprised. I had him believe that my mother never spoke about him, good or bad—but that was only to me, maybe because she knew in my eyes he did no wrong. To my other sisters, she did, especially to the one who was not his child. I told him that all she ever told me was that he was a "damn liar" and she said it with such pain and venom that I began to believe that about him too. Didn't tell him that I proved it to be true since I got to know him. He admitted that my stepmother was my mother's friend, yes, that they did each other's hair and my mother baked for her and her aunt and they went to church together and he believes that when my stepmother, who is a great upholder of moral values (he said this with a proud smile), left the country, my mother's barriers broke down and she began living "that way." Her friend was not there to show what was morally right or wrong. What crud, I thought. How dare he compare the two, even though his comparison is true. He said I should not blame her because they were not involved until they met again in England. Bullshit! He told me more truth than he ever did before. Maybe he felt the details of his life were his and not mine to interfere with, to know and to judge or make judgment. But it is not that I wanted to make judgment, but to clear up some facts. Believing that she was my mother's best friend and because of her I lost—was abandoned—by my father, was a heavy burden when I dealt with her and tried to love her as a stepmother. Although she was a witch of a stepmother. He apologizes always for her treating his children so badly, and claims to always defend us even though it was never outwardly visible to us. He said that he really bleeds because of my rejection of him. I told him I did love him, always have, always would, but from a distance. I do have problems with the closeness he expects. That's when it flares up for me. I cannot handle it. Never received it when I was a child. Not from him, not from my mother. That is why I have such a difficult time in my relationship with my husband, who is so loving and wants all this closeness. He said I should learn (ha) to have a better relationship and to love, not to be so cold and withdrawn. I said I was working on it because I did not want to grow old like my stepmother, a cold, withdrawn bitchy woman. He was not too pleased. We looked each other in the eyes all throughout conversation. I did not fidget or look down at my hands or feel embarrassed or ashamed. I felt like the woman I am and not like a little girl speaking to her daddy. Amen. I told him that I couldn't respond to his affection and his need for me to love him like a daddy and that I only pretended to in the past, which made me very angry with myself. He seem to understand and put on that "dear, you have hurt me" look. I also shocked him by telling him that my mother did tell my sister that he abused her physically and that is why she never returned home from the hospital after having my sister Jennifer, because he had kicked her in the stomach when she was pregnant with my brother before and said he was not his child. He was so stunned. He looked at me in wide-eyed shock and said in his most put-on painful voice. "I am so surprised she spoke badly of me. And to say that! There is no truth in that of course. Why would she say that!" And he laughed his British gentleman quality laugh.

Feel a part of me emerging again! A gay, joyful me with a colorful creative spirit and inspiration to dress up again. I feel so free. I want to wear colorful head-ties and dress in summery, tropical colors.

You know, Dear Diary, that we may never and would never have that daddy–little girl relationship or a father-daughter relationship, but maybe now we can respect each other as two adults. I beg my mother's forgiveness. I despised her unto death. My greatest regret. The book is dedicated to her, to make up in a way for not understanding why she lived so loose and free. Writing the book is helping me to understand. Amen.

Holding On and Remembering

The night has been a long one. The effort at sleep torturous. I am awake, and as yet there is no sign of dawn. I'm tired and restless and feel as if I have been fighting a calvary of demons all night and that the demons have won. I recall snatches of a dream and understand immediately *that my deceased mother's living spirit is angry. But mostly it is hurt. Saddened. I can feel her disappointment. In the portion of the dream that I could recall I had sat silently, a Peter-like witness to what felt like a public lynching or a witch burning, lacking the courage to stand up (before the hostile audience) for the accused, my mother's memory, or for myself.*

The context for the dream is obvious. The evening before I attended, along with Joyce Carol Thomas, my first "community" discussion of the movie version of The Color Purple. *The discussion, hosted by the Graduate Women's Forum at Berkeley's U.C. campus, included panelists: Barbara Christian, Luisah Teish, Quincy Troupe, Al Young, and Fran Beale. With the exception of Teish; the other panelists and a good portion of the audience (at least, that portion that dared speak) rabidly trashed not just the film but especially Alice. Throughout the discus-*

sion, I thought a lot about my mother. Her voice was conspiciously (and conspiratorially—it seemed) absent, from the panel and the discussion. I left the auditorium wondering what she would have thought about the attack, the discussion, the issues raised in the film and denied by the audience. Later, all night, I had terrible dreams and nightmares of betrayal.

Dear Maxine,

It is about five o'clock in the morning. I understand your anger. Mostly I feel your sorrow *and* your disappointment. I think the reason that I am writing this, is to let you know that *your* sorrow, *your* anger, and *your* disappointment are but dim reflections of my own sense of shame and guilt at my inability last night to stand and "bear witness."

I know that a great deal of your disappointment, comes from your knowledge that "the accused," in my dream, was one of the few people that I had been able to tell that "my mother was a victim of domestic violence." How statistically abstract and emotionally removed I had managed to make it sound in order to be able to say it at all. What I had really wanted to say was that you were murdered by your Baptist minister husband (my stepfather) and the Celie-like hardships of your life; all of which I knew she would understand. I also knew that I could trust her with my shame, my grief, my tears, and your memory. So, however badly, I had at least had managed to get it out. To reveal my deepest and darkest secret.

How hard I had struggled to "control" myself and not cry. Tears were after all a sign of weakness. Painful reminders to me of your weakness. After all, you were dead, they said, because you were weak. You must know, there were so many things about your life —including your death—that frightened me.

I remember (what was for me) the awkward silence following my announcement. Alice, because of my tears, was a watery blur,—but she was there. Quietly waiting in her rocker. How hard it had been to continue. But somehow her quiet presence communicated (in a way that I *felt* more than *understood* at the time) that the continuing, the remembering, and the tears were all part of the healing.

I needed to remember how it felt when I received the phone call at Old Westbury, where I was teaching, informing me that you were dead.

"I'm so sorry to have to be the one to tell you this, but your mother has been killed."

A prolonged, shocked, agonizing silence.

"She was killed in a car accident."

A profoundly sinking silence.

"Are you OK?"

And the barely audible, "I'm OK. I'll come right away."

And later on the plane. The numbness. The emptiness. The primordially familiar feeling of complete aloneness. But mostly the frightening familiarity. It was as if all my life I had been holding my breath, waiting for the other shoe to drop—and finally it had.

I remember arriving at the Phoenix airport with dreaded anticipation not wanting to be met by John.* It must have been obvious to you how intensely I had always disliked him. I hope it was also clear how hard, for your sake, I had tried. At the airport though it became instantly clear to both of us, as he reached to hug me and I surprised even myself by instinctively backing away, that with you gone there was no longer any need to pretend.

With what I later understood to be feigned tears and a trembling voice he explained how you had been, "traveling too fast on the road and missed the curve. The highway patrol said the speedometer was stuck at ninety . . ."

"Please," I responded, "I don't need to hear the details, I'd just like to see her—alone please."

After your funeral, as we sat around trying to deal with the your death, and the brief forty-four years of your life, one of your aunts (your fathers' youngest sister) said, loud enough it seemed so that I would be sure to hear (and hurt), "Well all I have to say is that anybody that's a big enough fool, to drive off a highway and kill

* Not his real name

themselves, I don't feel sorry for 'em." I sat there stunned and nauseated, beyond shock, waiting for somebody to say something.

Their collective silence I took to be collective assent. Even in death as far as they were concerned you were wrong. A fool . . .

As I stormed out of the house in tears. Your friend Miss Mabel* followed me outside.

"There is something I need to tell you," she said. "My house is just up the street."

I followed, my only thought being how to get the earliest possible flight back to New York.

Miss Mabel was in her sixties, and when we got to her house, she sat at her kitchen table for a long, long time without speaking.

Finally, she got up and went over to a nightstand and picked up a tin pan with a brownish-maroon-colored facecloth in it and brought it back to the kitchen table where we were sitting. "I'm not sure how to tell you this, or whether I should even be telling you. But your mother was very badly beaten the night she died.

"Beaten!?"

"Yeah, John had beaten her up pretty bad." She said quietly. "She showed up here at about two o'clock in the morning. She was crying hysterically. Really out of her head. Her clothes were all torn off. She barely had on enough left to cover her body. Her right eye was practically swollen shut. That poor child, her face looked like a piece of raw steak. This pan was filled with her blood. I had to empty it twice; and I still haven't been able to wash all of her blood out of this cloth."

The other shoe fell, but the edge that I was standing on was falling even faster.

Miss Mabel's voice broke as she gently caressed the cloth, "I begged her not to go . . . you know, I haven't been able to sleep really since she died. I begged her. She was in no condition to drive . . . I don't even know if she saw the cliff . . . she couldn't stop crying . . . she had lost so much blood . . . When she left here she could hardly stand up.

* Not her real name

As Miss Mabel talked, I was no longer there. I had gone where you had been. Last week you had been in the same room. Cried in the same room. This week, all that was left of your presence was a tin pan, a bloodied washcloth, some faded bloodstains on the kitchen floor and Miss Mabel's memories.

"I begged her to stay here . . . Ain't nobody gon' mess with you in here I told her . . . I could see how scared she was . . . but she just kept saying how she couldn't take any more, how she had a cousin in Phoenix that would maybe help her . . ."

Suddenly the ledge collapsed completely. And I vomited and retched until there was nothing left. Nothing. No tears. No bruises. No scars. No dried blood. No mangled body. Nothing . . .

This morning I very much need your forgiveness. Please try and understand why I couldn't stand before them last night and argue for your life. I was afraid. Afraid that I would not have been able to do it well enough to make them understand.

I'll ask Alice's forgiveness tomorrow.

And I do think you would have enjoyed the film . . .

Flashbacks and Wounded Children

PATRICIA BELL·SCOTT

These flashbacks and journal entries came to me nearly thirty years after "it" happened. It was a beating from my grandfather, the memory of which makes me cringe in chills to this day. Though I could not possibly have imagined at the time that I had been wounded or that this event would affect my relationships, my journal has helped me understand the child in me and the adult I am. Initially, I was curious about why my inner child decided to have me relive this experience at this particular moment. But I later realized that she had waited until I was in a relatively quiet and somewhat safe space. I am grateful for her patience and continue to write what she reveals. My journal writing provides soothing salve for both of us.

8/19/91—12:35 noon

Last night I had an emotional flashback. As I was ironing, I relived an incident when I was whipped by Granddaddy as I was ironing. I was being whipped because I hadn't ironed and wasn't holding the iron correctly. (With Granddaddy there was always a "right" way to do everything.) I actually didn't understand how to hold it. I didn't go to school the next day because I was so sore. As I remembered this, I started crying. I don't think I thought that much about it when it happened thirty years ago. I'm not sure I cried then. I have no memory of crying. I'm fighting back the tears now as I write. Maybe, I cried last night for the child who didn't cry out many years ago. Oddly, I don't feel angry with Granddaddy. I forgive him. What I am most encouraged about is that my spirit was never broken by this attempt to punish and control.

8/26/91 — 8:25 A.M.

On leaving the bookstore saw a Black man with a car full of Black children. Must have been at least six kids—but two of them caught my eye. One little girl—no more than five—who seemed to have spirit and a nice smile. She smiled mischievously at me. The other child with an arresting appearance was a male who appeared to have only one eye or there had been an injury or something and the eye was closed. I was shaken by the sight of him. He stuck his head out of the car window in such a way that it was an announcement of something wrong—like the roots of a plant searching for water.

3/11/92

Have thought about the oft-repeated family story about how my sister was left in the car by L.C. when he and Momma returned from the hospital. She was forgotten. She does not remember this I'm sure as an infant—but she may have some lingering sense of early abandonment. She told me that she felt abandoned when I left for college. She needs to know that I'm there for her.

3/12/92

Lately, I feel as if a floodgate has been opened. I'm feeling things, thinking about people like never before. I guess this is good, but I don't want to be in overdrive.

9/12/92

Thought again about the flashback of the beating. I remembered it, I felt the pain and cried. It created a wound that is still healing.

PART SIX

Fighting Back

I find love, power, and beauty in confronting and holding up to the clear light of day that which is good (or neutral) and yet which has been denigrated (race, color, etc.) by the social state of consciousness. I name it in order to reframe-transform-uplift it, and give it a seat of social ascendancy. **RISË COLLINS**
June 1992

Market women, those wide-hipped Mamas who haven't *seen* the inside of a school, have decided they're too busy to waste time standing on lines to turn old money in at the bank so they can collect new money later. In the self-same university city where armchair radicals docilely line up for naira, explaining that protesting government policy will give the new regime an excuse to jail them, unlettered women have sucked their teeth at military power. **ANDREA BENTON RUSHING**
April 29, 1984, Ile-Ife, Nigeria

Over tea at Jacsun and Iris's kitchen table Grainne asked me many questions. One of them was, "What are you a survivor of?" I answered, "Racism, sexism, and poverty." **RISË COLLINS**
December 25, 1992

Talked to Audre tonight. Her mother dead. From work. From neglect. From the racism and sexism of America and his puppets. . . . You must continue to live. Now. My sister. For her, For us. We need you. **SONIA SANCHEZ**
September 6, 1988

The Cancer Journals

AUDRE LORDE

There is a commonality of isolation and painful reassessment which is shared by all women with breast cancer, whether this commonality is recognized or not. It is not my intention to judge the woman who has chosen the path of prosthesis, of silence and invisibility, the woman who wishes to be "the same as before." She has survived on another kind of courage, and she is not alone. Each of us struggles daily with the pressures of conformity and the loneliness of difference from which those choices seem to offer escape. I only know that those choices do not work for me, nor for other women who, not without fear, have survived cancer by scrutinizing its meaning within our lives, and by attempting to integrate this crisis into useful strengths for change.

THESE SELECTED JOURNAL ENTRIES, *which begin six months after my modified radical mastectomy for breast cancer, exemplify the process of integrating this crisis into my life.*

1/26/79

I'm not feeling very hopeful these days, about selfhood or anything else. I handle the outward motions of each day while pain fills me like a puspocket and every touch threatens to breech the taut membrane that keeps it from flowing through and poisoning my whole existence. Sometimes despair sweeps across my consciousness like lunar winds across a barren moonscape. Ironshod horses rage back and forth over every nerve. Oh Seboulisa ma, help me remember what I have paid so much to learn. I could die of difference, or live—myriad selves.

2/5/79

The terrible thing is that nothing goes past me these days, nothing. Each horror remains like a steel vise in my flesh, another magnet to the flame. Buster has joined the roll call of useless wasteful deaths of young Black people; in the gallery today everywhere ugly images of women offering up distorted bodies for whatever fantasy passes in the name of male art. Gargoyles of pleasure. Beautiful laughing Buster, shot down in a hallway for ninety cents. Shall I unlearn that tongue in which my curse is written?

3/1/79

It is such an effort to find decent food in this place, not to just give up and eat the old poison. But I must tend my body with at least as much care as I tend the compost, particularly now when it seems so beside the point. Is this pain and despair that surround me a result of cancer, or has it just been released by cancer? I feel so unequal to what I always handled before, the abominations outside that echo the pain within. And yes I am completely self-referenced right now because it is the only translation I can trust, and I do believe not until every woman traces her weave back strand by bloody self-referenced strand, will we begin to alter the whole pattern.

4/16/79

The enormity of our task, to turn the world around. It feels like turning my life around, inside out. If I can look directly at my life and my death without flinching I know there is nothing they can ever do to me again. I must be content to see how really little I can do and still do it with an open heart. I can never accept this, like I can't accept that turning my life around is so hard, eating differently, sleeping differently, moving differently, being differently. Like Martha said, I want the old me, bad as before.

4/22/79

I must let this pain flow through me and pass on. If I resist or try to stop it, it will detonate inside me, shatter me, splatter my pieces against every wall and person that I touch.

5/1/79

Spring comes, and still I feel despair like a pale cloud waiting to consume me, engulf me like another cancer, swallow me into immobility, metabolize me into cells of itself; my body, a barometer. I need to remind myself of the joy, the lightness, the laughter so vital to my living and my health. Otherwise, the other will always be waiting to eat me up into despair again. And that means destruction. I don't know how, but it does.

There is no room around me in which to be still, to examine and explore what pain is mine alone—no device to separate my struggle within from my fury at the outside world's viciousness, the stupid brutal lack of consciousness or concern that passes for the way things are. The arrogant blindness of comfortable white women. What is this work all for? What does it matter whether I ever speak again or not? I try. The blood of black women sloshes from coast to coast and Daly says race is of no concern to women. So that means we are either immortal or born to die and no note taken, un-women.

10/3/79

I don't feel like being strong, but do I have a choice? It hurts when even my sisters look at me in the street with cold and silent eyes. I am defined as other in every group I'm a part of. The outsider, both strength and weakness. Yet without community there is certainly no liberation, no future, only the most vulnerable and temporary armistice between me and my oppression.

11/19/79

I want to write rage but all that comes is sadness. We have been sad long enough to make this earth either weep or grow fertile. I am an anachronism, a sport, like the bee that was never meant to fly. Science said so. I am not supposed to exist. I carry death around in my body like a condemnation. But I do live. The bee flies. There must be some way to integrate death into living, neither ignoring it nor giving in to it.

1/1/80

Faith is the last day of Kwanza, and the name of the war against despair, the battle I fight daily. I become better at it. I want to write about that battle, the skirmishes, the losses, the small yet so important victories that make the sweetness of my life.

1/20/80

The novel is finished at last. It has been a lifeline. I do not have to win in order to know my dreams are valid, I only have to believe in a process of which I am a part. My work kept me alive this past year, my work and the love of women. They are inseparable from each other. In the recognition of the existence of love lies the answer to despair. Work is that recognition given voice and name.

2/18/80

I am forty-six years living today and very pleased to be alive, very glad and very happy. Fear and pain and despair do not disappear. They only become slowly less and less important. Although sometimes I still

long for a simple orderly life with a hunger sharp as that sudden veg-
etarian hunger for meat.

4/6/80
Somedays, if bitterness were a whetstone, I could be sharp as grief.

5/30/80
Last spring was another piece of the fall and winter before, a progression from all the pain and sadness of that time, ruminated over.
But somehow this summer which is almost upon me feels like a part
of my future. Like a brand-new time, and I'm pleased to know it,
wherever it leads. I feel like another woman, de-chrysalised and become a broader, stretched-out me, strong and excited, a muscle flexed
and honed for action.

6/20/80
I do not forget cancer for very long, ever. That keeps me armed and
on my toes, but also with a slight background noise of fear. Carl
Simonton's book, *Getting Well Again*, has been really helpful to me,
even though his smugness infuriates me sometimes. The visualizations
and deep relaxing techniques that I learned from it help make me a
less anxious person, which seems strange, because in other ways, I live
with the constant fear of recurrence of another cancer. But fear and
anxiety are not the same at all. One is an appropriate response to a
real situation which I can accept and learn to work through just as I
work through semi-blindness. But the other, anxiety, is an immobilizing yield to things that go bump in the night, a surrender to name-
lessness, formlessness, voicelessness, and silence.

But on the day before my mastectomy I wrote in my journal:

September 21, 1978
The anger that I felt for my right breast last year has faded, and I'm
glad because I have had this extra year. My breasts have always been
so very precious to me since I accepted having them it would have
been a shame not to have enjoyed the last year of one of them. And

I think I am prepared to lose it now in a way I was not quite ready to last November, because now I really see it as a choice between my breast and my life, and in that view there cannot be any question.

Somehow I always knew this would be the final outcome, for it never did seem like a finished business for me. This year between was like a hiatus, an interregnum in a battle within which I could so easily be a casualty, since I certainly was a warrior. And in that brief time the sun shone and the birds sang and I wrote important words and have loved richly and been loved in return. And if a lifetime of furies is the cause of this death in my right breast, there is still nothing I've never been able to accept before that I would accept now in order to keep my breast. It was a twelve-month reprieve in which I could come to accept the emotional fact/truths I came to see first in those horrendous weeks last year before the biopsy. If I do what I need to do because I want to do it, it will matter less when death comes, because it will have been an ally that spurred me on.

I was relieved when the first tumor was benign, but I said to Frances at the time that the true horror would be if they said it was benign and it wasn't. I think my body knew there was a malignancy there somewhere, and that it would have to be dealt with eventually. Well, I'm dealing with it as best I can. I wish I didn't have to, and I don't even know if I'm doing it right, but I sure am glad that I had this extra year to learn to love me in a different way.

I'm going to have the mastectomy, knowing there are alternatives, some of which sound very possible in the sense of right thinking, but none of which satisfy me enough. . . . Since it is my life that I am gambling with, and my life is worth even more than the sensual delights of my breast, I certainly can't take that chance.

7:30 P.M. And yet if I cried for a hundred years I couldn't possibly express the sorrow I feel right now, the sadness and the loss. How did the Amazons of Dahomey feel? They were only little girls. But they did this willingly, for something they believed in. I suppose I am too but I can't feel that now.

The Years In Between

ELAINE SHELLY

My journal writing reaffirms the collage of colors that comprise my life. I reread these entries and am reminded of the washes of smoky purples, warm ambers, and crisp, cool blues that are with me daily. When I leave my journal for the outer world, I am constantly told that the colors I see are actually slate and ivory. Slate and ivory, that's all? It's confusing. Sometimes I wonder. Sometimes I think I will loose myself to slate and ivory, but my journal recalls the kaleidoscope.

A new color was added to my life in 1989 by multiple sclerosis, a disease of the central nervous system. These entries chronicle my journey through slate and ivory to recognizing and loving this new color.

Who I am and who I can be is not predetermined by what my body can or cannot do. This realization was liberating, but not the end of my trek. My greatest loss has not been the loss of muscle definition, but the loss of the gaze of my sisters. When I am out and about in my wheelchair, children will look in curiosity, men will look in pity, black women avoid my eyes. But sharing this piece of my life feels like a step back home. It feels like my sisters might want to make eye contact again.

October 2, 1989

The past few months have been a maze of depression and fatigue. After lots of tears, blood tests, and doctors, I found out today that I have chronic Epstein-Barr virus (EBV). It's a cruel disease because it robs physical and emotional energy. When that is gone, the spiritual energy, the life juice, can freely flow away, also.

I've read all this stuff about people with chronic and critical illnesses who never complain. Not me. I am relieved to know that I'm not crazy and that there is something actually wrong with me, but I'm also mad as hell. I have too many things to do to be ill. Too much remains unwritten and unseen.

I want my life back. Now.

October 5, 1989

One of my biggest problems with being ill is dealing with my self-image. I feel guilty for not working. I feel embarrassed that I'm not tough enough to just take a few days off and run back to work. I feel guilty that I wished a few months ago that I could take some time off. Got my wish, didn't I?

The truth is that this time away from work—two weeks exactly today—has given me a chance to listen to my body. For most of my adult life, I have run on mental energy regardless of how my body felt. Now the mental energy is low and the physical energy is even lower. I have to listen to my body for a change. I have to make friends with my body. It's not the enemy.

[I had originally planned to take only two weeks off, but after a week it became apparent to me that the illness would require more time. I don't go back to work until January.]

I also have a problem with telling people how I feel. I don't say that I feel fine because that's obviously a lie. I do feel self-conscious about my response, though. So how do I feel? This was a hard week. Fatigue is ever-present, but it had lots of company this week such as fever, upset stomach, muscle pain, and a very sore throat. Then there's the cognitive dysfunction. I can't remember anything. I've adopted a very structured way of thinking—I will do this after I do this—because of that. Chances are I will remember at least one part of the association and will piece together the rest. It's also hard to follow lengthy conversations. Fortunately, the problem is minimized by the fact that I've only had lengthy conversations with a few friends over the phone. I tune out and can follow subject headings, but details are gone. Besides, I'll probably forget the details anyway.

This illness and my body's reactions to it are amazing. At this very moment, sitting perfectly still, I feel fine. But yesterday I felt death approaching. Earlier today and quite frequently, I feel unbearably ill. Enough Body, I can't take it. I am amazed that my body can feel this ill and not be in the process of death. I find it hard to believe at times that Epstein-Barr is not fatal. I'm not afraid of dying. I just want to know that it's coming so I can say good night.

October 25, 1989

Couldn't finish my October 7 entry. It was just too upsetting. I had just found out that I would have to take three weeks of unpaid leave because I had used up all my sick days and vacation, plus I hadn't passed my employment anniversary date, October 31. I was told that I would have to pay for my health benefits during the three weeks, plus the company's benefit cost. I later found out that the company cost stuff was not true. Today I got a call from a secretary at work who was "just letting me know" that I would not get paid when I got back because the credit union would have to make up for missed payroll deductions. Thanks a lot! This, too, was misinformation.

What was so disturbing earlier this month (and led to four hours in bed with a fever) was I slammed face-to-face with how disposable and vulnerable I've become since being sick. Tough shit if I can't meet medical costs while on unpaid leave. Tough shit if the stress of financial worries prolongs my illness. Tough shit over how I might respond to bullshit misinformation. It is so sad and frightening that we try to survive beneath a system that is so dehumanizing and loveless. No wonder so many of us just die. No wonder that so often I feel the EBV is the embodiment of all the evil I have experienced in my life. It feels like death.

Speaking of how I feel, it seems I get a surprise each week. Since my last entry when I had the flu, I have had volcanic stomach upsets, misfunctioning legs and feet, and swollen salivary glands. I use a cane for balance in distances (when no grocery carts are available) or for jostling crowds. Oh, the final blow to autonomy—I can't drive.

When I first bought the cane, I thought I wouldn't be able to stand the look friends give when illness and pain are visible. That look that combines shock, pity, and fear. I find that I respond to that look by minimizing how I feel ("Oh, I'm just fine") or coming up with entertaining remarks about Sandy hitting me or that I just decided I needed an extra leg. I'm going to the Paramount Theater this weekend and I expect several people to be there from work. I am also expecting to climb stairs, which is particularly difficult. Part of me is dreading the idea of folks from work seeing me limping along with this cane. Another part of me is glad that they will see. They will see the EBV is very real.

October 26, 1989

There has been one black woman at work who has been extremely supportive. She seemed to understand how I felt. On Saturday, we had a long talk. I was feeling depressed and my body felt worse. Getting out of bed even just to shuffle to the bathroom was sheer agony. During the conversation, she asked if I was coming back to the newspaper as a reporter. I told her I was trying to keep an open mind. Maybe reporting, maybe editing, maybe not at all. I closed the conversation because I was getting tired, but I felt better. I got out of bed. I was surprised that she could be so sensitive. I hadn't really trusted her before.

I found out today that a few days after the conversation, she took my desk at work. She neatly placed my things at another desk. No wonder so many of us just die.

October 29, 1989

I'm wearing a cloak of sadness. I've felt it coming, but thought I could outrun it. I didn't or couldn't. Not sure which.

Yesterday I mourned in a very primal sense the loss of freedom. I mourned the loss of the physical freedom I've felt at times when I danced. After a day of vacillating, I decided that I'd better swallow my self-consciousness over my cane and get myself out of the house. I'm glad I went, but I am convinced that the lack of access for people with disabilities is the equivalent to Jim Crowism. I had to climb several flights of stairs. I am really surprised that I could get out of bed today.

Should find out this week about my medical leave of absence. There's no reason that it should be denied (which means the checks roll in again). But I am preparing myself for another assault. It seems that all's fair in love and work.

I don't sleep anymore. I nap a few hours here and there. It's 2 A.M. and I'm sure I'll be awake again by 6.

November 1, 1989

Yesterday was my one-year anniversary with the *Statesman*. It was such a glorious day last year when I was finally hired to work full time. It felt as if two years of campaigning to get on staff had paid off. I had attended numerous job fairs, just for the chance to talk to *Statesman* representatives. At one fair, I stood in line outdoors for hours in the heat. A woman in front of me fainted just before she was about to enter the hotel where the fair was held. At another fair, I ignored caution and common sense to drive from Wichita Falls to Arlington on icy Texas roads. At one point on the way there, my car involuntarily floated from one lane to another and gracefully pirouetted in front of an oncoming Mayflower moving van. The highway near Decatur, close to Arlington, was peppered with cars and trucks that had stalled or crashed. Today, the sweet victory tastes more like bile. Sandy has agreed to be my advocate. She is talking to the *Statesman* folks about my leave-of-absence request. I've gone several weeks without pay and they're dragging their feet on approving the request. When (and if) approved, the checks will resume.

March 20, 1990

[The doctor who was treating me for EBV told me that I would be fine by January, but December came and I didn't feel fine at all. So I decided to resign from the *Statesman*. I knew I couldn't be a reporter anymore and I doubted that I could work in that high-pressure atmosphere in another position. By a stroke of luck, I called one of my former sources, a woman who works with the Multiple Sclerosis Society, to talk about job openings with social service agencies. The MS Society needed an administrative assistant and I was hired. Immediately after I started with the Society, my supervisor noticed how I walked and how tired I got. She badgered me constantly about seeing a neurologist. I finally gave in.]

After weeks of waiting, the neurologist gave me a diagnosis of possible multiple sclerosis. At first when I learned that my spinal fluid was normal (which led to the diagnosis), I was happy. But the more I thought about it, the more upset I became. Possible? I can appreciate ambiguity, but possible MS? Possibly, I could be paralyzed. Possibly, I could be incontinent. [He couldn't give me a definitive diagnosis because he said there wasn't enough clinical evidence. I have brain lesions that appeared on a brain scan-MRI, but they aren't typical lesions. So we just wait. Meanwhile, he said to act as if MS isn't the problem. What does that mean?]

How am I handling this? By food and denial. I tend to vacuum up anything edible and nonmeat that doesn't clear my path. I keep having more symptoms of definite MS, but I tell myself that since I started working for the MS Society in January that I have learned too much about MS. I tell myself that my legs are stiff because I don't exercise enough. I tell myself that my hands shake because I need to eat. And when my bottom lip slides over toward my ear, I tell myself that I could control it if I wanted. I get no response from myself about my speech. I sometimes stammer and slur my words, so what?

A year ago, I could follow a parade up Congress Avenue to the

Capitol, stand around for speeches, then walk back several blocks back to work. A week ago I had to walk a block to the car. My legs nearly gave out. Is this the same body?

April 2, 1990

I think a good part of what bothers me emotionally about my physical condition is the unreliability. I have always hated that trait in others and myself, especially myself. I never know what's going to happen. It's baffling. One morning I stand in the cold for hours with relatively no aftereffects. Today my legs stiffen after walking less than an hour in a shopping mall. I couldn't take enough Tegretol to keep up with the facial spasms over the weekend. But I forgot to take one this morning before work and I was fine. I hate second-guessing.

April 3, 1990

My supervisor told me yesterday that she understood what I was going through and that my dreams had been spoiled. She said she didn't think she could be as strong as I am. I responded, "Neither could I." Don't think she got it.

April 9, 1990

My speech was slurring over the weekend and my legs have been weak for the past few days. This morning when I got out of my car to walk to work, I was moving so slowly that it felt as if I were walking backward. I finally brought home a potty lift and I am looking forward to the Newly Diagnosed MS Support Group meeting on Thursday. These two things are improvements, but I still panic when anyone mentions a wheelchair. I think a part of me sees it as the stopping point, the end. I sat in an electric wheelchair in February just to test it out. It felt wonderful and powerful. I guess I think about wheelchairs today because I know it's coming. Maybe not in the permanent sense, but it's coming. On mornings when my legs ache and are numb, I wonder until my feet hit the floor and my weight shifts down to shuffle (with or without the cane) to the bathroom—is this the day? I asked myself that question this morning. The answer was no. But what will

I do when the day comes? I have visions of peeing on myself in bed because I can't get up, then having to lie in it until someone comes to help.

April 10, 1990

Obviously under the influence of spirit this morning, I went swimming in Barton Creek. I was afraid. What if I couldn't get out of the water? What if I got in trouble in the water? What if there were too many swimmers and I couldn't swim close to the side of the pool area? But I went swimming alone in Barton Creek. For the first time since October, I had full range of motion in my legs. They didn't hurt. They weren't stiff. My arms felt strong. Two hours later, my extremities feel like hell, but I feel alive. I feel vital.

April 19, 1990

I haven't combed my hair since October. I stopped combing my hair to symbolically keep alive my unique creative self. Since my brain was too foggy to write, I grew hair. Since my hair won't dread, I am considering combing and cutting it this weekend. This means it's time to start back writing.

April 23, 1990

Yesterday I stayed too long in the sun at the finish line of the MS 150 Bike Tour. All these healthy bodies had spent two days biking 168 miles from Houston to Austin. Healthy bodies, as in flat stomachs and taut calves. Many of them didn't look that tired after the ride. Then there was John who sat watching in the shade from his three-wheel scooter. When John stood, his body bounded in an orgasmic rhythm, his legs protesting the weight of his thin body. And then there was Connie who couldn't complete her tasks at the finish line because her left side is dead. The wind blew papers that she couldn't catch. Her granddaughter took her place. And then there was me. Yesterday, I could have been mistaken for one of the bikers—no visible signs of disability. But today, I join the ranks of Connie and John. My body bounces from side to side in an attempt to steady and balance itself.

My hands shake, my legs refuse to pick up my feet and my speech and vision fuzz in and out. It's hard to believe that I am the same person I was yesterday. It's hard to believe that we—myself, John, and Connie—belong to the same species as the bikers.

May 8, 1990

On April 1, I had an appointment with Texas Rehabilitation Commission (TRC). What an awful experience! I felt handicapped (in the most negative sense) the minute I walked in the door. They had plaques on the wall for the most rehabilitated clients, kind of like those awards for the most hamburgers or vacuum cleaners sold. My counselor repeated himself for about forty-five minutes, made jokes about my catching MS from work and told me they don't fund graduate study unless I am catastrophically disabled.

May 10, 1990

Yesterday was the day. I used a wheelchair. My legs felt as if they were bending backward and the chair was sitting unoccupied in the office. My arms would have given out if I had to travel distances, but it was okay for my inaccessible office. The chair is too big, also. Perhaps I'll have to purchase a kid's chair one day. The most important thing I learned about the chair was that when it was time to stand up, the chair let me go.

July 30, 1990

The wheelchair is now sitting in the garage. I used it on a daily basis for about a month. After that, I just used it for distances. The last time I was in a chair was the Monday after July 4th. I went to Oklahoma for a family reunion and used a chair in the airports. Over the past couple of weeks I've needed my cane less. I just use it now for distances. Unless I'm tired, I don't even limp.

I am no longer an MS Society employee. They needed someone who could work a forty-hour week. I don't have the stamina for that, so I was discarded. My replacement does my job with such ease. It pisses me off. She has the energy to keep her desk neat and she can walk to the bathroom or mailbox with the speed of sound.

I continue to struggle with TRC. Since April, I have not convinced them that I have a disability. This is largely because of the noncooperation of my neurologist. Although I have two MRIs that show lesions on my brain and I have exhibited all these symptoms, he told TRC that there's nothing wrong with me. He told them that he couldn't verify my disability until I had a definite diagnosis. What? And of course, since he is male, he is white, and he is a doctor, he is also absolutely right.

The bright spots in my life are the things I'm doing to heal—acupuncture and counseling. Both are helping to heal the schisms, the division between mind and body; spirit and intellect; oppression and empowerment. I've also started back writing. I am participating in a women's theater production and am trying to connect with another theater group for a similar project.

George Bush signed the Americans with Disabilities Act last week. It's just like 1964. Some paper was signed, but I'm still oppressed.

August 31, 1990

I've been having trouble with my short-term memory this month. Sandy has mentioned a couple of times that she is afraid that I'll wander off and get lost. I told a friend yesterday that I don't get lost, I just forget where I'm going.

This makes me feel such an urgency. I feel that I better go on and do whatever it is I'm going to do. And do it now.

I still don't have a definite MS diagnosis. I went to another neurologist for a second opinion last week. He said that there's nothing physically wrong with me and that I have a psychological problem. He referred me for eight hours (yes, eight) of psychological tests.

September 20, 1990

I think I finally understand what risky living is. It is choosing to take the journey of reclaiming my humanity. Writing and having a chronic illness has facilitated this process. They help me and force me to break down the walls that stifle my own humanity. It is a risky, revolutionary journey to take. It can result in all sorts of dangers because when I become fully human, then I will know that I am good.

February 27, 1991

Thought today would be the day when the past two years would receive a name. I thought the illness, the disability would be explained. Not so. My spinal fluid is fine, X-rays are clear, and blood work is normal. Yet all my symptoms continue and a new one is added. Sometimes my legs shake so much I can't walk. I think of John's tremors the first time I saw them. I called them orgasmic. Mine are too. My hips swivel and Sandy says I look like I'm dancing.

I have found a doctor who is smart and kind. He believes that I am physically ill. Although he can't give me a label, he did write a prescription for Baclofen, a drug given to people with MS to relax spastic muscles.

March 16, 1991

I have been working since December. TRC finally accepted that I am disabled, but according to their records, my disability is emotional, not physical. Then TRC hired me to be a receptionist for a new office that handles training and resource coordination for the Americans with Disabilities Act. It is the mission of the office to expand opportunities for the people with disabilities, but the reality is they have a receptionist with a master's degree who has been passed over for professional positions with TRC. I wasn't even called for interviews.

Sandy and I went to a holy union at church last week. It was on a Friday evening and I was tired. At the reception afterward, I could tell my legs couldn't take the meet-and-greet much longer, but I leaned against a wall and kept going. When Sandy and I headed for the car, the tremors started in full force. My legs collapsed, so I ended up on the ground with my left leg folded neatly under me. I couldn't move and was too tired to try. Sandy started crying. At first I thought I had hurt her when I fell. I wouldn't let her try to pick me up, so I made her go get help. Two people had to drag me to the car. I think the tears were a mixture of frustration and feelings of powerlessness. I think she is finally beginning to feel what is happening. Maybe one day I will be able to cry with her.

March 23, 1991

Almost everything is in place. I have a therapist, a doctor I can work with, and access to physical therapy. I have medication and recommendations for equipment. The house will soon look like a medical-supply warehouse. While I am overjoyed that I have these resources, the starkness of the struggle is now so apparent. The struggle is mine. The responsibility is mine. I am the one who has to decide which appliance to use and when. And even with all the help that I may or may not receive, I am the one who has to get me from the car and into the house.

Physical therapy is hard and humbling. My body is so tired that I almost feel depressed. I am so tired that I have trouble controlling my left eye at times. Maybe that's why I feel so existential. I was expecting more goodness and light, not more struggle.

March 27, 1991

I found out today from my physical therapist that I get a walker on Thursday and will soon get a shower chair. I am going to apply to ride Special Transit, the public transportation system for people with disabilities. I guess that means I really have a disability, huh?

March 29, 1991

I received the walker today. It's not fancy, just an aluminum walker with wheels. I don't know how I feel about it, yet. It looks "disabled." How do I use it to get on and off a bus or across a busy street?

April 2, 1991

I went to the doctor yesterday. He prescribed Medrol, a corticosteroid to fight inflammation in my central nervous system. It's only a six-day course of 4 mg pills. I started yesterday with six pills and it decreases daily by one pill.

I'm going to physical therapy this afternoon. I don't want to go back to work tomorrow without some preliminary exertion. I want to see what my body will do after stress. I think I know what it will do. It will shake.

The major kicker about going to the doctor was the loss of driving privileges. My doctor told me that I was not safe to drive. I know he is right, but it feels like just one more thing to lose. I can't control body movements, I can't pick up my left foot, can't hold up my head sometimes and now I can't drive.

But it's different than the non-driving period in 1989. I have resources. I have friends I am willing to depend on. I made about four telephone calls last night and my transportation needs were taken care of for this week.

April 22, 1991

The MS 150 Bike Tour ended yesterday. I wrote a journal entry this time last year. It's strange to me that I could have been mistaken for an athlete last year. That wouldn't have happened this year. I had to use my walker yesterday. If I had gone out to the finish line, I would have been wearing a brace on my left leg and would have used some sort of wheelchair so I could stay out there for more than a few minutes. No one would have guessed that I was an athlete yesterday. They would have thought I was of the same species as Connie and John.

June 24, 1991

I think the adventure I've been on is nearing another stage. I heard the words today that I've been trying to hear for over a year. Today was my last day of physical therapy. I have a custom-made brace, a walker, and a three-wheeler. My left leg still shakes and stairs are difficult even on good days. It's so obvious to me what's going on with my body, but the physical therapist finally said it, "Your symptoms clinically present themselves as MS." There, she said it. And even though I know she is right, I still want to run and scream and hide. How can I be of the same species as John, whose tremors are so strong that he can barely feed himself? His short-term memory is gone and he had to stop working earlier this month. Am I the same as Helen, who was doing so well earlier this year but is now bowel-and-bladder incontinent? Are we the same? Will I have to wait two more years for a doctor to say yes?

July 17, 1991

I'm in the final stages of an exacerbation that started developing after I left my job at TRC at the end of June. It was, without a doubt, the worst exacerbation I've had to date. The tremors went wild. My whole body shook, including my head. It was like being a rag doll in the hands of a merciless child. I'm doing much better now, but am still dog tired. I can feel muscle fibers shrinking in my left forearm, the bottom of my feet, and the abductors of both thighs. My doctor saw last Monday that the muscles in the front of my thighs have atrophied. I had suspected this. I see bones and grooves where there used to be muscle.

The most amazing part of this exacerbation was my emotional state. The weaker I felt physically, the stronger and more centered I was emotionally, I didn't feel as if I was suffering, just feeling a part of myself. And that part of myself, the part that is sick, complements the other parts. It just is. So there's no need to be upset that it is—no more need to be upset than to be upset that I am black, lesbian, short, or all that I am. It just is.

[I told my counselor at TRC that I was leaving my job to be a free-lance writer. I didn't mention that the job is absolutely too strenuous and I didn't feel physically able to do it any longer. Therefore, I am successfully rehabilitated and the proud owner of a used three-wheeler.]

September 9, 1991

I'm in St. Paul now. Sandy is teaching and Patrick found a buddy the second day of school. I'm feeling my way around. It saddens me that I can't discover the Twin Cities the same way I've discovered all the new places I've lived. No energy, mobility, or wheels. That makes it a little hard. I'm disappointed that more buildings aren't accessible. I was expecting to see more ramps and curb cuts.

But dealing with agencies is simpler here. I call for information and I get it. I have a wheelchair from the MS Society and an independent living center is providing me with information on local resources.

I've been trying to get up early and write every morning. It's a short-lived discipline, but going quite well so far.

I haven't regained all the stamina I had before the last exacerbation. As a matter of fact, it looks like my legs are continuing to atrophy. It looks like someone took a chunk out of my left inner thigh. My abdominal muscles are still weak, too. Will I get some answers on Thursday? I have an appointment with a neurologist who is known for treating people with MS. I'm scared. What if he doesn't believe me? What if he does?

September 10, 1991

It is interesting that I'm approaching the end of this journal because I feel a new chapter about to begin. Randy Shilts (*And the Band Played On*) described it best. Before and After. What I have lived these past two years is Before. Thursday marks the beginning of After. It's terrifying. Even if it is MS, I almost feel as if hearing the words will cause me to stop breathing.

Now about poems. I am writing rhythms. One is an angular rhythm that pops with lots of explosive consonants. The other rhythm is a glide. It's sensuous and rolls like beads of honey. I want to start circulating my poems. Want to stay busy until After gets here.

September 12, 1991

This is the last day Before. It's raining. It keeps running through my head that this neurologist will listen to me, check some things, say a few "un huhs" and then tell me he's sorry, but there's not enough evidence, not enough proof, "I don't know what to tell you."

It occurred to me that I have already lived through an After experience. I've already written about it.

> The Morning After
> I mixed the dust of myself
> In a fearful fluid
> Hoping to dissolve and evaporate
> But when I awoke
> I found that the sun had taken the fluid
> Leaving the dust behind

I will survive After. I will have to rebuild, reconstruct, but the sun will rise on Friday and I'll go on.

September 13, 1991

The Morning After. I went to the doctor this morning. By the time I got there, I was so nervous that I felt sick. My left leg ached and felt collapsible. The MRI films from Texas were never sent to the doctor's office. Texas was Before. This is After. The first thing the doctor asked me was, "Why didn't they think it was MS?" He said that from looking at my lab results, it smelled like MS. He said that my coordination was a little off and that pointed to MS. I was right. He said I fit the criteria for MS. I was right. He said he wants to make sure it's MS and not something else, but it's definitely something. I have an MRI scheduled for tonight and evoked potentials scheduled Tuesday. Then I go see him in a week. This could be over in a week.

The main thing I feel is anger. I am angry that it has taken so long to get to this obvious conclusion. In the meantime, I have been lied to and patronized. The one who told me if I had MS, my lesions would change in six months. The one who told me that I didn't walk like someone who had MS. The one who said I created this illness to avoid responsibility and stress. The one who said that it was impossible to fake MS symptoms and that I probably had a stress disorder because my life-style was not mainstream. And although he was my only medical friend, the one who watched me for seven months and still knew nothing more.

I feel the kind of rage that needs to be outside in the streets. The kind of rage that smolders quickly then ignites and consumes streets, houses, neighbors. The kind of rage that makes the six o'clock news and makes white folks in the suburbs thank God that they moved out there. I could yell and curse at all the conspirators, the force of my words flinging spittle in their faces. And I could name names. The one who fired me from the MS Society. The one who told me I had to go a month without pay while on sick leave. The one who leaned back on years of experience and proclaimed I had a mental problem. The one who found a job for me and never read my résumé. The ones who were happy to have me overworked and underemployed. I hate you all.

September 14, 1991

I had the MRI last night. Pat was late getting home with the car and I drove to the hospital in about five minutes. I had to check in at the admission desk. The clerk was too slow for words. It was surreal with this slow woman in front of me and a teenager behind me playing in a hospital wheelchair. The MRI took forty minutes.

When they strapped me in the machine, I felt as if I was being helmeted for a long journey into space. Then the machine's knocking started and I went out to sea on a dinghy where it was a cool, cloudy day. I imagined wearing a navy-blue pea coat and knit cap. My hands were clasped as I leaned over the side of the boat listening to seagulls overhead. It was a peaceful feeling with just a hint of sadness. I was alone.

September 17, 1991

My scalp is still a little sore and I have sore spots near both collarbones. I have white flecks of glue in my hair. All this is because I had evoked-potentials testing this morning. Electrodes were applied to my head and collarbone area with glue, then scratched with a probe. [The test records how fast impulses reach the brain. It can detect damage to my optic nerves or lesions that aren't visible on the MRI.] The scratching was not pleasant, but at least the technician was personable. She apologized for the pain.

Now all I have to do is wait. I go back to the neurologist on Thursday and get the verdict. In the meantime, my mind is racing. I keep thinking about the times when I've felt like I was dying. Maybe I'll hear why I've felt that way. Maybe this is it. Maybe this is the beginning of more tests, more invasive tests, more waiting. But all I have to do is wait.

September 19, 1991

It's been almost an hour since I was told. I have multiple sclerosis. How anticlimactic, yet shocking. I looked at my MRI. The lesions, bigger than they were in Texas, are as plain as day. I think there are at least two in the cerebellum and one in the frontal lobe. I have MS. As long as I was fighting for a diagnosis, there was a possibility that I could be wrong. There was that chance that I really could be crazy and all this could just go away. Not so now. As of about 10 A.M. this morning, I have a preexisting condition.

Now what?

September 21, 1991

I've been writing letters the past few days and telling everyone I can think of about the diagnosis. The more I write it, the less large it seems. Not smaller, just less large. I have MS, I have MS, I have . . . The thought slips from my consciousness.

I dreamed of myself as being able-bodied last night. I gave a big party. All of my Austin friends were there. There was no cane, chair, walker, potty lift. There was only a yard and house filled with people who wanted to socialize and eat.

September 28, 1991

I've started an accessibility campaign. Every time I can't get into an arts event or have trouble with access, I write a letter. It takes so much energy and concentration to get to the car, out of the car, to the building. Many times it is just not worth the effort. I stay home.

It seems that MS has taken it's proper place in my life. It is like one of the books on my book case. Sometimes I pick it up and read it. At other times it just blends in with the other books, barely noticeable as a separate entity.

Ambiguity is so much a part of MS. What about my bladder? What about my vision? How disabled will I become? I can spend October getting parts of these questions answered, but the full answers will only come with time. Now it's on with the rest of my life. Is this what it means to get my life back?

A Small Place

JAMAICA KINCAID

This personal narrative offers a political analysis of the exploitation of this writer's birthplace by Europeans and Americans. She writes of the Antiguan's daily struggle for dignity and freedom.

The Antigua that I knew, the Antigua in which I grew up, is not the Antigua you, a tourist, would see now. That Antigua no longer exists. That Antigua no longer exists partly for the usual reason, the passing of time, and partly because the bad-minded people who used to rule over it, the English, no longer do so. (But the English have become such a pitiful lot these days, with hardly any idea what to do with themselves now that they no longer have one quarter of the earth's human population bowing and scraping before them. They don't seem to know that this empire business was all wrong and they should, at least, be wearing sackcloth and ashes in token penance of the wrongs committed, the irrevocableness of their bad deeds, for no natural disaster imaginable could equal the harm they did. Actual death might have been better. And so all this fuss over empire—what went wrong here, what went wrong there—always makes me quite crazy, for I can say to them what went wrong: they should never have left their home, their precious England, a place they loved so much, a place they had to leave but could never forget. And so everywhere they went they turned it into England; and everybody they met they turned English. But no place could ever really be England, and nobody who did not look exactly like them would ever be English, so you can imagine the destruction of people and land that came from that. The English hate each other and they hate England, and the reason they are so miserable now is that they have no place else to go and nobody else to feel better than.) But let me show you the Antigua that I used to know.

In the Antigua that I knew, we lived on a street named after an English maritime criminal, Horatio Nelson, and all the other streets around us were named after some other English maritime criminals. There was Rodney Street, there was Hood Street, there was Hawkins Street, and there was Drake Street. There were flamboyant trees and mahogany trees lining East Street. Government House, the place where the Governor, the person standing in for the Queen, lived, was on East Street. Government House was surrounded by a high white wall—and to show how cowed we must have been, no one ever wrote bad things on it; it remained clean and white and high. (I once stood in hot sun for hours so that I could see a putty-faced Princess from England disappear behind these walls. I was seven years old at the time, and I thought, She has a putty face.) There was the library on lower High Street, above the Department of the Treasury, and it was in that part of High Street that all colonial government business took place. In that part of High Street, you could cash a cheque at the Treasury, read a book in the library, post a letter at the post office, appear before a magistrate in court. (Since we were ruled by the English, we also had their laws. There was a law against using abusive language. Can you imagine such a law among people for whom making a spectacle of yourself through speech is everything? When West Indians went to England, the police there had to get a glossary of bad West Indian words so they could understand whether they were hearing abusive language or not.) It was in that same part of High Street that you could get a passport in another government office. In the middle of High Street was the Barclays Bank. The Barclay brothers, who started

Barclays Bank, were slave-traders. That is how they made their money. When the English outlawed the slave trade, the Barclay brothers went into banking. It made them even richer. It's possible that when they saw how rich banking made them, they gave themselves a good beating for opposing an end to slave trading (for surely they would have opposed that), but then again, they may have been visionaries and agitated for an end to slavery, for look at how rich they became with their banks borrowing from (through their savings) the descendants of the slaves and then lending back to them. But people just a little older than I am can recite the name of and the day the first black person was hired as a cashier at this very same Barclays Bank in Antigua. Do you ever wonder why some people blow things up? I can imagine that if my life had taken a certain turn, there would be the Barclays Bank, and there I would be, both of us in ashes. Do you ever try to understand why people like me cannot get over the past, cannot forgive and cannot forget? There is the Barclays Bank. The Barclay brothers are dead. The human beings they traded, the human beings who to them were only commodities, are dead. It should not have been that they came to the same end, and heaven is not enough of a reward for one or hell enough of a punishment for the other. People who think about these things believe that every bad deed, even every bad thought, carries with it its own retribution. So do you see the queer thing about people like me? Sometimes we hold your retribution.

And then there was another place, called the Mill Reef Club. It was built by some people from North America who wanted to live in Antigua and spend their holidays in Antigua but who seemed not to like Antiguans (black people) at all, for the Mill Reef Club declared itself completely private, and the only Antiguans (black people) allowed to go there were servants. People can recite the name of the first Antiguan (black person) to eat a sandwich at the clubhouse and the day on which it happened; people can recite the name of the first Antiguan (black person) to play golf on the golf course and the day on which the event took place. In those days, we Antiguans thought that the people at the Mill Reef Club had such bad manners, like pigs; they were behaving in a bad way, like pigs. There they were, strangers in someone else's home, and then they refused to talk to their hosts or have anything human, anything intimate, to do with them. I believe they gave scholarships to one or two bright people each year so they could go overseas and study; I believe they gave money to children's charities; these things must have made them seem to themselves very big and good, but to us there they were, pigs living in that sty (the Mill Reef Club). And what were these people from North America, these people from England, these people from Europe, with their bad behaviour, doing on this little island? For they so enjoyed behaving badly, as if there was pleasure immeasurable to be had from not acting like a human being. Let me tell you about a man; trained as a dentist, he took it on himself to say he was a doctor, specialising in treating children's illnesses. No one objected—certainly not us. He came to Antigua as a refugee (running away from Hitler) from Czechoslovakia. This man hated us so much that he would send his wife to inspect us before we were admitted into his presence, and she would make sure that we didn't smell, that we didn't have dirt under our fingernails, and that nothing else about us—apart from the colour of our skin— would offend the doctor. (I can remember once, when I had whooping cough and I took a turn for the worse, that my mother, before bundling me up and taking me off to see this man, examined me carefully to see that I had no bad smells or dirt in the crease of my neck, behind my ears, or anywhere else. Every horrible thing that a housefly could do was known by heart to my mother, and in her innocence she thought that she and the doctor shared the same crazy obsession— germs.) Then there was a headmistress of a girls' school, hired through the colonial office in England and sent to Antigua to run this school which only in my lifetime began to accept girls who were born outside a marriage; in Antigua it had never dawned on anyone that this was a way of keeping black children out of this school. This woman was twenty-six years old, not too long out of university, from Northern Ireland, and she told these girls over and over again to stop behaving as if they were monkeys just out of trees. No one ever dreamed that the word for any of this was racism. We thought these people were so ill-mannered and we were so surprised by this, for they were far away from their home, and we believed that the farther away you were from your home the better you should behave. (This is because if your bad behaviour gets you in trouble you have your family not too far off to help defend you.) We thought they were un-Christian-like; we thought they were small-minded; we thought they were like animals, a bit below human standards as we understood those standards to be. We felt superior to all these people; we thought that perhaps the English among them who behaved this way weren't English at all, for the English were supposed to be civilised, and this behaviour was so much like that of an animal, the thing we were before the English rescued us, that maybe they weren't from the real England at all but from another England, one we were not familiar with, not at all from the England we were told about, not at all from the England we could never be from, the England that was so far away, the England that not even a boat could take us to, the England that, no matter what we did, we could never be of. We felt superior, for we were so much better behaved and we were full of grace, and these people were so badly behaved and they were so completely empty of grace. (Of course, I now see that good behaviour is the proper posture of the weak, of children.) We were taught the names of the Kings of England. In Antigua, the twenty-fourth of May was a holiday—Queen Victoria's official birthday. We didn't say to ourselves, Hasn't this extremely unappealing person been dead for years and years? Instead, we were glad for a holiday. Once, at dinner (this happened in my present life), I was sitting across from an Englishman, one of those smart people who know how to run things that England still turns out but who now, since the demise of the empire, have nothing to do; they look so sad, sitting on the rubbish heap of history. I was reciting my usual litany of things I hold against England and the English, and to round things off I said, "And do you know that we had to celebrate Queen Victoria's birthday?" So he said that every year, at the school he attended in England, they marked the day she died. I said, "Well, apart from the fact that she belonged to you and so anything you did about her was proper, at least you knew she died." So that was England to us—Queen Victoria and the glorious day of her coming into the world, a beautiful place, a blessed place, a living and blessed thing, not the ugly, piggish individuals we met. I cannot tell you how angry it makes me to hear people from North America tell me how much they love England, how beautiful England is, with its traditions. All they see is some frumpy, wrinkled-up person passing by in a carriage waving at a crowd. But what I see is the millions of people, of whom I am just one, made orphans: no motherland, no fatherland, no gods, no mounds of earth for holy ground, no excess of love which might lead to the things that an excess of love sometimes brings, and worst and most painful of all, no tongue. (For isn't it odd that the only language I have in which to speak of this crime is the language of the criminal who committed the crime? And what can that really mean? For the language of the criminal can contain only the goodness of the criminal's deed. The language of the criminal can explain and express the deed only from the criminal's point of view. It cannot contain the horror of the deed, the injustice of the deed, the agony, the humiliation inflicted on me. When I say to the criminal, "This is wrong, this is wrong, this is wrong," or, "This deed is bad, and this other deed is bad, and this one is also very, very bad," the criminal understands the word "wrong" in this way: It is wrong when "he" doesn't get his fair share of profits from the crime just committed; he understands the word "bad" in this way: a fellow criminal betrayed a trust. That must be why, when I say, "I am filled with rage," the criminal says, "But why?" And when I blow things up and make life generally unlivable for the criminal (is my life not unlivable, too?) the criminal is shocked, surprised. But nothing can erase my rage—not an apology, not a large sum of money, not the death of the criminal—for this wrong can never be made right, and only the impossible can make me still: can a way be found to make what happened not have happened? And so look at this prolonged visit to the bile duct that I am making, look at how bitter, how dyspeptic just to sit and think about these things makes me. I attended a school named after a Princess of England. Years and years later, I read somewhere that this Princess made her tour of the West Indies (which included Antigua, and on that tour she dedicated my school) because she had fallen in love with a married man, and since she was not allowed to marry a divorced man she was sent to visit us to get over her affair with him. How well I remember that all of Antigua turned out to see this Princess person, how every building that she would enter was repaired and painted so that it looked brand-new, how every beach she would sun herself on had to look as if no one had ever sunned there before (I wonder now what they did about the poor sea? I mean, can a sea be made to look brand-new?), and how everybody she met was the best Antiguan body to meet, and no one told us that this person we were putting ourselves out for on such a big scale, this person we were getting worked up about as if she were God Himself, was in our midst because of something so common, so everyday: her life was not working out the way she had hoped, her life was one big mess. Have I given you the impression that the Antigua I grew up in revolved almost completely around England? Well, that was so. I met the world through England, and if the world wanted to meet me it would have to do so through England.

Are you saying to yourself, "Can't she get beyond all that, everything happened so long ago, and how does she know that if things had been the other way around her ancestors wouldn't have behaved just as badly, because, after all, doesn't everybody behave badly given the opportunity?"

Our perception of this Antigua—the perception we had of this place ruled by these bad-minded people—was not a political perception. The English were ill-mannered, not racists; the school headmistress was especially ill-mannered, not a racist; the doctor was crazy—he didn't even speak English properly, and he came from a strangely named place, he also was not a racist; the people at the Mill Reef Club were puzzling (why go and live in a place populated mostly by people you cannot stand), not racists.

HAVE YOU EVER WONDERED to yourself why it is that all people like me seem to have learned from you is how to imprison and murder each other, how to govern badly, and how to take the wealth of our country and place it in Swiss bank accounts? Have you ever wondered why it is that all we seem to have learned from you is how to corrupt our societies and how to be tyrants? You will have to accept that this is mostly your fault. Let me just show you how you looked to us. You came. You took things that were not yours, and you did not even, for appearances' sake, ask first. You could have said, "May I have this, please?" and even though it would have been clear to everybody that a yes or no from us would have been of no consequence you might have looked so much better. Believe me, it would have gone a long way. I would have had to admit that at least you were polite. You murdered people. You imprisoned people. You robbed people. You opened your own banks and you put our money in them. The accounts were in your name. The banks were in your name. There must have been some good people among you, but they stayed home. And that is the point. That is why they are good. They stayed home. But still, when you think about it, you must be a little sad. The people like me, finally, after years and years of agitation, made deeply moving and eloquent speeches against the wrongness of your domination over us, and then finally, after the mutilated bodies of you, your wife, and your children were found in your beautiful and spacious bungalow at the edge of your rubber plantation—found by one of your many house servants (none of it was ever yours; it was never, ever yours)—you say to me, "Well, I wash my hands of all of you, I am leaving now," and you leave, and from afar you watch as we do to ourselves the very things you used to do to us. And you might feel that there was more to you than that, you might feel that you had understood the meaning of the Age of Enlightenment (though, as far as I can see, it had done you very little good); you loved knowledge, and wherever you went you made sure to build a school, a library (yes, and in both of these places you distorted or erased my history and glorified your own). But then again, perhaps as you observe the debacle in which I now exist, the utter ruin that I say is my life, perhaps you are remembering that you had always felt people like me cannot run things, people like me will never grasp the idea of Gross National Product, people like me will never be able to take command of the thing the most simpleminded among you can master, people like me will never understand the notion of rule by law, people like me cannot really think in abstractions, people like me cannot be objective, we make everything so personal. You will forget your part in the whole setup, that bureaucracy is one of your inventions, that Gross National Product is one of your inventions, and all the laws that you know mysteriously favour you. Do you know why people like me are shy about being capitalists? Well, it's because we, for as long as we have known you, *were* capital, like bales of cotton and sacks of sugar, and you were the commanding, cruel capitalists, and the memory of this is so strong, the experience so recent, that we can't quite bring ourselves to embrace this idea that you think so much of. As for what we were like before we met you, I no longer care. No periods of time over which my ancestors held sway, no documentation of complex civilisations, is any comfort to me. Even if I really came from people who were living like monkeys in trees, it was better to be that than what happened to me, what I became after I met you.

And Still Risë

RISË COLLINS

Today is Wednesday, March 31, 1993. It's 11:00 A.M. Over the past two years while completing an MSW program at the University of Houston, recovering from a divorce, turning forty, surviving the deaths of two close friends, training to be a therapist/activist, and trying to be conscious about the unfoldment of myself as soul—I have written monthly life letters. And, after a winter of flying in the face of no seeming possibility—that which didn't kill me made me strong. Now, spring is coming. And I—a wild woman of color, a snake-eyed dragonflower, a renegade queen—am whole. I am well. I thrive. And I love.

October 1992
Wound Walking

When my maternal great-grandfather, an Irishman, married his part-Moroccan maid, after the death of his white wife, his ten white children never associated with his ten black children / when my mulatto great-aunt became a nun in the Catholic church she was housed in a segregated convent / another great aunt was institutionalized in a place where she was given electric-shock treatments and about which she repeatedly blathered that she had been raped by white men / my grandfather a World War II purple-heart veteran, was captured and held prisoner in a German concentration camp where he was fed only potato peelings / he told war stories of bombing Catholic churches and finding baby skeletons in the basements / my growing up without a father, brother, or uncle / having a father who has approximately eleven children by ten different women and he's been married once—a blueprint left over from slavery / my mother being paid $28 a week for doing the same job for which a white women earned $85 a week in a downtown Houston retail store in the 1950s / my mother saying in a moment of anger when I was very young, "You can marry anybody when you grow up except a Chinaman" / a man breaking into our house while we slept, killing our dog, and entering our bedroom when I was eight—all this on a night when my baby sister and I were supposed to be at home alone while my mother worked her second job—but that night she had been too tired to go / being poor, hungry, and cold in inadequate clothing and run-over shoes during a Cleveland, Ohio, winter in grade school / being told in 1966 at Yates, an all-black Houston high school, that I was too dark to be a cheerleader / and at Lamar, the all-white high school across town, having an American history book with only one paragraph in it about black Americans—and that one paragraph being a lie / having the Lamar drama coach discourage me from entering speech tournaments because of her fear of racial backlash / my entering anyway and winning first place in women's poetry fourteen times consecutively, being called into the principal's office to have him say, "You are a credit to your race," when I'm a credit to the human race / being told, "It's too bad you're black, girl," by one of my classmates / being summoned to the dean's office and asked if my change to a natural hairstyle was an attempt to make a radical statement (and later having my ex-husband say that he didn't like my dreadlocked hair because it reminded him of slavery) / listening to my father tell me when I was fourteen, "If I could change from being black to being white, I'd do it in a splinit—and that's faster than a minute." And learning that his ideal of beauty, in 1966, was Angie Dickinson / insisting, during an out-of-state high school speech tournament on eating with my class-mates in a Louisiana restaurant where the proprietor did not want to serve me and fearing, as I ate, that the food had been poisoned / hearing a white woman in the lobby of a River Oaks bank where I worked when I was a teen repeatedly screaming, "Angela Davis! Angela Davis!" as she pointed at me / and a policeman rushing over to arrest me when I looked *nothing* like Angela Davis / hearing a wealthy seventeen-year-old white classmate, who lived in River Oaks, greeted as "Miss Lily" and fawned over by smiling fifty-year-old black maids whom she called by their first names / this same friend telling me that I wouldn't be able to go to Carnegie-Mellon, the expensive university she was going to attend in 1969, because I wouldn't be able to afford it / deciding on the spot to go there, and arriving in Pittsburgh to experience a car of young white men who circled the block many times to hurl racial slurs at me / where one of the few black male seniors in the drama department said to my black sophomore roommate who was enamoured of him, "The only thing that a black woman can do for me is show me the way to a white woman" / where I was stared at by white people when I entered a church near campus / and where the school psychotherapist, who had sex with people who later broke confidence and bragged about it, did not want to treat me / standing in line twenty minutes for water to have a policeman in Jackson, Florida, put a billyclub in my face, tell me the water fountain was closed, and allow everyone else in the line to drink / graduating from the most prestigious acting school in the country to be offered, by Nina Vance of Houston's Alley Theatre, the opportunity to come back home to Texas to play a maid on stage / having a white female friend in New York City tell me, "I exclusively dated black men for many years because my self-esteem was low, and I knew that being white, with my blond hair and blue eyes, black men would accept me" / hearing repetitions of that theme from white women again, again, and again / fearing like my friend Cynthia S. ending up old, black, female, poor, and ill in America like our mothers and like one of my heroines—the brilliant black writer Zora Neale Hurston / hearing my mother say, "I am the tree and my daughters are branches on the tree, and the tree will always be bigger than the branch," and "I have already learned, forgotten, and flushed down the toilet more than you will ever know"—because a woman who lives in an environment and under a system that has not supported her in realizing her power seeks, in unaware moments, to usurp the power of those near and dear to her / visiting the National Museum for Peace in Hiroshima; seeing the devastation done by American warfare; and being identified with those Americans in power who dropped that bomb / being taught to drive by the owner of a Cleveland, Ohio, driving school who turned out to be a white, male ex–race car driver from Holland, who on my first lesson showed up in a sports car with no "student driver" sign on it; who had forgotten to bring his driver's license; who got in the car, turned on the radio, chewed gum, and talked incessantly; then instructed me to enter the freeway—first lesson—where I slammed on the brakes when I saw orange cones and road work in front of me and a fast-approaching eighteen-wheeler behind me; and the man in the eighteen-wheeler, who had overdriven his ability to stop, and in an effort to avoid hitting us, overturned his truck / my mother disowning me when I was twenty-nine and thirty-nine / my sister saying to me, "You are the most uncouth person I know" (that is the *only* hurtful thing she has ever said or done to me) / not having adequate math, technical and mechanical training and skills / my ex-husband's reply to my suggestion of marriage counseling three years before the divorce, "I don't have a problem, and since you see the problem, you have the problem, and you need the help" / his unwillingness now to lend me money to finish graduate school, though, during the last year of our marriage when he went into business for himself, I loaned and gave him money / having to file banckruptcy after the divorce / the effects of the Vietnam War / Desert Storm / present-day South Africa / learning that American Airlines has ten thousand pilots out of which approximately three hundred are women, and of those three hundred maybe ten are black women / a woman friend telling me that I am so strong and so powerful and so beautiful that she doesn't know if I'll ever be able to find someone to love . . . wound walking . . .

Late October Check-in

I'm tired, weary even. It's Saturday. After a week of four classes, eighteen hours of free labor at the jail; after Dialogue Racism on Tuesday
night, the women's Empowerment Group on Wednesday night, meditation on Thursday, right after five friends dying, another two approaching divorce; after reading the crime alert in the lobby which
says that yesterday it was reported that a man followed an intended
victim into the hallway and forced entry into her home; after seeing
growing numbers of homeless people gathered between cardboard
boxes near the bayou by the jail en route to Spaghetti Warehouse
where I sometimes eat lunch; after wondering what miracle Spirit is
going to work so that I'll have the money to finish school; after my
check for $32.32 bounces for insufficient funds; after knowing I'll have
to refuse Anu's invitation to visit India with her this December;—after
five back-to-back calls from some unknown, white-sounding man at
2:30 A.M. saying, "This is your secret admirer. What a sexy voice you
have. Can I have some pussy? Huh? Oh I want to eat your pussy!";
after loco Hispanic children call twelve times a day screaming "Pow
pow pow!" or whimpering "Mommmyyy," or shouting "Fuck you,
you nigger!"; after realizing that I have forgotten to give the dogs
heart-worm prevention tablets for four months in a row; after the
arrival of Xhosa (pronounced "Kosa"), a scruffy three-month-old
black, tan, and silver Yorkshire terrier who tends to lose her lunch in
the car; and after giving my word that I'd actually go out and vote
for Clinton, or Bush, or Perot—I'm in bed till 4 P.M. reading *Bullwhip
Days—The Slaves Remember*, an oral history edited by James Mellon;
wondering if James is a Mellon as in Carnegie-Mellon University,
where I went to undergraduate school, and what he did with the pro-
ceeds from his book; while I try to figure out how to use my "call
blocker" service; while I keep my third eye on my grade-point
average—'cause a colored woman needs all the credentials she can get
to keep life from chewing her a new asshole; after this I am lost in
space, floating in darkness, and I feel as if I am drowning . . .

The Election

As I stood in line for early voting at K-mart on Friday, October 30th, two men approached me. One held a microphone and the other a television camera. The one with the microphone walked forward and asked me, "Do you think it'll be a close race?"

I answered, "Whether or not it's a close race is not my issue. My issue is that our only choices are three rich white men. My issue is that I'm forty years old and this is the first time I've ever voted because I've not felt I had anything for which to vote. I don't feel represented in these elections. These candidates do not reflect the racial or gender makeup of this country. Neither of them has, to my knowledge, selected a person of color or a woman as a vice presidential candidate. America has a long, ugly, and painful racial history—the effects of which are still reflected in our limited choices for leadership today."

I mean no irreverence toward Clinton. He is probably a good man. I only wish that we had had the chance to elect him (and that we will have the chance to elect future presidents) from a wider and more representative variety of Americans that includes Hispanics, Native Americans, Asian Americans, Afro-Americans, poor Anglos, women, everybody. . . .

The Boston Murders

BARBARA SMITH

The following entries are excerpts from the journal I wrote in on a regular basis in early 1979. These entries were selected because they focus upon the murders of twelve Black women in Boston, which occurred from January through May of that year. That winter and spring were a time of great demoralization, anger, sadness, and fear for many Black women in Boston, including myself. It was also for me a time of some of the most intensive and meaningful political organizing I have ever done. The Black feminist political analysis and practice that the Combahee River Collective had developed since 1974 enabled us to grasp both the sexual-political and racial-political implications of the murders and positioned us to be the link between the various communities that were outraged: Black people, especially Black women; other women of color; and white feminists, many of whom were also Lesbians.

One of the frustrations we faced was that the murders initially received no media attention. Eventually, because of collective pressure and protest, that changed in Boston, but the wave of killings never received national media coverage, unlike the murders of Black children in Atlanta about a year later. The Combahee River Collective was the first group to produce a pamphlet addressed specifically to Black women which was originally titled, "Six Black Women: Why Did They Die?" Eventually tens of thousands of copies of the pamphlet were distributed and they served as an important catalyst for organizing.

The murders marked a watershed in my development as a Black feminist. They demonstrated exactly what the stakes are—our deaths —which I'd already known. They also demonstrated that our politics as radical Black feminists and Lesbians are key to addressing all Black women's oppression and that in a crisis, various elements of the Black community, including homophobic ones, are able to recognize and value our leadership.

February 1, 1979

I had two very disturbing dreams last night. The one that woke me up just now concerned Aunt Rosa. We were in Cleveland. There was going to be a big family party (Aunt Bert's family). Susan ———— had done a story about all of Aunt Bert's sisters. It was even in the *New York Times* with a color picture. I said something about how it wasn't just in the *Plain Dealer* and also talked about how I had asked Susan ———— about being paid a commission for giving her the information she used in the story and she of course brushed it off, as in real life.

Then Aunt Rosa and I and this little girl, all dressed up, were waiting for a bus. Aunt Rosa had a cane. While we were standing waiting she did something to her foot/ankle. I asked could she actually ride the bus and she said she could. One bus passed us by. I had to go flag them. One finally came and stopped but as we approached very slowly it began to close its doors. I yelled. Please wait, please wait. Over and over again. And it did. We got on the bus in the back and I went up to pay our fare and also to tell off the bus driver. I was going to say something to him about how Aunt Rosa was so old and would only be here for a few months and that the least he could do was wait. But when I got to the front I saw he was a white man and I didn't want to say anything. I was looking at the fare list and didn't see anything listed for senior citizens or regular fares.

The little girl in the dream was very fair and pretty. When we crossed the street at one point she didn't hold onto my hand. I told her she had to do that. I also said to Aunt Rosa at one point, "Wasn't she the cutest little girl she'd ever seen?" I had to take care of them both.

I woke up furious.

The second dream I remember less clearly, but know that it was about the murders of young Black women they've been discovering this month. (In my dream) a new one had happened on Park Drive near where Ellie lives. It was very upsetting. When I woke I was haunted by these murders and thought about my conversation with Lorraine who wants to "do" something. This morning I want to do something too.

Two dreams about Black women's oppression and powerlessness. Goddamnit I'm sick of this world.

February 7, 1979

. . . Then there are the murders of four of us right here and the most frustrating meeting I think I've ever attended on Monday at the Blackstone school. Sexual and racial politics with a vengeance. I don't have the strength to write about it. . . . Perhaps I'll tape some thoughts.

March 19, 1979

Random thoughts: Violence against us is overwhelming. A sixth woman was murdered last week. Racism from white women and homophobia from Black people is a vice that will choke the Black feminist movement.

April 28, 1979

I've been awake since 5:54 and didn't go to sleep until around 2:00.

An eighth Black woman was murdered yesterday. There is going to be a demonstration this morning, a march from the common to Pig

Mayor White's house. It is an action planned in one night. I think there will be hundreds of women there. Practically everyone I called last night already knew, some had gotten four or five calls. But I talked to at least five women who didn't know.

There was a meeting last night in the South End at Harriet Tubman. There were around fifty or sixty women there. Over half of them feminists and Lesbians. Actually more like three-quarters. The word got out. When I called up Calvin Street Kathy ——— answered the phone and before I could say anything she said, "Are you calling about the meeting?" It's happening. This is the third meeting about this violence I've been to this week and at every one we were there giving vital input. The meeting Thursday night at Amaranth was beautiful. So well planned. At least sixty women.

The meeting at Harriet Tubman last night was so intense for this very reason. We were a powerful presence. It just occurred to me that I'm saying we, (meaning feminists and Lesbians), but I am as a Black woman a part of both we's. Before the issue of race came up Charlotte whispered to me her concern about the action being predominantly Black and my forehead furrowed even deeper than it was before. I felt so in the middle. Eventually Charlotte spoke about this and more of that feeling came out. At one point a young Black woman responded to a white woman's suggestion that a group of people take responsibility for security, and that it be someone from the Black organization she belonged to. She said she saw no reason why women in her group should take the weight for this totally and then made some statements indicating her distrust of the white women there, talked about the bad faith that had occurred in other movements.

This is the major issue. Trust and following through. If white feminists ever needed to have their act together it's now. I have faith in a lot of women, because I know their politics, their commitments. But it all has got to be proven.

One idea from that young Black woman and others is that this kind of coalition had happened before and failed. But this is *new*. Black and white, feminist and non-feminists, women have never come together to work on a woman's issue, an issue of racial-sexual politics, at least not in this era. I'm thinking about the anti-lynching movement at the beginning of the century as the nearest parallel—and that of course was different. So this has never been tried before. It could work.

I think about sitting up at Harriet Tubman House three or four years ago in CESA [the Committee to End Sterilization Abuse] trying to figure out how to involve Third World women in our work. And now it's the other way around. White women taking leadership from Black women around one of those "universal" issues we as Black feminists have always said would pull in everyone.

THEN THERE IS the emotional level of this, the level so much harder to write about. We are dying. Again the truth I've always talked about that at bottom Black feminism is about keeping Black women from dying, is made frighteningly real.

When Lilly called me yesterday besides being devastated I got scared. I felt cold inside and was afraid. It is an epidemic. When I spoke to Demita about this she said to remember that most of the women who have been killed are very poor and in the streets more. I told her I knew how we lived might be different, but still. We have to tell ourselves something, tell ourselves why we will not be the next victim. And they are arresting Black men. Who knows what it all means, but that's who's getting arrested and we've got to deal with that. Who over time has been the most likely to violate and kill Black women, at least in urban ghettos for the last twenty years? I remember the *Call & Post* in Cleveland. The horrors of sexual politics, particularly that one grisly life-size picture of the dead infant (found in a trash can perhaps?)

I thought about what I was doing yesterday as our sister was dying. Waiting in front of the Harvard Coop for Beth. Eating quiche, but talking to her about the murders too. Lord help . . .

May 7, 1979

Now it's eleven Black women and one white woman. I am numb and aching. They found two on Friday and Saturday, one this morning in Back Bay beaten to death. Naked? Sexual fodder. I'm afraid.

June 26, 1979

I'm sitting by a pond, surrounded by woods listening to birds (and suddenly the inappropriate disturbance of a helicopter). I cannot believe that I got away, that where I am is real and that I am real in this place. I've had such fantasies already about being here after less than two hours. Fantasies about the kind of writing I could do away from the distractions of oppression. Not just city life, which I need and love, but pain. Terror. Knowing from moment to moment that who I am is on all counts hated. Black, woman, Lesbian, my breathing from moment to moment inevitable fear.

I came here on many levels to get away from the murders. To escape death. So they're "over" now. The pressure has "died" down. Not so. Every other phone call that I get concerns them. The poetry reading benefit with Adrienne and Audre, leafleting last week at Dudley station, random conversations . . . For me the deaths of these women has shaped six months of my life. There has never been forgetting. There has been other activity, other moments, definite joy and laughter, but always, always, always, the tragedy. The certain irrefutable and demonstrated knowledge that my Black female life is worth nothing. That my most appropriate fate here in white-boy patriarchy is to be beaten beyond recognition. *Beyond recognition.*

I am furious as I write this. Furious perhaps that the escape will be so temporary. Consciousness does not permit it. But I will rest here and explore.

I wonder how many Black women have *ever* had the chance to do the simple thing that I've just done. To go away by oneself to write.

Milwaukee Uncle

QUO VADIS GEX-BREAUX

Victimization of any kind bothers me on a deep and personal level. When I heard the news story about the young man who had been killed by police in Milwaukee in 1958 I was singularly struck by the irony that I had been sent there as a child to live with my uncle and his family to escape racial violence in New Orleans. Maybe that wasn't why I was sent. But that was what I was told. As an adult, twenty-two years later, I realized that the incident in question happened sometime around the time my relatives made their protective move.

On November 13, 1980, Sherry Lynn Singleton was killed in New Orleans in what became known as the Algiers Fisher Incident during a hot police raid fueled by the unsolved killing of a police officer. The incident was so like the news accounts of the incident in Milwaukee that surfaced at the same time that I wrote the following piece and a poem about Sherry's killing.

This piece seems especially interesting now, given the Rodney King beating. Unfortunately, it, like so much of our loosely recorded history, speaks volumes about how little we have traveled toward the proper meting out of justice in this country.

1981

In your Milwaukee, Uncle, twenty-two years ago, one year before Mama sent me away with you to escape racial upset here, a black man was shot down by a cop with nothing better to do that night than hunt human game.

In 1958, two white policemen gave chase because this man's car had a broken tail light and one of them shot him standing only one foot away. This is 1980 now but we are still being killed in much the same fashion. Three people were gunned down in the Fisher Housing Project in Algiers, New Orleans, at around three in the morning. Our lives are not valued highly enough to have anyone make attempts to save them. We are indicted, found guilty, and executed all in one fatal swoop by policemen who have been granted license to kill.

Twenty-two years ago, just shortly before I was sent away to your Milwaukee, Uncle, because integration "worked there," there were black men being beaten up and down elevator shafts as a matter of routine in your land of the free.

Now, November 17, the Ku Klux Klan has been granted the right to kill too. In North Carolina the courts said it was okay. They let the murderers go.

It's not working now, Uncle, it has never really worked and certainly not twenty-two years ago in your Milwaukee.

I'm thirty now and things are still the same. Your Milwaukee cop came out of his alcoholic closet to tell his story to the world. He got his buddy sent up for a taste of what he had gotten over those years, to get what he hopes to be a clearing conscience. The man who was shot had a knife planted in his right hand. Even though his sister said everyone knew he was left handed and that she had said so at the trial.

Now twenty-two years later, because a white man cannot bear to look at himself in the mirror, her testimony and the evidence of a burned jacket, which showed this young man was shot at close range, is finally admissible. We cannot afford to continue losing people to a world that admits our existence and our right to it twenty-two years after it has been taken away. There has to be another way. How are we to prove (and honestly, why must we?) that we belong to the species *Homo sapiens*, that those inalienable rights folks talked about so long ago should also be ours.

When will our voices be heard, make a difference? The third to die in the Fisher Project case was heard pleading for her life, yet a gun was produced as evidence against her. It seems more than strange that *all* three of these people would have guns, be able to find them at three in the morning, and be brave enough to insist on trying to use them after others had been killed. It seems more than unlikely. It is unreal. And if that were the case why was there no injury reported by the police? Is the gestapo, black American extinction, Milwaukee-style, at work?

Where are the answers to the pertinent questions? Will we have to wait twenty-two years before people believe that Sherry really screamed, begged for her life and died as her four-year-old son stood watching? Will we have to wait twenty-two years for some white cop or other official to decide he can no longer live with this deep, dark secret? That he must tell? Will her screams then be admissible evidence like that woman's brother's left-handedness twenty-two years later in your Milwaukee, Uncle?

Night Raid

There was one witness
but the papers did not say so
neither did the police
perhaps he was too small to mention
so small so small
hardly there at all
peering out behind the bathroom door

He simply was not that important
not worth shooting that night
he had not pushed dope
or been accused of cop killing
his biggest worry till now
was the pain of having his hair combed
before nursery school

He was easily taken care of
tossed inside the next-door neighbor's living room
as some closing act of kindness
an end to a bloody sacrificial feast

What could he say in court
that would be believed?

No one would listen to the recurring nightmare
of a four-year-old
who could have fantasized
his mother's cries for mercy
her pleading for her life
before her bath became her blood

It really doesn't matter but
there was one witness.

PART SEVEN

Claiming a New Self

We are the hyphenated people of the Diaspora whose self-defined identities are no longer shameful secrets in the countries of our origins, but rather declarations of strength and solidarity. We are an increasingly united front from which the world has not yet heard.

AUDRE LORDE
Spring 1984

I was me with everyone. Me felt good—it also leaves no concern about the impact of who I was and must be in the future.

PATRICIA BELL-SCOTT
9:10 A.M., July 31, 1992

I'm ashamed to tell anyone this, but sometimes I sit in the bathroom and pretend that I'm being interviewed. "Did you ever feel that you would make such an impact on the literary world?" . . . "Why do you write?" I'm thinking up all my answers just in case.

PAULA OBE THOMAS
1991–92

Being alone with myself is a good feeling even though it is kind of new. . . . I have nothing to prove or disprove. I've stop worrying about the things that have no answers.

CATHARINE SMITH JONES
March 12, 1989

Starting Over

MIRIAM DECOSTA-WILLIS

After thirty-odd years of domesticity—as wife, mother of four, grand-mother of three, and professor at a small, historically Black college in Memphis, Tennessee—I decided to start over, to reinvent myself as a desiring woman, Dolores of the Wayward Ways, and to set out on an adventurous journey in quest of a new way to be in the world. I had just emerged from what was, perhaps, the most difficult period of my life, the three-year illness and death of my husband, "A" (Archie); and I realized that I could not remain in that time and place because our life together was over, gone, and I was now alone, at fifty-three, with the second half of my life spreading out before me like a dark stretch of asphalt in the distance. My journal entries during this period reflect my constant struggle to balance the contradictory impulses of my life: memories of a traditional past countered by fantasies of a nonconven-tional future, love of family coupled with a wish for separation and distance, commitment to teaching but a need to do more research and writing, and desire for independence with a longing for compan-ionship.

September 3, 1989

Whoever would have thought last year that August 1989 would find me speeding through downtown D.C. on the back of a Yamaha motorcycle behind a tall, muscular, dark brown man, my hair flying in the breeze, the dark night lit by bright-white monuments, the city iridescent in the dark water of the Potomac. What a summer this has been! I feel as though I'm caught in the eye of a tornado, swept here and there across mountains and rivers with little control of my destiny. I just wonder when the incessant movement will cease . . .

September 17, 1989

These past few weeks, I have felt very disoriented, uprooted, and un-centered because of the hectic pace of the city: traffic, noise, crowds, expressways. Maybe once I get settled I can spend long, solitary hours just reading and writing.

January 8, 1990

I've been reminiscing about my Sunday biscuits-and-country-ham breakfasts with A. Rich food is symbolic of the textured life we lived: full, complete, sensuous. How hard it would be for me to live that kind of life now—without him. I can imagine the loneliness of living in our house on Goodland, seeing the bed where we made love, the sitting room where we sat on dark, snowy nights watching movies, the pool where we swam alone together on so many nights . . . Now I have a totally different life-style—I'm alone and sometimes lonely. I'm free, independent, and vigorous with such boundless energy that it scares me sometimes. Would I go back to that old life? Definitely, if I could have A back with me. I wonder how he'd like the new me.

I ran across the passage in Wells's 1885–87 *Diary* where she wrote about "the demon of [her] unrest." Of course I thought about myself, because I have the same restless energy. It's tiring but exciting, and no day is like the last. I'm on a roll and I love it.

August 22, 1990

I'm back in D.C. after a very tranquil and unhurried drive on Monday. I left Memphis a little after 7:00 A.M., and reached my apartment by 9:00 P.M., after wandering off Route 66 down dark, lonely roads, looking for food and an AMOCO station. I was not tired or stiff, but didn't sleep as well as I'd wished. Too keyed up, I guess. Phillip woke me up early the next morning and invited me to lunch at his place. We had such a good time: hugged four or five times, talked freely about our former and present lovers, played touch football in the living room, and just enjoyed each other. Afterward, I drove him to the airport for a 1:50 flight. The vibrations were there for the first time, and I wondered what it would be like to make love to him. Convenient, for one thing, with no strings attached. He looked so good: tall, lean, brown, ready! He kissed me in the mouth at the airport. I think we're going to be real good together, however it flows.

September 16, 1990

The keynote speaker at the Women's Studies Symposium spoke about the discontinuities in a woman's life that contradict the paradigm of the "ladder of success." Explaining that most women's lives are marked by downswings, valleys, and nonevents—the job we didn't get, the man we lost, or the school we didn't get into—she said, "We're living out different scripts." What a remarkable idea! I went home and reached for Carolyn Heilbrun's *Writing A Woman's Life*. I started it yesterday afternoon, sitting in the little park across from my apartment, comfortable on a bench under the trees, looking up from time to time at the pond and the people passing by. And thinking. Thinking. Thinking. The idea of women writing new scripts for their lives—throwing out the patriarchal scripts that were handed to us, the domestic scripts about being a wife and mother and nurturer—and choosing a different kind of life, a revolutionary life, was mind-blowing. One reviewer wrote, "Heilbrun celebrates women who do not make a man the center of their lives: adventurous, pioneering women in search of new story lines such as going it alone or living with a younger, less accomplished mate; women who wish to make an impact in the public domain; women who wish to live a 'quest plot,' like men."

Heilbrun points out that often women writers use a pseudonym as "the mark of a private christening into a second self, a rebirth into linguistic primacy." That's what I've done with the name Dolores da Costa under which I've published my erotic writing. I've deliberately created a whole new persona. I was telling Paula about that today, how after A's death, I sold the house and fashioned a new *mise en scène*—and then I shaped a new person to inhabit that world. It sounded like me that she [Heilbrun] was describing: the older woman who threw away the scripts. "Neither rocking on a porch, nor automatically offering her services as cook and housekeeper and child watcher, nor awaiting another chapter in the heterosexual plot . . ." That's exactly what I told my children: "I'm not going to sit around and rock grandbabies. I'm going to enjoy my life." And so I created this new me—Dolores—thirty pounds lighter, gorgeous in sexy lingerie, off on sixteen trips in four months. Moving. Moving to the rhythm of my own heartbeat.

September 24, 1990

Robert left last night at 10:30, and I was exhausted. I came to the conclusion over the weekend that I don't want our relationship to develop into anything more permanent because we have a number of basic differences. First and foremost, we have radically different biorhythms: he stays up half the night and sleeps late in the morning, while I turn in at 10:30 and am up very early. Also, he is cut out of a very traditional and patriarchal mold that comes through in his tone of voice (loud, animated, domineering, critical, overbearing), his body language, and his assumptions that I am going to wait on him: make up the bed, fix the meals, and clean the kitchen. I told him straight out that I'm not into nurturing and domesticity; I've had thirty years of that and I'm *sick* of it. I've let him know over the past couple of months that I love my life just like it is, treasure my freedom and independence, and have made my work the center of my life. I know that if we were seriously involved, he would always expect my work and life to be secondary to his. Then, too, there is a neat orderliness to my living space that I don't want to change. I like—no, I enjoy, delight in, am thrilled with—my life!

November 2, 1990

The day after my fifty-sixth birthday, which was spent doing interesting things *alone*. Perhaps the most fascinating part of the day was attending the play, *Hidden: A Gender* at GMU. It was a wild and controversial play, which dealt with the "gender blur" (a new term to me) and which asked the question: When it comes to gender, why can't we count higher than two? Written, directed, and acted by Kate Bornstein—a wonderfully talented, transexual lesbian (also a new concept to me), who calls herself "a shameless art slut"—the play had three characters: (1) the narrator/playwright/doctor, played by Kate, (2) Herculene Barbin, based on a nineteenth-century French woman, raised in the Catholic faith, who was a hermaphrodite, and (3) Herman Amberstone, a man who grew up feeling that he was a woman, a character based on Kate's experiences. The play was a funny, touching, animated, sharp-witted exploration of gender, which focused on that gray area between male and female, where the lines/distinctions/differences are blurred. It was a very provocative work, which raised more questions than it answered. The audience was warm and responsive, laughing loudly at the ribald humor and the dialogue—peppered with words like "dick," "cunt," and "fuck"—and sighing audibly when the doctor placed four live leeches on Herculine's wombless cavity. Kate explained during the question-and-answer period that there is a difference (or can be) between one's gender and one's sexuality because she *was* a man who fucked a lot of women (a real lady's man!) and now she *is* a woman who still fucks women. Now that seems strange to me.

Coincidentally, when I got in that night, my wonderful gay friend Carl called to wish me a happy birthday, and the first thing he asked was, "Have you ever done it in the kitchen?" I had to think a minute, and then I answered, "No, I don't think so. Most of the other rooms in the house, but not the kitchen," to which he responded, "That's a real turn on." Then he proceeded to tell me about his new lover. "I can't stand him," he explained, "but we have the greatest sex together! The best I've had." I love Carl dearly, but sometimes he can get very graphic about his sexual experiences.

Back to the play . . . One of the things that I love about teaching at a university and interacting with young people is the constant exposure to new ideas—new ways of examining the world. Those ideas don't necessarily change *me*, but they do change my ways of thinking. I know that I'm—to quote my Atlanta friend—"hopelessly heterosexual," but I think I'm learning to accept people who have different sexual preferences.

December 21, 1990

Snapping my fingers to the beat of Stevie Wonder grooving "Never in Your Sun" and boogeying down the highway doing seventy-five— passing everything in sight—flipping to a natural high, when suddenly I look to the right and read CHATTANOOGA big and bold. Oh, hell, I'm on the wrong road. All the signs are there: the sun to my right (so I'm heading south instead of west) and up ahead a flat, unfamiliar highway with stretches of nothing in the distance. Forty-two miles out of the way! So, I back up to Knoxville and take Forty going west. Before I know it, the sun has dropped and darkness is coming on fast. Trucks zooming by, their headlights sticking pins in my retinas. I'm sleepy and tired and stiff. Doing fine until I realize I've eaten up a whole hour going nowhere *fast*. Pissed off at myself. But Stevie's sounding good. Now I put George Michael in the tape deck and don't even think of Josh. Good! Let's me know that's over. To hear Michael's "I want your sex" and remember those Wednesday nights and not get funky blue is an ACCOMPLISHMENT. But I gotta thinka someone, so my mind rolls over onto Robert and gets stuck in third gear. Nina's on now, low and guttural. Sounding high or stoned. Mississippi deep mud, goddamn. "Now you got my love and gone," but not quite. Rolling on into Memphis, stiff but still able to push another hundred miles. Feeling good and young and cute. Proud of myself to have done it again—nine hundred miles straight with only three stops for gas.

Unfamiliar again, this place—my space—that I used to love. Shall I defamiliarize the text—my life?

January 13, 1991

I'm ready to roll—ahead of schedule for a change—and I finished my paper—eighteen pages in all—at 9:30 this morning. What a relief. I plan to Xerox about ten copies to distribute, but then just talk informally about my work. That way I can do what I do best—communicate my enthusiasm, excitement, and commitment to my work, which students have always said is my strong suit. I hope I have everything that I need to dazzle administrators and faculty—short skirt, bottle of L'Air du Temps, flashy new earrings, clean-cut outfit that shows off my cute figure. If I don't get 'em with my brains, I intend to knock 'em dead with my body! How's that for professional decorum. Girl, you know you shame!

April 4, 1991

Whenever I walk into my apartment and look out on the water, boats docked at the marina, cars streaming across the Fourteenth Street Bridge, airplanes flying low into National Airport, I feel so peaceful, so at home. My spirit is renewed. When I come in late, tired and tense from so much work, I turn the lights out, light a scented candle, burn incense, sip wine, and gaze at the night-lit city, pinpoints of light, stationary and bright; cars and trucks in the street below; and boats in the water. It's the serene counterpoint that keeps my life in balance.

July 3, 1991

Boy, little children can wear you down! I kept the three grands last night, and those little devils didn't go to sleep until 10:30. I fell into bed along with them, exhausted! Of course they laughed and screamed, and kept up a racket, but they have such a good time when they get together. It's now almost 8:00 A.M. and they're still asleep, so I have a few minutes of peace and quiet.

August 3, 1991

I wondered when I woke up this morning if my children will ever be solidly on their feet so that I won't have *any* responsibilities. Parenting is a lifetime proposition, and sometimes I get *so* tired. My brain just fogs over and I feel so emotionally drained. I'm beginning to look forward to the return to D.C.—if for no more than to put *geographic* distance between me and my children's problems. All the talk, talk, talk. And worry, worry, worry. Not to mention the money. Oh, well, off to the library.

August 7, 1991

On the road again—this time to Holly Springs to do research on Ida B. Wells. I went, first, to Rust College, where I found an interesting paper on the early history of the college, written by a grad student from Michigan. He wrote a detailed description of the Methodist evangelism and New England Victorian (Puritan) values that were inculcated into the Black students by the White missionary teachers. I now have a good "feel" for the foundation that enabled Wells to develop her independence, morality, and religious beliefs. I spent two hours there in the small, hot room on the second floor, which houses the Rust archives. What a pitiful collection of documents the college has, primarily because of a series of fires, in 1879, 1884, 1887, and 1940, which destroyed valuable historical papers, as well as buildings. Afterward, I headed toward Court House Square, stopped briefly by the tourist office to pick up maps, and then spent an hour and a half at the Marshall County Library, conducting a futile search through nineteenth-century cemetery lists. From there, I went to the Marshall County Museum, where I found four photographs from the nineteenth century that the curator will copy for me. She was very southern with "cute" southern belle manners and a delightfully soft drawl, though she must be close to fifty. I ate a sandwich in a café on the square and drove by Asbury Methodist Church (Black) before turning toward Highway 70. It was hot as hell down there in that Mississippi town, and I felt drained after all the moving around and exertion.

November 3, 1991

This domesticity bit is a mess! A man enters your life and right away you're into the nesting thing again—cleaning, cooking, looking for pretty nightgowns, and getting all feminine! I'm going to fix salmon and grits for breakfast (for the first time in four years). And I don't even believe that shit about "the way to a man's heart." Fuck that. But this thing must be in the genes because it's hard as hell to eradicate. Already (and I hardly *know* the man), I'm thinking moonlight and roses, even honeymoon and walking into the sunset together. I'm *surprised* at myself . . . after all that talk about being free, loving myself, and being happy with my single life.

February 22, 1992

I'm determined to enjoy myself. Take time to see some sunsets and moonrises. Hang out with my women friends. Forget Larry. Forget Robert (who's been calling and sending notes). Forget Josh (who wants me to join him in New Orleans next week). Forget Phillip (who can't take a hint). Live each day. Love myself. Enjoy being a "fuck you woman"—hands on hips, mouth stuck out, eyes blazing. Uppity as hell. It's my LIFE and I intend to go with the flow! End of journal (volume XIII). Now on with the rest of my life.

On Turning Fifty

JUDY SCALES·TRENT

When I was in my mid-forties, I took a leap into the unknown . . .
well, several leaps, actually. I changed my name, and I traded in the
life of a practicing attorney in Washington, D.C., for the life of a
writer and teacher in Buffalo, New York. I left a bustling, exciting
city where I had old friends, family, lovers, for a quiet town where I
knew no one. After years of hesitation and fear, years of not knowing
exactly what to do to make my life work better, I was hoping to find
a life that was a better fit.

As you might imagine, the process of making these decisions and
transitions involved a lot of thinking about what we gain and what
we lose as we make changes in our lives. How do the accounts tally?
Had I done the right thing, or not? I suppose the process of making
these assessments goes on all the time, but I think that there are certain
times—momentous occasions, important birthdays—which bring that
process to the fore. I also think that the tally becomes more painful
as we get older because, despite the eternal promise of America, we
do not get to start over again and again, forever and always.

I wrote this essay the week before my fiftieth birthday, in the last
few days of September 1990. I was absolutely compelled to write,
obsessed with writing: my thoughts were so powerful that I had to

write them down in order to move them outside of my body, in order to manage them, in order to transform painful feelings into marks on paper. And as I wrote and rewrote, as I polished and smoothed out the phrases of the essay, I also polished and smoothed out the feelings in my heart.

I had thought that I would live my mother's life. I suppose all girls do. Like my mother, I would have a dignified and successful husband, one who would take care of me and our children, who would provide a life of status and comfort. I would be involved in my church. I would take classes and volunteer in my community. I would passionately enjoy my garden and my sewing.

This has not been my life. It has been more the life of my sisters. Like my mother, they are married, each with three children. My eldest sister now has four grandchildren: there will be more. In my eyes, they live a life of comfort—trips to far-off places, a summer house in the country.

This has not been my life. I live alone, with one small dog. A university professor, I do much of my work alone. I am no longer married. My teenage son lives in another state, long miles away. If I am to have any security or status or physical comfort, I must give it to myself.

It is at times like this, reckoning times, that I wonder where I went wrong. For I long for family—a husband, children, grandchildren. And this is not a mild longing. At times like this when I allow myself to feel it, the longing is so fierce that I close my eyes to hold back its power. I started down the path of my mother's life, but somewhere along the way I walked away from it. Where did I go wrong? Or did I go right? For it is at times like these, reckoning times, that I also remind myself that the life I now lead is the right one.

There was a moment, one morning, when I understood its rightness. It took place during the frenzy of my move from Washington, D.C., when I flew to Buffalo to sign closing papers for my new house. Isabel, a new colleague at the law school, picked me up at the airport and made me welcome as an overnight guest in her home. And it was the next morning, as I came downstairs, on my way to go to the attorney's office, that I was struck by something, something not yet clear in my mind. I remember the moment. I can see it clearly. I walked into the living room. The sun was streaming in through a stained-glass piece hung against the window. High ceilings, richly colored rugs on wooden floors, plants spilling over in profusion on a low, wooden bench; mugs and coffee and bread and jam on a coffee table in front of the sofa; stacks of books everywhere. And Isabel, sitting on the sofa, drinking her morning cup of coffee, reading a book. The sun made a golden picture. I stopped and stared, overwhelmed by the beauty and the quiet. "Is this what my life will be like?" I asked. She smiled. "Yes."

I must have longed, without knowing, for this—the sun and books, a quiet room, the generosity of friends. And that is my life now. For the very first time, my life is a seamless piece of fabric. There is no sense of working or not working. For the very first time, I do what I am. There is profound joy in this wholeness.

But there is no denying that this wholeness has come late. I will soon be fifty. The number feels important. Life does not go on forever. A friend and I once talked about this getting older. I told her that sometimes I felt as if I could see the end. Did she feel the same? "No," she answered, "but sometimes I can *feel* the end." The end. Feeling the end. This is a powerful thought. I see the signs: the eyes that do not work so well during the day, and even less well at night; the bones that complain when I push myself up out of bed in the morning; the skin that softens and sags. Fades.

My father has just turned eighty, my mother seventy-eight. They have been in good health all their lives. Now age makes them vulnerable and frail. My father is impatient. "Why should I no longer be able to drive," he rails, angry at life's betrayal. He has always been active—tennis, swimming, long daily walks. Now that he can no longer go for his walks around the neighborhood, now that he can no longer swim, he does not give up. He goes to the Y six days a week, and walks back and forth across the pool, buoyed and strengthened by the water. He counts the steps—precious steps, and calls me in

Buffalo to tell me how many miles he has walked. My mother still gardens and sews and goes to her classes. And she, who never exercised before, now takes daily exercise classes at the church. They have a morning routine. She drives my father to the pool and waits while he walks. Then she drives them both to the church, where he waits for her.

I am moved by my parents' courage and their devotion to each other. Soon they will lose each other. Soon I will lose them. And still they teach me. Still, I learn from them. Just as they once taught me how to tie my shoes and to count, just as they once taught me to write thank-you notes, now they teach me how to suffer loss after loss with dignity and grace.

I am more interested in death now. It seems more familiar. I see and read things in a different way. Sometimes I remember a phrase from a spiritual, and hope that someone will sing it at my funeral:

> Steal away,
> steal away,
> steal away to Jesus.
> Steal away
> steal away home.
> I ain't got long to stay here.

Sometimes I come across words which I read with new meaning, like this Indian death song:

> From the middle
> of the great water
> I am called by the spirits.

Through the words I feel a broad and generous grace. There is calm, peacefulness, rightness. Homecoming.

There is a special poignancy to this fall. I do not want it to come. More than usual, I hold on to summer. This fall feels different. It feels like the announcement of the fall of my life. I accept and deny at the same time. For the first time, I want to plant bulbs. I want to store away the promise of spring, to make sure that its sweetness will return. This fall I will dig in the ground and plant daffodils and jonquils of all different kinds—daffodils and jonquils, and crocuses to announce their coming.

And as I plan this latest addition to my garden, I think that in many ways I am indeed living my mother's life. She is an independent woman who can work alone, contented, joyously, for days and weeks at a time. And she is passionate about her work. She creates her own projects in her garden and in her sewing room. She plans, she designs, she works and reworks until it suits her. She takes classes to refine her art. I used to consider myself a failure because in my family the women sew, and because I do not have the patience to sew—to pin and baste and stitch and then take it out and start all over again if the shoulder is off-line, if the dress doesn't drape just so. But in reality that is also how I work. For I too am passionate about my work. And I can work alone—joyously, contented, for days and weeks at a time. And when I write, I too pin and baste and stitch, and then I take it apart and do it over again if a phrase is off-line, if a sentence doesn't fall just so.

It pleases me to find this similarity between my mother's life and mine. I rejoice in my work. It is a good life.

It is not enough.

That day, my fiftieth birthday, is coming soon now. I am getting ready. Friends in Washington and Buffalo are giving me parties. I am having a dress made—short and red and silky. I am looking for dancing shoes. My parents will fly from Greensboro to the Washington party. I will go to these celebrations, as I go into my fiftieth year, embraced by family and friends. And I will look at these days the way life teaches me to look—with one eye laughing, one eye weeping.

Going Through
My Changes

LOIS FLORENCE LYLES

When I get up, before I break the night's fast I pull from my dresser drawer what is more necessary to me than food: the cheap, spiral-bound, drugstore notebook which is my journal. I begin communing with my own spirit by scribbling down whatever thoughts I have—of a sensation, of an emotion, of a belly laugh, of a crying jag, of one of yesterday's street scenes, or of the dream I had that ended just before I awoke on this day at dawn.

I write to try to make sense of the hurts and fears, of the frustrations and disappointments, of the lusts, joys, and excitements of life. I write to savor the salt-and-vinegar tang of the words themselves. I write to feel lightning crackle down my spine when the right words come.

"Going Through My Changes" was written while I was at home recuperating from the surgery I had in the summer of 1991 to remove my uterus, which had become engorged with massive fibroid tumors. The journal entry records my attempt to understand and accept the changes (including the cessation of menstruation) which followed the loss of my womb. Writing helped me define what it means to be a

woman at different stages of a woman's lifelong struggle to become herself and to locate herself in the world.

August 8, 1991

Yesterday afternoon I explored my stomach and pubic area with my fingers. The surgical tapes over the wound had started to come loose, so I could see some of the cut straight down the middle of my belly. The incision begins with a sickle-shaped, one-inch cut just below my navel; then it runs vertically, bisecting my stomach, and stopping about four inches above the lowest part of the V which outlines the doorway to my secret regions—the vulva. The doctors shaved my pubic area while I was anesthetized, so that the wide part of my V is bald, and the wiry black hairs begin only a couple of inches above my labia.

A few days ago, when I was just back home from the hospital after the hysterectomy, the shaved places prickled a whole lot, especially where the chopped hairs were fighting to get new growth under the bandages. Luckily this intense itching eased off after a day or two. Nevertheless, my whole pubic area still itches—my stomach, too. I called nurse Diane and asked her what I should do about it—a lotion, perhaps. She told me to cure the itch by scratching my head. I laughed in amazement. She explained that I should not have a medicinal cream on my stomach, because this might loosen the bandages, and they needed to be there to help me heal. The itch was a normal part of the healing, Diane said.

I still itch pretty bad, though; and scratching my head doesn't seem to solve anything!

The flesh around the incision is healing cleanly, without pus or inflamed tissues. Running my finger over the longitudinal part of the scar, I feel a tiny ridge like the crest of a miniature mountain. The flesh of the scar is thick and hard. It is as though somebody had cut a seam down my middle, stitched a zipper in there, and then zipped it up. Parallel to each side of the incision line is a line of tiny scar holes. I remember the surgical staples put in my belly right after the operation; I also remember the scissors-like tool which Claire, a friendly medical student, used to pull the staples out after the wound began healing. I'd been trussed up like a Christmas turkey.

Now my pubic region looks just like the boys' haircuts nowadays, only upside down. My son has a thick bush on his crown, but midway down his head, proceeding all the way to his nape, he is closely shaved, so that only the shadow of dark hair is visible on the lower half of his skull.

I haven't felt much sexual arousal since the operation, and I've been wondering if I'll still be able to feel the pulsing light and heat of orgasm in my brain and belly. I remember how my uterus used to send me "go" signals of sexual energy right before and right after a menstrual period. I feel sad to think that never again will I feel those thrilling waves of blood rising and falling like a heartbeat magnified one hundred times. Will I inhabit a desert of feeling (all its cactus flowers of desire stunted and unlovely) from now on?

I have really enjoyed the experience of a bodily cycle—of different types of smells and sensations, of different kinds of secretions—at various times of the month. Now I *have* lost a complete inner world with its own laws; a whole inner magic-lantern show; a whole inner whirl of seasons, accompanied by blizzards, hail, mild rain, and the heat of summer sun.

I do not wish to indulge in self-pity. After all, I did not have surgery to remove a malignant tumor. I will be fine, especially since I have been relieved of the fibroid growths that made me need to piss as frequently as a pregnant woman. On the scale of things, I have not lost that much by having my uterus taken out.

Yesterday, on the campus where I am employed, I saw a tall young fellow with a prosthesis on each arm. He'd lost, in addition to the left forearm, both hands. Instead of hands he wore steel claws. It hurt to look at him. What must it be like to face years and years of not touching anything or anybody with your hands! What must a strong-looking amputee (like this student) feel when he wants to make love—wants to stroke his girlfriend's face!

Change is omnipresent in life. This man lost his hands. I would have become infertile in several years' time, anyway, as a result of menopause. The only defense a person has against change is to learn to step out and face each new wave of life in time with its approach. Whether the waves are surging whitecaps or calm ripples, they must be breasted.

The first day I was home from the hospital, I tried to act as though nothing had happened to me. I walked a long ways to the grocery store and toted back heavy bags full of groceries, even though it was less than a week since I'd been in surgery. I wanted to prove to anybody and everybody that having a hysterectomy didn't mean a thing.

But it *did* mean something. I *am* different.

One thing I believe I must do is find new sources of strength through using my body in new ways: dance, calisthenics, or karate. Slowly, I am learning to let go of a former self.

Yesterday I called Judy to ask if she'd like to have my stock of unused tampons and sanitary pads. "There are three women in your house; why should the stuff go to waste?" I asked. When Judy replied that I should not throw my old gear away, but save it until she could pick it up, I was very glad. She has two beautiful, smart, lively girls, home now from preparatory school.

When I first got my period, at age thirteen, it was a nuisance; I had headaches and bad cramps. It was a mess. But after I gave birth, at age twenty-three, to my son (now nearly grown), menstruation no longer hurt. I grew to accept and even like this part of my being.

Once I had an Italian landlady who referred to the menses as a woman's "friend." A Black woman I once knew called it her "changes." And now a woman's menstrual cycle makes me think of chord changes. Just imagine—the center of a woman's body, tuned, like the heart and womb of a guitar, to the rhythms of the human spirit!

I will miss my "friend": for all of two decades and the greater part of a third, a vital part of me.

Jive Talk and Random Thoughts

PEARL CLEAGE

I think the best thing about my journals has been that they gave me an easily accessible, nonjudgmental place to try and figure out the things that were driving me crazy. For that, I am grateful. The worst thing about keeping them is the danger of becoming an observer of your own life. There were times when I found myself watching myself with the detached alertness that is required when I'm going to write about IT later. It was that constant need to watch and write down everything that has lead me away from my journals these last few years. I realized that I wanted to see what happy felt like, not just what the fantasy of it looked like on the page. I wanted to make a move, not craft a perfect paragraph to describe the projected motion. I wanted to wallow in the real thing with no thought of remembering the details to be carefully recorded later on secret pages meant for my eyes only. I decided to try and write some pages for the outside world and see how it felt. And I liked it, and I like it, but still my journals sit behind me even as I type these lines, and they are still smirking a little, knowing that I am always cocky when I think I have figured IT out. Knowing how long that usually lasts and that when it turns out that IT is still in a state of flux, as IT always is, knowing I'll be back, scribbling frantically, trying to see out by crawling far enough in to know that there is no way to go but up toward the light.

Besides, if I hadn't been so obsessive about writing down all that March 27, 1981, stuff, how would I have remembered that the small ballerina was spinning to the Viennese Life Waltz and the moon was full outside my window?

March 27, 1981

Of course I'm still stoned. It's moving day. I've been carrying Henry Miller around as if he was a talisman to ward off bad spirits. Evil eyes. Boring lives. This morning I moved some critical stuff into the place. Then I sat down in front of all of it laid out neatly on my green shawl. Smelled the incense. Listened to the traffic and the occasional bird, opened *Tropic of Cancer* and read this: ". . . no one to whom I can communicate even a fraction of my feelings." First private time in my new space. I hear how loud the traffic is on Peachtree and I panic. Is it too loud? Is it the wrong apartment? Is it too far/too dear/too little/too old/too unsafe? It is my own. This is my own private choice. (Yesterday, bringing D. here, pressing my palms against her child hands. Rituals for good luck, long life, and her eyes as round and hopeful as the full moon through my window. I am the only mother she has ever had!)

This is what I have brought in this first load: photographs of my father/my mother/my great-grandmother/both sets of grandparents/ both great aunts; the postcard of Niagara Falls, shimmering with the green and pink of artificial and determined spotlights; the doll Kris made of me with rosey nipples and pubic hair, a tiny tuck of navel; a publicity sheet from Madame Walker's cosmetology school; candles; incense; a photobook of Georgia O'Keefe by Alfred Steiglitz open to the page filled with her breasts and her legs spread open/open/open; the butterfly book I bought in L.A. in defiance; a bottle of Amaretto; a pink shot glass which was an inspired Christmas present from my four-year-old middle neice to my five-year-old only daughter, the collage Kris made for me with the butterfly wings sprouting from my shoulders; my green Mexican shawl from Georgetown; four photographs of myself; a flea-market music box that plays the Viennese Life Waltz while the ballerina rises and falls, dips and swirls; an orange paper lantern from the road to the other coast; a blue plastic frog; a pair of smiling pink satin lips; a travel clock in the shape of a stack of gold coins; a set of photos from the four-shots-for-a-dollar machine at the zoo; the quilt Kris made; a snap of my daughter at Sweetwater Creek and one of me kissing the Pueget Sound salmon; an envelope of letters to and from: *China Men, Don Juan, On the Road,* Anaïs Nin's photo supplement to the diaries, Toni Morrison's *Newsweek* cover; Henry Miller by Norman Mailer; a hanging charm and the San Antonio candle; the black Madonna pointing at her baby; the fishing weight from the Sound; the goat bone from the farm; a shell from Ossabaw; postcards of Christo's running fence and Dalí's *Woman at the Window*; scented soap in blue paper with a flowered seal; four perfect joints in a green plastic cigarette case circa 1920; paper; and a pen. Welcome home/Welcome home/Welcome home . . .

Looking

QUO VADIS GEX-BREAUX

Journal keeping is often cheap therapy. "Looking" is one of those truly personal therapeutic pieces. The notion of want, wanting, and having wanted left over from childhood is haunting. Many life choices are determined by leftover feelings of need.

It was important to note my expression of need after I recognized its passing. I wondered about the genesis of such a strong sense of lack and the need to find a solution outside myself. As I moved to a different space internally, I found I no longer had this driving need for succor from some undetermined but magical exterior place. I suppose the journal entry served to examine the death of this feeling by analyzing its origins.

Like all parents who reach a point of total frustration with the adolescent animal, my mother had taunted that she wished she could be a fly on the wall to see how I handled having a family. Sometimes, I find myself in that juxtaposed position in her memory, thinking in ways that she might have thought about what I'm doing, thinking, saying. So this piece is also a bit of appreciation for the trials she experienced as a mother simply trying to do her best.

May 6, 1984

I have spent a lifetime looking for money, food to eat, and shelter. One of my most vivid memories from childhood focuses on maddening searches into the crevices of secondhand upholstery for coins or bills that might have fallen there by chance. These frenzied searches were family affairs. Everyone participated because, after all, we were working to find enough change to buy a pound of red beans, a pound of rice, and a thirty-cent piece of pickled pork—a meal, for less than a dollar then. I have spent many waking hours not listening to birds chirping, eyeing exquisite shrubbery, or admiring unique architecture, but watching the ground, grass, or curbside, woefully hoping to find money—dollars, I'd fantasize, in rolls, that someone who needed them less had lost.

We had many lean days but only one absolutely breadless one. It was a sorrowful event. I had never seen my mother so heartbroken and helpless. I realized later, when I became a mother myself, what a gut-wrenching feeling not having a thing to feed your children must be. In the past, we had always been rescued. Some relative would clean out her refrigerator and/or pantry sending us home with a bag of rejects that would soon become a wondrous or several wondrous meals for us. Sometimes a kind cousin would send us a few bail-out dollars. Or we would scrounge up enough change from those hidden places in the couch and living room chairs to feed us. The sense of glee at realizing the bottom stretch of cloth on the sofa or chair actually clinked with coins is indescribable.

I didn't realize what a lifetime occupation this looking had become until I was thirty-three and suddenly realized one day that I was not scrutinizing the pavement, curb, and street beneath me hoping to find a stray bill or two or that "pot of gold" rainbow illusion of the tidy but lost wad looking for a needy spender. My sense of amazement and release was unbelievable.

On "Going Home"

DEBORAH E. MCDOWELL

*When typing this entry for inclusion in the present collection, I thought
curiously of Robert Frost's poem, "The Death of the Hired Man,"
which contains what must be one of the worst, or certainly the most
awkward, lines in the history of poetry: "Home is the place where,
when you have to go there / They have to take you in." Despite the
awkwardness, the dialogue between the two speakers in the poem over
the meaning of "home" has always made me pause. It's the repetition
of "have to"—twice in the space of two short lines—that gets to the
heart of the matter of "home" for me. "Have to," with all that it
evokes about urgency and obligation, duty and necessity, with all the
complex mix of feelings that all these terms arouse. Although my
words and explanations have failed me, time and time again, I still
feel I "have to" make my beloved Alabama family understand why I
just can't pick up and move back home. One afternoon while reading
Edward P. Jones's short story collection from his volume* Lost in the
City, *I seemed to find a temporary answer in "Store." Explaining why
he left the safety and danger of home, the narrator says, "I was making
room in my soul for more than one neighborhood."*

Sunday, 27 July 1986. 5:10 P.M.
Bessemer, Alabama

I am at home. I see the effects of the Alabama drought on Auntie's grass. It's brown, dry, patchy. Rain is in the forecast for today, but I see no sign of clouds. At least it's cool enough to sit here in the backyard and take more notes for the essay on *Sula* that I have promised Nellie for her volume.

The trip down was uneventful. On the way to Portland I kept driving behind assholes going 50 mph in the pass lane. One woman kept braking, just to be spiteful I felt, so I pulled into the right lane. She honked her horn and gave me the finger. I fingered her back. A few miles down the road, I started laughing out loud—at myself, at her. What was the point of all that rage about the speed of a car? I made it to the Portland Jetport to find a mob at the People Express counter, but I managed to get on board.

Today I went to church with Cindy and Auntie. Because it's so hot and the elderly members can't climb the thirty steps to the main hall, the service was held in the basement. As Cindy and I walked around the side of the church, down the little stone path, we saw Miss Mattie Mae Wills. I was surprised to see how much she's aged. I guess I had left in my mind the picture I had of her when I was a child. Her long, coarse, thick and wavy hair made many a woman find reason to hate her. Now her hair is almost completely gray and she sports a stingy row of curls turned up stiffly around the nape of her neck. She no longer struts, the pleats of her skirt swinging from side to side. Now she tips, trying hard to stay balanced on the three-inch heels of her patent-leather sandals.

The church service was dry. The new minister, whom I've never met, was ill and the service was run by Reverend Precious Hopson and Mrs. Barron, two old faithfuls. Mrs. Barron actually preached the sermon, and, though I was very glad to see a woman in the pulpit, the sermon left me cold. It reminded me of so many others that I'd heard all my life. It had that generic theme: Satan's temptations are powerful, but we must be strong in the Lord.

After church, several people came up to me and I was glad to see them. Even Daddy's old card buddy, Mr. Matt, was there and seemed just as I remembered. He had left Mount Zion for our church; his wife, Miss Mavia, stayed behind.

Since this was a trip to pick up any little pieces that might fill the huge gaps in my memory of my early childhood, I was touched when Mrs. Emma Merriweather just volunteered a story about me. She said I was a reporter (not exactly an image of myself that I relish), and that one day at church I came to her and said, "Mrs. Merriweather, please excuse my socks, but Stanley [one of my age mates] is getting out of hand." I hadn't asked for that detail, but given my search, it was a precious tidbit. It gave me a clue as to why Papa called me Miss Priss. What could have been wrong with my socks? Why should they be "excused"? I was apologizing for myself, my imperfections early on and ever since.

Even despite all the warm and lusty greetings and the deliciously sweaty hugs, I still felt odd. Odd because I can never make my choices seem sensible to all the folks back home. Mrs. Young, who used to smooth down my can cans and sneak me nickles for ice cream cones, wants to know why I'm not married. Why I don't have children. I must be too fussy she says. Auntie wants to know why I don't move closer to home. Aren't there good jobs in Alabama? in Tennessee? Why must I live all the way in Maine. Isn't that near Canada? Then I might as well be in a foreign country, as far as she's concerned.

I laugh and indulge them. Ever the "good" girl, even if a childhood tattletale, I am not dismissive, defensive. I smile, knowing that I will never reveal what I truly think about the idea of moving back home. When I left home and discovered that life could be more than getting drunk and having fights on weekends, gossiping about the neighbors, and fending off creditors and the insurance man, I experienced blessed relief. I swore then that, if I could help it, nothing, no one, would ever threaten that relief. But even as I write this, I feel guilt and fear. I even hear Grandma's thunderous quotation from the Scripture, which I always thought she saved especially for me: "Pride goeth before a fall."

Monday, 28 July 1986. 12:05 P.M.
Bessemer, Alabama

Why does the thought of moving back home scare me almost shitless? Coming home would mean sitting on porches in sweltering heat or indoors in the daylight darkness with all the curtains drawn, the din of the air conditioner fighting it out with the buzzers of "The New Price Is Right." If I came home I would be constantly saddened by the destruction that this economy, combined with their own bad habits, is heaping on the people that I love.

Here, there is a drugstore on every corner to suppress the symptoms that result from a lifetime of poor diet and great stress. This morning we went to Food Town to get cranberry juice for Auntie. She's complaining of painful urination. Right next to Food Town is the druggist. On the way from the drugstore we stopped by Mr. Honey Pop's to get some information about Daddy's discrimination pay. Apparently all the while Daddy worked at the Pipe Shop (the U.S. Pipe and Foundry), he, along with other black men, was paid much less money than white men for the same job. I'm first furious, then deeply saddened, when I hear this. Daddy died at fifty-one, felled almost instantly by a massive brain stroke, the result of drinking, smoking, worrying, and womanizing. Would pay equity have prolonged his life I wonder?

As it turns out, Mr. Honey Pop didn't know too much. He's now retired and feels too exhausted to take on this fight. After all, he says, his house is paid for and he has food to eat. He gave me the name of somebody who was a union official. He could tell me what I needed to know.

We left and rode through the streets of Pipe Shop. I sat huddled in the back seat of Auntie's Rambler and cried. Cried out of sadness, fear, anger, guilt, relief. Relief and guilt at having "escaped" this place. Sadness for everybody left behind. Fear that I will have to come back here, and against my will to a gutted and desolate community. All but the poorest have gone to the white housing developments, now that they can move in without fearing a cross burning. Pipe Shop School is gone. Oddly, nothing remains but the room that used to be my first-grade, then fifth-grade class. The houses along the street need paint and repairs, need grass, flowers. Children playing hopscotch step out of the road to let the car pass by, a passing car with unfamiliar faces which they watched until we were out of sight.

Natural Monuments

MÉLINA BROWN

My journal has been my sounding board. *Rather than subjecting my friends to political ranting or losing my thoughts through speech to the fragility of the air, I often prefer expounding on paper—making my thoughts concrete. This process gives them shape and validity and often sparks new ideas and action. Through my journal I can work out plans and solutions to problems that may be too controversial to discuss with others without coming to blows.*

My journal has also been my therapist. When no one else was around, or when I couldn't pull myself together enough to talk to anyone, I could release my thoughts and emotions without worrying about being judged. My journal would accept it all, and save my words until I was ready to read them.

Never has my journal served such an important role as when I experienced the difficult dissolution of my marriage. Being able to record my mercurial moods helped stabilize me. I would vent much of my sadness and frustration at any time of the day or night without worrying about disturbing anyone. I would read my words later and my situation would crystallize before me. I was then able to sort things out and make changes, or simply accept my predicament. Even though I would disbelieve I had ever written some of the entries, seeing my handwriting in the journal helped me recognize all facets of my personality. Without my journal it would have been difficult to gain the kind of self-knowledge I now possess.

December 26, 1989

I feel bizarre, empty, and sad. I wanted to cry all weekend and I actually spent a good portion of the weekend doing it. Things with Ian and I are pretty much over. Today I didn't know what to do with myself. I wanted to keep busy to keep my mind off of things. I didn't want to go shopping or see my parents. I still feel pretty bad about everything. So I went outside—had to be outside. I went to the Oakdale cemetery and looked around at all the monuments to the dead for the living. The snow was coming down hard and it was colder than I thought. I froze my face; it was completely red—almost as red as my scarf. My feet and fingers froze as well. I thought I would feel weird walking among the elaborate tombstones, like spirits of the dead would overcome me or something. Nothing happened. I just felt cold, empty, alone but alive. I could feel the pain of the cold and the loneliness. I felt very alive.

I then drove to Mounds Park to see the Indian Burial Mounds. More monuments, although simple, to the dead, overlooking the river and the city. Because of the snow I couldn't see the supposedly beautiful view. All I saw was bleak, empty, whiteness. I felt like the only human alive as I left my small footprints on the snowy trail.

Sunday, March 11, 1990

It has been about exactly a year now since Ian left. I feel so sad and confused and helpless. It's not fair; I hate feeling this way. He said today, that he's ending the chapter in this book because we're not being true to ourselves. It's just so hard to deal with. I'm still so scared of ruining my life and ending up alone and lonely down the road.

Tuesday, August 14, 1990

After the divorce hearing last Wednesday, I couldn't really cry (although I wanted to) until I got in my car after having walked through West. After that brief sobbing, all I could think of was going to the beach. I changed, and went to Fort Snelling with a book because it was so beautiful outside. I read a little, slept a little, cried a little bit more, and reminisced about my childhood. Hearing the happy (and sometimes sad) voices of all the little kids playing in the sand and water made me long to be back in that promising, innocent age—only for awhile. I don't lament my life too often but the thought of reliving certain periods held great appeal at that moment. But I just got up, took a dip in the refreshing water and lay back down in the sun to enjoy its warmth. It felt good.

Later Patty and I went and gorged at Billy's on Grand, where we'd been the last time just the two of us had gone out to bear our souls.

I kind of wish Patty, Momma, and Daddy, or anyone else I know and love had been with me on the bench this evening, watching the sky. The huge, biblical clouds had captured the oranges and peaches of the setting sun and through them, hot flashes of silver-white lightning were bounding around, the sound of thunder only barely audible in the distance. The background sky had split so that above the clouds the sky remained bright baby blue while below them the sky became ominously dark. It was so incredibly beautiful, uncommon, and electric that I could've been having a religious experience. Maybe I was.

PART EIGHT

Writing from a Different Place

Watching market woman at work, I rethink how, enslaved African women took their spiritual powers to and through the Middle Passage with them, they lost their awesome economic power in the Americas, colonized by sexist Euro-Americans who *knew* "a woman's place was in the home."

ANDREA BENTON RUSHING
January 11, 1987, Ile-Ife, Nigeria

I really love this country, which is strange, when you think that it doesn't suit my personality, I mean the fast pace and the obsession with the whole materialism thing—nevertheless I feel very close to Japanese in my heart, like they're cousins of mine. I feel some hint of recognition when I see them, although some of them would rather die than admit this, as they are trying so hard to be as close to white people as they possibly can.

VIKI RADDEN
June 2, 1991, Kōbe, Japan

Folks are surprised that I know anything about respecting my elders, sucking my teeth, or getting caught up in the Holy Spirit. And can't believe I grew up eating sugarcane, avocado, black-eyed peas, okra, and hot sauce and sucking meat off bones.

ANDREA BENTON RUSHING
January 30, 1988, Ile-Ife, Nigeria

African art, Egyptian art, mummies . . . stolen from our ancestors by the British. It was a sight to see.

DOROTHY WILBANKS
Sunday morning, September 8, 1991, London

Ubud, Bali

ALICE WALKER

This journal entry, which first appeared in Living by the Word: Selected Writings, 1973–1987, *is part of this writer's map "to find [her] old planet."*

February 12, 1987

Another rainy night. I am in bed, where I've been for several hours, after a long walk through Ubud to the monkey forest and then for lunch at the Lotus Café—entirely inhabited by Europeans and Americans and one stray very dark and pretty Indian girl in a vivid red dress. Then the walk home, stopping in a local shop—where the woman proprietor is sweet and sells wonderful flowing cool and colorful pants. (Rebecca, on seeing them hanging near the street, immediately exclaimed, "Miss Celie's pants!") Anyway, the pants I liked, knee length, with the flowing grace of a sarong, she no longer had, but she urged me to try a kind of flowered jumpsuit, very long—before she showed me how to adjust it to my shape—and Western-influenced Balinese. It looked great, so I bought it.

But the rain threatens to get me down. In the mornings there is a little sun—nothing direct; in the afternoons there are quite heavy showers, which, even if they are warm and we can walk right through them, I find a little overwhelming after the third or fourth day. Also feeling down because I've drunk so much beer, since the water is considered unsafe except here at the house. And, Robert says, this is the week before my period!

Anyway, *very* out of sorts, for me. It's true I overheard the housekeeper (who travels everywhere with an umbrella against rain and sun) tell Rebecca she "don't like black," as Rebecca was saying how much she wants to "brown"; and I resent always being perceived as just another "rich" American tourist and importuned to buy at every turn when we are walking and even here at the house. But Ubud is beautiful! I've never seen anything like it. The green rice paddies, the soft bluish-gray skies, the people who've created the landscape, and themselves, graceful, friendly, amazingly mellow.

So much so it is a shock to realize that as recently as 1965 more than 100,000 of them killed each other after an attempted Communist coup in Jakarta.

Bali makes me think of Uganda. The same gentle countryside and gentle people; the same massacres and blood baths.

Robert wondered aloud why you don't see middle-aged people, only the young and the old. A lot of them would have been among the 100,000.

I have many bites! The ones on my feet are especially maddening. In my gloomier moments this morning I thought: If it's going to rain all the time and I have to suffer mosquitoes as well, I might as well be in Mendocino. (Not knowing that Northern California was experiencing the worst flooding in thirty years!) I felt very homesick, which Rebecca found astonishing. She has taken to Bali—the people, the landscape, the food—like the trouper she is. She is one of those old, old transparent souls the Universe radiates through without impediment, and so, wherever we go, within a week everyone seems aware of her presence. She walks in the rain as if it is sun.

Have been reading *Dancing in the Light*, by Shirley MacLaine; much of it is true, as I have experienced life, and a lot is straight Edgar Cayce. But it is sad to see her spirituality limited by her racialism.

Indians and Africans have a hard time; especially Africans who, in one of her incarnations, frustrate her because they're not as advanced as she is! It is amusing to contemplate what the Africans must have thought of her.

But I don't care about any of this. In the kitchen, Ketut is making dinner, chicken satay. Rebecca and Robert are at a fire dance, to which I declined to go—pleading aching joints, footwear erosion, and mildew of the brain. The rain is coming down in torrents. Lightning is flashing. The house we've rented is spectacular: it faces a terraced hillside of rice paddies, two waterfalls, and coconut trees, and is built in Balinese style but is huge by Balinese standards, I think. Two large bedrooms downstairs and an open-air one upstairs, with another great wooden hand-carved antique Balinese bed at one end. The roof is thickly thatched.

Two days ago I celebrated my forty-second birthday here, with the two people I love most in the world; we talked about my visit, before we left home, to a very beautiful Indian woman guru, who spoke of the condition of "judness." A time of spiritual inertia, of feeling thick, heavy, devoid of light. Yet a good time, too, because, well, judness, too, is a part of life; and it is life itself that is good and holy. Not just the "dancing" times. Nor even the light.

Thinking of this, hoping my loved ones are dry, and smelling dinner, I look up straight into the eye of a giant red hibiscus flower Ketut just placed—with a pat on my head—by the bed. It says: Just *be*, Alice. Being is sufficient. Being is All. The cheerful, sunny self you are missing will return, as it always does, but only *being* will bring it back.

Standing Alone with Myself

FAITH ADIELE

In 1985, at the age of twenty-two, I became the first black Westerner to live as a Buddhist nun in Thamtong Temple in northern Thailand. During the process of researching how nuns are marginalized in the Buddhist church, I decided to take a sabbatical from the university and ordain for a temporary period. I shaved my head, donned white robes, and took vows which included not killing any living creature and no contact with men. Thamtong, a retreat in the forest renowned for its caves, was one of the few places in the country that allowed women to practice the rigorous Forest Tradition. I had no previous meditation experience and did not realize that the Forest Tradition placed heavy emphasis on austerity, isolation, strict discipline, and meditation practice. The other inhabitants and I rose at 3:30 A.M., ate a single daily meal, forsook money and shoes, and spent nineteen hours a day in some form of spiritual practice. I was not allowed to receive letters or visitors, and could break silence only during my daily lesson with the head nun. My first day I was only able to sit in meditation fifteen minutes; eventually I worked up to seventy-two hours at a stretch.

15 January 1985

Jim asked me why I'm ordaining. Now that it's down to the wire (only eleven more days!), why have I decided to go through with it? I don't know. At first, while planning in the abstract, I thought becoming a nun would be different. An experience that would be beneficial both for me (to learn to develop discipline and peace) and for my research (to understand those whom I presume to explain). Something to look back on. Something to make me brave. However, the instant I saw the temple, I wanted to ordain. It was more than the physical power of the place. I just wanted it.

23 January 1985

This is the third day I've made it on a single meal. I've snacked a lot, however—usually due to social situations. It's odd, but except during the after-school snack hours, I'm not hungry. When I *am* hungry, three bites of food completely satisfy my hunger. If I were dieting, I wouldn't have such control; but here, now, for this—it's easy. A minor concern. I now understand what Head Nun Roongdüan meant the first time I met her, and she used eating to illustrate how we misplace our energies.

"Try it," she had said. "Eat a single daily meal purely for sustenance and note the difference in suffering. You are saved from having to think about whether or not you are hungry yet, what and how much you're going to eat, whether it is the most delicious food that will make you the happiest. Saved from preparing, serving, and spending the time eating, and from washing up afterward. All this, three times a day!"

At the time, the idea had seemed interesting but not entirely clear. If one loves to eat, where is the suffering? But now, already I feel so clean, so free. Sometimes I think: I don't have to worry about the issue of eating all day! I feel free and full of energy. I have so much more time. I begrudge the time even spent on one meal; for if one thinks about eating and concentrates on the actual act of chewing and chewing and chewing, one soon tires of it all.

24 January 1985

Today, all of a sudden, I caught sight of myself in the bathroom mirror and was seized with a panic that made my knees buckle. Why have I agreed to shave my head? Is it to prove my strength of will? Is it out of shame at appearing to care about my hair? Since I'm not Buddhist, why am I doing it? They keep telling me I can stay in the temple as a layperson, dressed in white and following the same rules.

Looking in the mirror, I felt my attachment to my hair, and fear. Plain fear. I am most afraid of future ugliness, that my hair for some reason will not grow back. But I am willing to take the chance for this experience. The victory is not that I am brave enough to "deface" myself, but in my release from the fear of ugliness. In a way, I forever free myself.

25 January 1985

Today was sunny and still. A faint breeze. Perfect. I wrote letters, coordinated things over the phone, had fun with my Thai mother. A long, slow, lizard-green day.

At 7:00 P.M., feeling slightly apprehensive, I took my scooter to pick up Chong. We went to Scott's, where the whole gang was waiting. Spirits were high. We had Thai stick, chocolate chip cookies from Jim's mother, and Jiffy Pop popcorn (as much fun to make as it is to eat!) sent by Aunt Freda. They were all raring to go, but I was frazzled. Everyone gathered around, gave me a big communal hug, then practically threw me into the barber's chair. Scott got giant bottles of Singha beer, and I begin to relax. As the hair started coming off, the fun began. My curls gently whispered by my ears and the back of my neck, tumbling into my lap. I felt vulnerable yet light and free. It surprised me how quickly it shaved off, how quickly it fell away, how quickly it was gone. Once the sides were done, we started clowning for the camera. It was odd to touch places on my head, never before revealed. To hold my entire scalp in the palm of my hands.

"Do it!" Scott shouted, and the barber shaved a road down the middle of my head. I looked like Groucho Marx. At this point I was hysterical with laughter, but as soon as I became entirely bald, we all fell silent and serious. Then the barber laid me down and, with old-fashioned hand razor, delicately scraped away my eyebrows. Finally I began to look different: calm and sleepy like a nun.

26 January 1985

I ordained this morning at 8:30, though I still have no idea of what ordination signifies or will entail. After the drive to the forest, all the preparations for my stay and the leave-takings, I was left alone in a meditation hut at the furthest edge of the temple near the forest entrance. Head Nun Roongdüan gave me a brief lesson in the simplest levels of walking and sitting meditation and promised to return in a few hours.

I am supposed to clear my mind and concentrate only on my breath, inwardly noting the rising and falling of my diaphragm. Any distractions—internal or external—should be noted as they arise. Eventually I will progress to higher levels. For seated meditation that means focusing on an increasing number of key points on my body. For walking meditation it means focusing on each tiny action or movement involved in walking, such as lifting the heel, swinging the foot, touching the ground . . .

She said, "At first you will be bored: Everyone in their huts. No one to talk to. All day and nothing to do. You'll have to "note"—to focus on all that you do and all that you intend to do. And when you become bored, note it. You will see that it rises and falls, comes into being and fades—just like everything else. If you see this, you see the dharma. You have to live in the present, be aware only of the present."

She told me to do walking meditation for twenty to thirty minutes at a time, and sitting for fifteen to twenty. As she left she said, "If I tell you the truth, you will forget it. But if you experience it, touch it for yourself, you will never forget. You are here to prove the truth of the Buddha's dharma yourself." For the first time I realized that I am not going to observe women's monastic lives—rather, she intends to make a nun out of me!

I began my first walking meditation at 3:40, determined to last the twenty minutes assigned. Immediately I felt peaceful, nothing on my mind other than my breathing and walking. This disappeared as my steps and breathing slowed, and there was more time to think. I don't know *how* to think only about walking. At times I spaced out, coming to a standstill, numbly droning the litany, *standing, standing, standing* . . . I'd have to jolt myself into awareness.

An itch developed on the left side of my face. Head Nun Roongdüan had said that if one focuses on distractions rather than giving in to them they fade away. As I focused, the itch became so painful that my entire face was twitching violently. I came to a halt, clenched my fists, and concentrated with all my might to keep from crying out. Eventually the pain subsided, and the few incidents that followed were much less intense.

I became obsessed with knowing the time, terrified at the prospect that only a few minutes had passed. Fear and desire nagged over and over. I resolved not to stop until the urge to stop had passed. How much of one's mind can be occupied with the actual act of walking? Roongdüan had said that being overly serious the first day could lead to headaches and stiffness. Already my shoulders were very sore. Eventually I became calm, though thoughts still flitted through my head: people's reactions upon my return to lay life, whether or not my face would glow with peace and wisdom like other nuns, the color of my Thai brother's sweater this morning, the look on Scott's face as he left the temple.

I became aware of the sensation as one foot comes down and the weight shifts onto that leg, and the other foot lifts up, poised to move ahead. It's wonderful, smooth. I became suffused with happiness. I felt I could do this "boring" activity indefinitely! I stopped and went inside to check the time—forty-five minutes! Though proud and eager to do more, I felt drained.

An hour later, Roongdüan came for my second lesson, bringing with her two books in English. I had been doing walking meditation a little incorrectly: I must feel the steps. Noting the feeling should correspond to my breath. She cautioned me to work gently into "mindful life," sleeping and eating little. I should be aware in all four postures: standing, walking, sitting, even sleeping. Kneeling down, touching the mat, spreading out the body. The rise and fall of the abdomen as one waits for sleep. Upon waking, one should take a deep breath and note, *knowing, knowing, knowing,* thereby becoming aware to oneself and one's body at the instant of awakening.

She said, "Meditation is simply training the mind to become alert and aware. At first it seems difficult and picayune. [She *actually* used the word picayune!] Soon it will become automatic. Until then, note everything, gently. You do not need to try to think of 'truth'—it comes on its own once the mind is cleared."

After her lesson, I felt a bit discouraged. When could I rest? How would all this time pass if I am always slow, precise, aware? Going to the bathroom is an ideological act! I longed to sleep.

Later I read one of the books. I didn't really understand all of the phrases that intrigued me, and at times I scoffed at the Hallmark greeting card approach. Yet I had to admit that much of it was compelling and true.

> Every day you are responsible for how you feel; no one can make you unhappy or nervous.

> The untrained mind is so vulnerable to circumstances: Something good happens and it is happy . . . something bad happens and it is in pain.

> Irritation is natural. Don't deny anger—understand it.

> An immense amount of fear is created as we spend our lives dodging pain.

> Our relationships are unfree to the extent that we demand things of others.

I went to bed.

Night. Can't sleep at all. Mind wild with thoughts and the fear that 3:30 A.M. will sneak up and find me asleep.

Moths crawling up my sarong. Finally couldn't stand one that fluttered over my face, into my shirt. Grabbed at it, trying to brush it away, perhaps killing it. First sin of my new life. When I open my eyes, it's as if they were still closed: it's that dark. No city lights. The absolute blackness of night in the forest in a country halfway around the world from home. I'm quite alone.

27 January 1985

The nun next door woke before the 3:30 bell but is silent. Must be meditating. I got up with the bell because I had never slept. Had something to drink and washed my face. Found a large, brilliant-green beetle floating in last night's bowl of water. Am I responsible for the death? I had forgotten to wake up mindfully but sat down to meditate.

Had a great meditation! At first my body was plagued by itches, back pain, a sleeping foot. I realized I was forcing my breathing, keeping it slow to accommodate my internal notation. Not knowing what to do, I concentrated on the pains, hoping the breathing would even itself out. It did; and when I returned focus on my breathing, the result was instantaneous. Always before when I have closed my eyes, I saw light and dark splotches of red and felt my eyeballs twitching beneath the lids. But, for the first time, this was not the case; there was smooth, even darkness. I was inside a large, empty, peaceful dark space. I felt I had become part of my breathing, which was so shallow as to be barely noticeable. It was as if I were in a foreign landscape, a different existence. All the while, I could hardly believe it—it happened so quickly. It felt fragile, and I was terrified that the experience would quickly evaporate. I concentrated on my thoughts, on my fear. Then a light blue hue dripped down my vision like a top coat of thick paint. This happened several times, in several layers. I knew something very important was happening.

Finally relaxed after a sleepless night, I began to feel tired. The itches returned with my thoughts. I concentrated on them and then came out of the meditation. Only twenty minutes had passed. I went to sleep, a deep, refreshing sleep, from 4:10 to 5:00, then from 5:00 to 6:00, then from 6:00 to 7:00. Each time I woke up promptly, realized that I needed more sleep, and returned to the same refreshing sleep.

The mealtime is horrible. Thankfully it only comes once a day! They ring the bell at 8:30 A.M., and we line up according to ordination seniority. An old nun with betel-stained teeth is first; Head Nun Roongdüan is third. One woman coughs a great deal and seems to be recovering from bad burns or a skin disease. The nuns are interested in me as much as they can be, considering the thick ritual of the meal. We walk with mindfulness in a procession to the front of the temple grounds. We leave our thermoses outside and wash our feet in the stream before entering an open pavilion. The monks and nuns are separated by a waist-high partition. We sit on three long mats, again according to rank. I am the last nun but ahead of two resident laywomen.

When everyone is seated, the senior nun rings a small bell, signaling to the abbot and monks. We chant—one prayer I know and one I don't—before pouring glasses of water for everyone. Then all the monks carry their alms-bowls to the table outside and slowly serve themselves with awareness. When they are done, the nuns serve themselves according to rank. We put the entire meal in a large enameled metal bowl. There was regular rice, brown rice with peanuts, beans and soy, glutinous rice, oranges, finger-size bananas, sweet dark glutinous rice, two raw vegetables (leaves), chilies, and three side dishes, mainly vegetable, one with meat. Several nuns remained in the kitchen, filling our thermoses and attending to their business. The senior nun rang the bell and an exquisite chanting began. The nuns, their voices guttural and Islamic-sounding, harmonized with the monks, playing off their part, weaving intricately through it. This lasted quite a while, though not long enough, and then we all began to eat with awareness.

Needless to say, there was no pleasure involved in the actual act of eating. I had to eat slowly, since it is too difficult to be noting *chewing, chewing, chewing* if one is already starting to *take a spoonful, take a spoonful, take a spoonful.* The food was good and I ate until the act of eating seemed passé. Having taken among the smallest portions, I was still the only one who left food in her bowl. We passed our bowls behind us, drank water from the tray of glasses and continued sitting. My legs felt as if they had long since fallen off. When everyone was done, the senior nun again rang the bell; we gave thanks once more, prostrated ourselves to a picture of the Buddha and got up, rolling up the mats and removing the trays. It was 10:00 exactly. Inadvertently I held everyone up and had to be told to get in line. Then we walked slowly back to our huts. Outside of the chanting and the whispered summons for me to rejoin the line, not a word was said the entire time.

Head Nun Roongdüan came and helped move me into my apartment hut. On short stilts, situated in the center of the nuns' side of the temple. It's built for life without furniture, with five shuttered windows low to the floor. Dim wooden interior. Moths and grasshoppers fluttering through. White gauzy mosquito net floating in the breeze. Outside is a tree with a circular meditation bench built around it. Flowering plants everywhere. A private stone bathroom. Next to it a bench and open drain for washing clothes and dishes. Water is piped into the bathroom and drain from the small stream that runs in back of the hut. Everything is cool, green, and white: the thick greenery, silent nuns in white, drifting slowly through the shade.

Our huts face the monks' side of the temple, and I was struck once again by how different their side is from the nuns'. The temple is in a narrow gully between high rock walls. At the edge of the forest is a waterfall that turns into a large stream flowing out toward the temple entrance, slicing the grounds into two opposing camps. The way the mountains are positioned, the sun misses our side, storming instead onto the monks' side of the stream, where red soil stains huts, trees, the mountain wall the color of brick. Against this fiery backdrop, the monks in their bright saffron robes bustle about doing chores. They wear only their underrobes, leaving their arms, shoulders, upper chest, and calves bare, their overrobes meticulously pleated and draped over their shoulders. They stand above the stream, sweeping the red earth or rinsing out their black-and-gold alms-bowls. The water falls onto the bank below with a great splat, staining the earth dark copper. Large, golden dogs run back and forth, barking in frenzy.

At night my hut is even more fantastic—all cozy with bright fluorescent light, the sound of cicadas and grasshoppers in the woods. I turn on the golden light to my little stone bathroom and take a shower in the cold stream water. The white towels are soft, velvety, and sweet-smelling. Without hair my body is easier to clean. It feels somehow cleaner when washed with cold spring water. Then I put on my simple, loose white cotton clothes and go barefoot out into the night.

I wasted all day, impatiently trying to reconstruct the meditation experience I had this morning. I tried to force it and got impatient. Help! You have to try hard but not too hard. Your mind has always to watch itself.

My back hurts so much it's difficult to maintain concentration during meditation. The only thing that helps is to be lying down, but it is forbidden during the day. The monastic way of life is not so terribly different from the military: no sleep during the day, the careful maintenance of greenery and walkways, control, habit, regularity, ritualized eating, rank, summons by bells, early rising, an abhorrence of sloth. I think that the army targets the body, monastics the mind. The latter have more freedom. I now see what nuns mean when they say that, outside of their many restrictions and chores, they have all the freedom in the world. Freedom of movement in lay life is merely a way to compensate for the lack of freedom while standing alone with oneself. In a sense, these nuns have such restricted, sleepy lives—but in another sense—it is freedom, freedom, freedom.

Unlike most nuns other places, we have to wear a long overrobe that wraps around the body twice, under one shoulder, and over the other. It's hot and often cumbersome, but it's soothing to be swathed in so much rough, off-white cotton, and one feels more like a monk. Two monks (a tall young one with a smaller, older dark one leading) were on our side today and had to pass by me. They hugged their side of the path, going single file. Is there actually *no* interaction at all? No one seems to interact with anyone, but the monk-nun situation is particularly acute. The monks seem to be quiet, meditating gardeners. All visitors are received by the nuns.

28 January 1985

Today I am supposed to do twenty minutes each of the first and second levels of walking meditation, and sit forty minutes at a time. I awoke carelessly at 4:45 A.M. Then I scrubbed the toilet, impatiently cleaning up some gnats in the process. Two sins, day three begins.

Breakfast was better today. The walk was marvelous—cool, our feet firm and soundless as we move along the pathway. Blind to all but the spot on the path six feet in front of me, I can *feel* the beauty around me. Far below, streams slice the vegetation—tangled greenery ranging from fragile celadon to black pine, from iced orchid to glossy crimson. Long bugs skimming over the water. After we cross the wooden bridge we come to the gravel. The leader falters a bit and we think about the pain, crunching our way through. Today there were two animals (owls, I assume) weeping in liquid tones at each other, louder than our chanting, louder than the grandfather clock in the kitchen.

Today I took even less food, barely covering the bottom of the bowl. When it turned out to be delicious, I regretted it, but by the time I had mindfully chewed every bite, even that small amount was too much. I am still less mindful than the other nuns so move more quickly. This makes me appear lost and without purpose, as if dog-paddling in air to kill time. Also, I sleep too much. Maybe it's a way of avoiding mindfulness.

Much of Buddhism doesn't concern me, especially the rejection of the body. Where do my own personal beliefs and values come in? My goals:

- to develop my concentration
- to overcome the suffering due to emotions and desire
- to recognize my emotions and understand them
- to think and know before I act
- to overcome fear and anger
- to be content with myself
- to interact constructively with people
- to train the mind for its full potential
- to take control of my life
- to have realistic goals and values and be able to live up to them
- to be able to accept failure
- to demand less from relationships

- to be able to find relaxation and solace within myself
- to be less attached to food and sleep
- to judge others and myself less harshly
- to understand people better.

Are these Buddhist goals?

I made the long climb up to the caves at 2:30 to do walking meditation. A group of tourists showed up to view the caves, which was distracting until I found the correct posture, and it felt glorious. Eyes six feet in front of me; the smooth rise and fall of my steps. I think I was smiling. Roongdüan says that walking meditation generates thoughts, while sitting meditation calms the mind, but I find walking calming and pleasurable.

We cannot go into another nun's hut; and when we can talk, we have to do it outside. I wonder if it's forbidden to read outside. There's all this beauty and no opportunity to appreciate it. When I'm outside, I feel as if I should be doing walking meditation, eyes on the ground, or sitting in meditation with my eyes closed, or doing my laundry. Why, then, are the plants so carefully tended? Do we do it to keep busy? For the tourists? Or just so we *know* beauty is present?

As it happened, I was reading outside—which, while not *forbidden*, is a waste of daylight better spent meditating. Head Nun Roongdüan suggested I go meditate. I was on my way up to the cave and saw that nice-looking nun who sat in front of me today at breakfast looking down at me. Another nun, with an eager, shiny face, grinned and waved me up. She turned out to be only seventeen years old! She was delighted that I could speak Thai, though the other one did most of the talking (the ol' where-are-you-from routine). She kept wanting to know what level I was at and whether I could practice a lot yet. I didn't know how to answer her.

I was standing with one foot up on the lower rung of the bench next to me. The seventeen-year-old grabbed my leg with a worried exclamation, saying that nuns had to stand up straight. Then she laughed. "Being Thai, being a nun—there are *lots* of rules!" she said. They kept looking over the side of the wall with distracted expressions.

The newest resident, a young laywoman whose vow taking I had participated in last evening, stood staring over the wall toward the mountains that surround us. Four mats lay on the ground beside her; it must be group instruction for the newest members. Head Nun Roongdüan appeared and, looking fierce, rebuked the seventeen-year-old for wasting time talking. As I sheepishly descended the stairs, the girl smiled behind her hand and whispered, "time's up." She's always turning around and grinning at someone during mealtime. What is this high-spirited thing doing as a nun?

I am now supposed to be mindful of all my actions—noting everything I do—so that every task is a mini meditation. Roongdüan compares this form of meditation to filling a basin with a slowly dripping faucet, whereas other forms of meditation are making a container, walking to the river, and returning with the water. She said, "some people bore a hole in their meditation hut for the light to shine through and concentrate intensely on that light; after they have developed their powers of concentration they seek the truth. But our meditation is for those who seek knowledge right now, those who are in pain. No one hits us, no one scolds us, but our thoughts make us unhappy."

Being mindful is what I find most difficult. I am used to being completely undisciplined when alone. It is difficult to watch oneself. It is hard to want something so tedious and boring. I lack humility. I lack a twenty-four-hour kind of dedication.

29 January 1985

At 3:30 A.M. I opened my eyes then remembered that I should be mindful. When the bell rang I was able to note *knowing* . . . and *wanting to rise* . . . I tidied up, washed my face and dishes, and made coffee. I tried meditating and felt supremely calm but was so sleepy that I couldn't remember to watch my breathing, which made it no more than sleeping upright.

Did walking meditation until 6:30, when it got light. Refreshing. Then helped with the sweeping. Invigorating yet odd to be sweeping dirt and leaves. Head Nun Roongdüan said, "Do it slowly, not as if you wanted to finish it. The leaves fall; it is natural. Every day they will fall, and every day we will sweep them. Our work is for the meditation." Then I scrubbed my bathroom and cleaned my hut. The meditator doesn't need to do exciting things—the ordinary acts of survival are wonderful enough.

During the walk today I noticed that the nun's feet in front of me are beautiful. I can just see her heels and a hint of the side when she lifts them up and firmly puts them down, arched and turned slightly outward. When she leans forward, poised to take a step, her heel rises up gracefully, her clean white robes skimming her ankles. When she goes down the stone steps, the robe hovers just centimeters above the moss-covered stone. This soft white descending into a little pool then quickly rising to reveal strong ankles, a determined foot! And all the different colors and textures of white! Thick, rough, slightly wrinkled off-white. Crisp, glowing, smoothly woven white. Bluish gauzy floating cheesecloth. Suddenly we run into sunshine on the path, the sun still low in the hills. The path glows red-gold and warms our feet.

I meditated during the serving and was fascinated by the rich sounds all around me. The stately ticking of the grandfather clock. One of the owls. A faint cough, drowned in white cotton. The clear call of birds in the trees outside. Someone scrubbing white cloth with lots of soap. Someone quietly filling all the hot water thermoses. Plastic lids being screwed on and off, picked up and put down—as if there were no hands involved.

Is it really Tuesday, the twenty-ninth? Time moves so quickly and yet so slowly. One week, which seems like a mere fraction of time while going to school, is forever at the temple—one could learn an incredible amount. And yet, it goes incredibly quickly. I can't *imagine* being here months, and yet I feel I could drift into it. I'm filling my journal at the rate of ten pages per day!

After my first vision today, I felt peaceful—but isn't it the same kind of peace I experience after spending a day at a temple as a layperson? At first I felt I had freedom here, but as a nun, there's so much one can't do. The simple act of reading. As a layperson, it's calming to read at a temple; for nuns, it's normally forbidden. We think peace is somewhere in the temple, but we are wrong. This place is too intense, a summer camp gone berserk. This is not an ordinary temple, a community. One nice thing, though: if you don't mingle but stay near your hut all the time, it's considered good—at summer camp that would be labeled abnormal or antisocial.

At times I'm a bit impatient with life here. What *am* I doing here? The city with all my friends and clubs is only an hour away. But when I slow down, I'm okay.

30 January 1985

I am supposed to be mindful of everything touched and of every desire. "Taste, smell, touch, hearing, sight, mind are the six senses," said Head Nun Roongdüan. "And the six elements are earth, fire, water, wind, space, and consciousness. Consciousness is essential to the senses. Take sound, for instance. You have always the ear and its nerves, and you have always the sound of the stream; but only at certain times do you *hear* the stream. Only when your consciousness is with the ear. When you are reading the book, you do not know the sound of the stream, anymore than you know the pain of the mosquito who bites you. You must note, to see where the consciousness is at a given moment. It cannot be two places at once, but it moves quickly, like waves of electricity, so that one receives the impression of a continuous flow of light."

I have to admit this idea of consciousness being the third element in sensory awareness is seductive and seems to make gut-level sense.

She continued: "And be aware of every desire, every time you want to open a door, stand up, pour water—every common desire. We note common desire as practice, because it is easy, because it is difficult to note our emotions. Like anger: you cannot touch it. But eventually we will be able to note it, and then we can deal with it."

At 7:00 that cute little nun with the big grin and crooked teeth who is always with Head Nun Roongdüan came to get me to "go see the monk." It felt like a surprise spot check at camp; hastily I took off my stocking cap and put on my overrobe. We went to the kitchen, where some nuns were acting very casual. The older laywoman who sits behind me and always treats me very respectfully was there in civilian clothing. It turned out that she would be returning home later in the day. The second-senior nun, a dark, frail woman, came in. She too would be leaving today to return to her temple of residence. She was the one who got up to meditate at 3:00 A.M. in the room next to me my first night. She seems extremely dedicated. She leans to the left and her little body seems at all times on the verge of collapse.

What a face! She has large, round, protruding ears and a full plum-colored mouth. Though at first she gives the impression of being old, it would be impossible to guess her age. Her skin is flawless—it's smooth, delicate, glowingly translucent. Tight yet without lines or stretches. Looking at that wonderful skin, I got the impression that she was a woman who has achieved incredible peace, whose face has gotten younger until even the normal lines of life were erased. And her eyes! Long, liquid, dark. Shaped like inverted tears—oval at the top, then drooping down to the side in a long tail. The longest eyes I've ever seen. I couldn't see the whites, only long darkness. I could have watched her face for hours! It reminded me of a certain *feeling* I couldn't place.

The temple she came from was near Bangkok and had thirty nuns. "Was it a 'supporting temple'?" my companion asked, and I think she answered wanly, no, nuns had to find their own food. She answered these questions shyly, eyes downcast, only occasionally raising her head to smile faintly.

Prostrating herself to us beautifully, the laywoman served us a tray with hot Ovaltine and a plate with a heaping portion of biscuits. I couldn't eat so early. The sun was just coming up in the direction of the road to Chiang Mai. No wonder we never see it, stuck back in our narrow gully to the west. What a pity!

The sky was the softest, purest shade of pink imaginable, neither garish nor faint. Perfect soft pink. A darker pink sun, ringed with gold, hung at midlevel in a soft blue sky. The three colors hung separately and distinct in the still, cool morning air. This landscape is amazing; it has a life of its own. It changes every hour and one can feel it. Every time I step out of my hut I am overtaken with admiration. Each time of day is distinctly beautiful and, in its own way, more intriguing than the last.

We climbed cement steps up the hill leading to what looked like a school. The nun unlocked a door and we went into what turned out to be the church. It was small and surprisingly ugly—even the Buddha statues were second rate. On the wall were garish paintings of scenes from the Buddha's life and the history of the temple.

I talked to my companion, who's been ordained four years, over three of them here. She said the temple is thirty to forty years old. She pointed to the landscape painted behind the main Buddha figure and laughed ruefully. She explained that once many birds flew into the church, thought that the painted trees were real, and crashed into the wall, falling dead at the foot of the Buddha statues.

I asked her how many monks lived here, and she laughed sheepishly and said she had no idea. "They come and go, sometimes many, some-times hardly any. Just like the nuns—sometimes thirty or forty, some-times seven or eight." It turned out that most of the temple's nuns were like the long-eyed one and the laywoman—just here for a tem-porary period of intensive meditation and retreat.

We sat down to wait, and soon the very young, pale, round-faced monk I've seen crept in, shoulders hunched, eyes painfully on the ground. (I've never seen such humble-looking monks in my life!) He climbed onto the platform and we waited for him to prostrate himself to the Buddha before prostrating ourselves to him.

Speaking with a lisp that sounded as if his mouth were full of too many teeth, he launched into an hour-long discussion on something —life, pain, the universe—I don't know. It dawned on me that I was witnessing something like an exit interview for the two departing women. At first I was pleased that I was sitting like a proper nun—that is, made of stone. Then I tried to understand what he was saying but couldn't understand his lisping monotone. What was I doing here? The others were meditating or asleep, who knows. My leg and back were in such pain I thought I'd scream. I kept considering shifting my position but something always made me stop: momentary relief, a great surge of interesting pain, the urge to cry, but mainly pride—and the desire to maintain the pain and thus my anger.

Finally, when we could hear the mealtime chanting begin, the monk realized how late it was. He told us he had studied one year in England and one in the United States. His parents wanted him to return to help with the family business, but he "had found the real happiness without problems" as a monk. "People who travel . . . that's not real happiness. It's just chance, luck, that they have the opportunity to go around."

I thought this was interesting but didn't quite see his point. Why isn't travel valid happiness, for that particular lucky person? Or was he referring to someone like me, who derives pleasure in the actual *act* of travel, because it fills the senses and provides concerns that transcend the mundane? Yes, for me, it *is* easier to be happy in a new landscape. If I fail, it's culture shock; and when I don't, the scenery's breathtaking. I'm not *that* superficial, *that* much on the run, but in a sense, I guess it's not real, pure, down-home happiness at the foundations. It's superficial happiness, dependent on the locale. If he were a mother, he would say, "go back to America, deal with being a black woman who goes to Harvard." But he's a monk, so he says "give up the world and be mindful of yourself."

He apologized for running into our mealtime and left. I asked if I could skip the meal, being improperly dressed and not up to more motionless sitting on rubbery legs. Immediately the nun said no problem, my food would be brought to me. As we passed by the kitchen area, a lovely monk came out. Smiling and pointing, he said, "partake of the meal."

Embarrassed, I nodded. "Please never mind," I said and scurried on.

"That was the abbot," the nun told me.

I was stunned. The monk was a small man, very young-looking, handsome, but most striking for the pure "goodness" and "kindness" that seemed to radiate from him. His face was so pleasant, so alive. It inspired love and trust. These nuns seem nice and gentle, and are always friendly and kind, but they seem somehow otherworldly. The dynamic ones, like Head Nun Roongdüan, seem in a way taut—as if their core had turned to iron from years of brilliance, restraint, and determination. Other older ones seem to be amazingly good and wise. But none seem as vital and steeped in the present as this monk. He clearly loved striding around the temple, fetching water and feeding the dogs. Why are the good monks like this? Is it that the temple offers them a full life where they can cultivate *all* their talents and energies, whereas it only offers women a timeless escape *from* life, where they spend their energies cultivating their minds and erasing the rest?

31 January 1985

I was a very bad nun. I slept maybe one hour last night; otherwise, I spent the entire time dreaming about every man to whom I was ever attracted. The dreams were quite simple. In them, these men come to my Harvard dorm room one at a time and we have sex and then eat chocolate chip cookies (not just any chocolate chip cookies, mind you, but bittersweet chocolate with macadamia nuts at $5.00 per pound!). Of course I was exhausted when 3:30 came. So it would look like I was meditating, I turned on the light, strategically put on my clothes —just in case of surprise summons—and went back to sleep. When I got in line at 8:30 I noticed the nuns were smiling. I know I must seem strange and bedraggled. Every day I tie my overrobe differently and every day it's wrong. They must think I'm seriously slow. I started tying it at 8:15, I was sure it had to be correct, but five minutes out of my hut, I realized I was having serious breast trouble. So, feeling like Julie Andrews in "The Sound of Music," I tried to struggle un-obtrusively with my breast-wrap on the walk. I feel so un-nunlike today!

I know there is talking going on somewhere. Last night in my hut, I distinctly heard it—talking—someone with someone else. (Just as I finished writing this, two nuns walked by carrying laundry. They were talking their heads off and one said, "this one, with the blue sandals," referring to the bathroom sandals outside my hut. "Oh!" the other said, laughing, "what huge shoes!")

The entire lower part of my face is chapped or bug bitten, and all I have is that tiger balm which burns. My ears are scabbed, my neck has all sorts of welts on it. I have mosquito bites all over my scalp! I've never seen so many stupid, creepy bugs in my life! No matter how often I scrub the toilet, there are gnats that live there. It makes sense to say "don't kill animals" when you live in civilization and people are swatting anything that gets in their way for no reason at all, but I get very bored of coaxing nineteen ants out of my glass just to be able to have a simple sip of water, of dribbling warning water all around the toilet, so that the gnats finally get the idea through to their teeny-weenie brains to fly off so I can pee without committing a sin, of concentrating on *pain, pain, pain*, all the while knowing another creature is sucking my blood at the very moment I am trying to cultivate compassion, of feeling bugs crawling up between my legs just as I am drifting off to sleep. What is the point of bugs? I'm not a particularly good nun, but I'm not a bad one, either, I don't think. How does one be a bad nun, anyway? We don't have the resources and power of monks—so there's not much potential for abuse besides killing bugs on the sly.

Today it was so cold when I went to take my shower. The bathroom was gray. I was trying to remember all the movements that go into the stupid little action of scooping water from the basin and dousing myself with it (*lifting, reaching, dipping, lifting, pouring, feeling cold*, etc.). I was getting them all mixed up and saying them too late. I wished I were anywhere else.

I was in the middle of soaping my shivering body, when suddenly I was struck by the way the soap lather was gleaming faintly, coolly on my body in the dim bathroom interior. It was 4:00 in the afternoon, so the daylight was pure—clear and transparent—not gold, bright, or heat. It crept unevenly through the slatted roof into the stone room, giving my wet skin a dull finish like fine wood. The lather was thick and rich like real cream. I looked at my palms: soap bubbled up in thousands of swirls against a porcelain background. My right shoulder was covered with perfect droplets of evenly spaced water. The scene had the quiet perfection of a still life—one moment captured from thousands that somehow manages to say it all.

Life is no more than this—a series of brief recurring moments—but therein lies the beauty. In impermanence. In moments of simplicity that cut through the confusion and complexity. One stumbles onto something—a painting of apples, the clarity of breath—and brings order to it all.

As ridiculous as it sounds, everything changed. My depression was out the window; I was delighted and intrigued. It made sense to be mindful while I showered, it was a joy to be able to go slow and appreciate all the marvels of the shower. I wanted to see everything, and as soon as I slowed down and thought about it, the notation was easy and smooth. There was some joy in identifying every little action I made (some for which I didn't even know the words in English) and satisfaction in performing the action in tandem with the "chanting." I noted everything: brushing my teeth, drying off, dressing, putting tiger balm on my mosquito bites, and drinking water. I went outside; it was 5:00 and the air was perfectly still, cool, new.

Head Nun Roongdüan called me outside and said that she would be visiting her sick aunt tomorrow and that my new task was to note and record all the time of the day spent either mindfully or in meditation. This is much worse than a simple locker check—it's the Thought Police! I shuddered and crossed my legs, hugging myself. "You can't sit like that," she said immediately. I careened dangerously toward tears. She asked if I needed anything and, suddenly, there in the dark, I felt a great wave of loneliness sweep over me.

I'm so lonely, I wanted to say; *it's so hard. In one day, I'm supposed to give up my friends, family, freedom, way of life, conversation and become not only a yogi but a proper Asian woman! I never said I wanted to reach* nirvana—*I'm here for the sociological aspect.*

Seconds later I noticed to my chagrin that was noting the feeling—*lonely, lonely, lonely* in Thai!

I said, "I'm very tired after I meditate, is that natural?" I wondered how in the world I could come up with the six to ten hours of daily seated meditation she expected!

"Yes, it is," she assured me. "Don't be too serious about it—you are just the beginner. Are your bowels okay?"

She left and I crept inside. After turning on the lights, I knelt down, arms wrapped around myself, and quietly, mindfully cried until there was a little clear puddle on the mat before me. When I looked up I noticed something on my left cuff. It was a moth, less than an inch long, absolutely flat. Its exquisite, elongated wings were like faded lace. As soon as I saw it, it lifted straight up with long, flat strokes as if made of paper, and disappeared.

1 February 1985

Atmosphere distinctly relaxed with Roongdüan gone. During the breakfast chanting I felt so *clean*, physically clean, even though I hadn't yet showered. It's the seventeen-year-old who has that startling voice—deep, nasal, passionate. I can see her thin shoulders rise and fall jerkily with the movement of her diaphragm.

My first hour-long meditation! I sat in the back of the cave, no mat, my back didn't even hurt. Quiet, cool. Once I thought people came up and waited for quite some time; when I thought one of them was standing on the edge of the mats in the cave, my face began to tingle, and the fear I have of my eyes just POPPING open, breaking my concentration and exposing me for a fraud, threw me deeper into concentration. My tingling face seemed to drip off in layers, leaving a softer, expressionless one beneath, and my breathing disappeared. Nothing much happened; I just felt *good*.

From 5:30 to 7:00 P.M. had an amazing talk with Head Nun Roongdüan about her life and the decision to ordain. Then she started talking about the importance of developing compassion toward all creatures, especially dangerous ones. This made me nervous because so far every issue she's brought up has been perfectly timed for me to use in my meditation practice. *Oh no!* I thought, please *don't tell me about snakes falling off doorjambs onto your head in the morning.* But she did. Once as a student she woke covered with white ants; they swarmed all around her, on the pillow, everywhere. Unable to move, she switched off the light and began to meditate, praying they'd leave so she could sleep and make it to her class the next morning. After a while, she turned the light back on; they had all disappeared.

She was impressed that already I could sit for one hour at a time.

She said the reason she discouraged talking was that we still thought like laywomen and would thus speak without meaning (e.g., the food was good, your hair is beautiful). She is not without a sense of humor, this powerhouse nun! She compared meditation to the desire to catch a fish. One wades into the paddy up to one's calves in mud and searches for the fish. At last the hand grasps what seems to be a fish, but upon withdrawing the hand, one realizes instead that it is a snake. What to do with the snake? Bare-handed, one cannot kill it; stuck in the water, one cannot fling it away for fear that it will twist back and bite. So, one whirls it around and around above the head until it is tired, then flings it away and runs in the opposite direction.

Then she talked about the use of noting everything. Mindfulness or awareness serves as a dam to desire. By realizing our desires, we allow them to cycle and cease. By ignoring desire, or by judging it ("I don't want to think about that—it's not good"), we allow it to fester, then we act explosively, without consciousness or control. For example, if a nun develops the desire to go to the movies, she must say "wanting to go to the movies," then she will know herself, her desire and the futility of it. Eventually the desire will increase then pass away. Notation gives us the time to establish volitional intention *before* action.

After this talk, I went back to my hut, opened the door, turned on the light, and, there, lo and behold, as I had expected—though not quite *this* soon—on the wall above my sleeping mat hung a huge black spider, some four inches in diameter. I sank to the floor before it and tried to calm the panic rising within me. I focused on the spider, in order to become aware of what exactly it was and how irrational was my fear, but it remained an ugly, mythic creature whose very shape made me want to run screaming into the night or to cry with the sinking realization that from now on we would be roommates, sharing this refuge. When I felt a bit calmer, I began to meditate, fighting, albeit sometimes unsuccessfully, the urge to pop open my eyes and keep tabs on my visitor.

I heard a loud thumping and looked up to see the planks of the wall connected to the bathroom contracting in and out in a row, as if something heavy were being rolled across the wall. Perhaps the wood expanding with a weather change?

Hurrying through the dark, I entered the bathroom then stopped short. A muscular blue iguana, a full foot long and some three inches thick, clung to the wall above my head, staring down at me unblinkingly. The Thai said that iguanas locked their jaws during attack and nothing short of burning them off of their victim could loosen the grip. *I'm in a Buddhist temple*, I mumbled, *none of us could burn it off without breaking our vows! This thing is going to be latched onto me for life!* I thought about its weight as it had moved across my wall—the thing was pure, cold-blooded muscle and teeth! I approached it, hoping to get it used to me, and it immediately raised its tail straight up. I stopped breathing. Was it warning me, about to attack? How to interpret the actions of a reptile? How to anticipate them? Would it attack out of pure malice or only if provoked? What constituted provocation? I slid by and returned to my hut, thoroughly disheartened.

I often find myself wondering why we have to be braver than other women. Isn't it enough that we're different?

13 February 1985

Often in meditation, I get quick, vivid images of people I don't know—foreign couples buying coconuts in the market, people drinking water, the tail-end of nonsense conversation—as if I had plugged into a short-wave radio or am flipping through a constant procession of TV stations.

There is a cleanliness in knowing the body so well, in one meal a day—without spices, grease, or sugar—just fresh vegetables and fruit, rice, tofu and occasional poultry, in a single bowel movement every one or two days. No distractions to delude me, no shoes, no furniture, no money. The need to have perfect posture. I know exactly who I am, what my body is. If I have too much coffee, too much sugar or cream, if I neglect to do my back exercises, if I'm sitting in a careless slumped position, this all becomes obvious. Cause and effect are quite clear.

Deterrents in ordinary life are the very motivations in this life: You cannot say, I would love to sit for an hour and meditate but my legs are asleep, my back throbs, I keep falling asleep, and mosquitoes are bleeding me dry. In regular life, those are each reasons enough to stop; in this life, they are the precise reasons to continue—for the notation itself. If you hurt, you sit and continue meditating until you don't. If you want to stop, you continue until you don't. If you're afraid of snakes on the path, you walk on the path until fear subsides. I never realized religious life was so connected to bravery.

16 February 1985

I finally feel like a nun and not someone pretending to move slowly, just dog-paddling in air to kill time. When I catch a glimpse of another nun—a silent, white figure—I am reminded of something mysterious, not quite human nor ordinary. I feel light, indistinct, something people can't quite look at or see.

Differences and Blurred Vision

TIJUANA MURRAY

Jobless, languageless, and virtually friendless, I voyaged across the ocean to live in Rome after finishing my B.A., armed with only my imagination and my youth. My aim was to "get in touch with my creative voices" and I envisioned myself bathing year-round in the warmth of Mediterranean hospitality and "frolicking naked through fields of green green grass." However, my transition from U.S. college student to world citizen proved to be a much more arduous and exacting experience than I had anticipated, particularly when issues of gender and color were factored in.

3/5/92

When I called home the other day, I was talking to my granddaddy and he asked me, "You see any of ya'll folks over there?"

"What you mean?"

"Blacks. You see any blacks over there in Rome, Italy?"

I told him, "Yeah."

Europe '92 is full of immigrants from everywhere. But the funny thing is that I've begun to question how to even define "black" or identify "black people" (in the communal sense that we African-Americans understand it) in the world, outside of the U.S.A. I see so many people in a day now. The first time I came to Italy, three and a half years ago, I didn't think it was so complicated. When I saw other people I thought were African or of African descent (and sometimes other "people of color"), I spoke. But then again I saw less foreigners here then and plus I was different (than I am now) and my motives for being here were different also. There was this one time Diego and I had gone to the zoo and I had my head wrapped up in this purple Indian scarf. And these Indian women kept smiling at me. They were very gentle and familiar with their eyes, as if they thought I came from where they came from too. Of course, I'm projecting but I was so afraid that they would speak to me in their native tongue and realize that I was not what they thought I was. Anyway, now things are different on the street. If you happen to meet the eyes of a dark-skinned foreigner—African or not—there's always some hesitation.

So, how does one . . . define "black" in racial terms? By dark skin? Well, dark is relative. By kinky hair? Kinkiness comes in different degrees and is also relative. By blunt features? These aren't necessarily restricted to people of direct African descent. . . . or identify people as "black" in the loaded sense that we (African) Americans understand blackness? By possession of all of the above physical characteristics? By possession of one or two of them at the very least? Or by possession of just one drop of African blood in one's family tree?

Ethnic identity is something we don't understand well in the United States. That is why it is possible for us to get wrapped up in a color vacuum as if racial categories—black, white, yellow, red—made any sense and really accounted for people's ethnic differences and how people actually perceive themselves. What's interesting though is that these categories really say much more about how people identify themselves as Americans, as citizens of the United States, than anything else. Of course the United States isn't alone in "dividing the races" but

I find the rationale behind such at least understandable there. Merging different cultural experiences is not easy. And these divisions are useful in redirecting the hostilities that are involved in a merger. But here in Europe, I'm always a little astonished when people start to talk about identity in terms of race as opposed to nationality or ethnicity. Because here people are really sensitive to national, ethnic, regional differences. A German is not the same as an Italian is not the same as a French person and so on. It's just understood. And again for this reason I am always surprised when an Italian calls me *una ragazza nera* (a black girl) and points out to me the differences between us based on "color." But the differences between us are based on cultural orientation, not the amount of pigmentation in our skin! And then when people refer to me or are talking about me and they use the collective forms of "you" (*voi*) or "they" (*loro*), I don't understand. Who is this "you" or "they" that they are talking about? I don't know. Maybe I shouldn't be so surprised. This stuff goes very deep.

3/12/92

Living in the city is hard. I think I must be dreaming my life. No way did a man just spit in my face. And no way did a man shine a light on his penis and masturbating hand yesterday—through the windows of two trains—for my eyes only! No way. No way. No way.

Saliva blurred my vision for one whole minute and I had to rub and rub and rub my left eye to see clearly. It was a dark-alley kind of street and something within told me not to walk there tonight. Something within told me I had no business walking through dark alleys alone after nightfall. But it was only seven o'clock and I wanted to get home in a hurry. He drove up on his vespa passing up another man to ask me "Che faresti per trenta mila lire?" (What would you do for 30,000 lire?) I thought he was going to ask about the time. Instead he was saying something about money. "Vaffanculo." (Fuck you.) And I walked past the only two shops on that street with people inside. Something told me to stop, to stand near one of the shops, or to run to the main street. But I continued walking. When I heard his vespa behind me, I switched my briefcase to the other hand.

"Mi parlavi cosi? Perche?" (You were talking to me like that? Why?)

"Vaffanculo." I was very calm even as the saliva hit my face and blurred my vision. I never knew what the sensation was like before. I tried imagining that I was a part of a movement or a disobedient slave woman with hot saliva staining my face. My skin doesn't really feel like mine anymore. But I told him what I wanted to tell him.

3/13/92

I've been lying in bed paralyzed for hours. Thinking and thinking and thinking. I really have no great love for Italy right now. I didn't get the student from La Spina. A man was masturbating in the next train for my eyes only. The near fist fight I almost had on the bus. And hot spit blurring my vision for one whole minute. I'm tired.

I keep telling people in my mind. I keep telling all of my friends as if something could be done, as if one of them would challenge my story and call me a liar. And in fact, my stories would dissolve into untruths, nonsense, bold-faced lies.

But you know what the killer was? The man was so angry. I thought perhaps as the droplets of saliva clung to my hair and forehead I had misunderstood. I thought I had done the man a great injustice. In fact, he had the same look the bitch on the bus had. Crazy with anger. Outraged by my nerve.

Damn. Here I sit alone in Roma, Italia, at my kitchen table smoking cigarettes and drinking beer. Listening to oldies from before my time. Not a telephone to use on the block.

I miss being drunk and being sensual, seductive in a dark, cloudy room lit by candles in bottles and littered with bottles of beer, vodka, tequila, or rum—if it was summer. I miss sitting on the floor of a little kitchenette, rubbing feet and sliding out of my clothing. It's only 11:30 A.M. I have a long day ahead of me.

3/23/92

Jocelen sat on the metro today legs spread wide in a short skirt and spit-shined her high-heeled shoes with her fingers. In class, she is loud and rambunctious. Outside of class, she is quiet and the heaviness underneath her eyes is very deep. She is a country girl from Santo Domingo who's come to Rome to marry, to be opportunity's bride. What does she know about life in this cold European city? I think she's lonely and homesick. But Ginger won't have anything to do with her. She can't stand Jocelen for being so loud and mannerless. And that's what makes me so mad at Ginger. She has no imagination. She can only sympathize with people if they are just like her. If we had met in the United States, I'm sure I wouldn't have even wasted time getting to know her and she wouldn't have even seen me. What with the way she's labeled Jocelen "simply intolerable" and how she'd like for everyone in the class to give Jocelen the stiff back and ostracize her. It's just sickening. Every time I see Jocelen, leave Jocelen, I feel heavy. "Skin the color of dusk," like Toomer's Karintha. She is very beautiful. I see the heaviness beneath her eyes, hear the desperation in her loud abandoned laughter. I feel even the heaviness of her silence and I think: Yes sister, I have weight too. I hear what you're not saying. And I'm here if only to smile and say "cammina" so that you keep up. I know that outside of class and even during class we are both foreign women here in this country with no money, no friends, and no blood.

3/26/92

I don't know. Ever since that man spit in my face . . . Something broke, something snapped inside of me then. And what's ironic is that I was lucky. I know that worse could have come of the situation.

4/6/92

I had a dream that Tara visited Italy for one day and one night. I was very happy. I haven't written anything in a long time. But what is it that I am writing when I do write? Keeping a journal. I can tell myself that I'm taking notes, recording my "special" thoughts and feelings, keeping my brain alive, working problems out, relieving tensions . . . I can tell myself all of that as if I'm actually getting any work done. I need to be writing characters, situations, stories, articles, using my imagination creatively—I'm too self-conscious about my writing and living my own life. I'm always searching searching searching for the right way to be. I'm twenty-two years old. There's time in which to make mistakes, to grow up, to become wise.

4/14/92

I'm so unhappy. No matter what I do, how I feel, I am unable to find work. Maybe I should buy myself a one-way ticket home. To one city and travel through my "beloved" United States of America. But you know really, I'm not sure if I could find work there either. Anyway, the key words were "buy" and "travel" (with what money?). Italy is not more humane than my country. It's just different. I think my ears are better than they used to be. My hearing is more adequate. I feel so low. I've been half-heartedly considering suicide except I think I'd be betraying my people's history. I would like to call my family, my friends, any of the people who love me and who would share some of this misery with me. I don't need for anyone to send me money. The rent is paid and I'm not hungry. I just can't find work and my self-confidence is rock bottom. It's a combination of things: bad luck, Italian randomness, being practically languageless, and finally, the normal seeking employment runaround. Everything is at least three times harder to do here in Rome. But sometimes I really wonder if it's me. What do these fucking Italians see when they look at me? Is it something personal that makes them not want me? What I really want to ask is, is it me, is it racial, or is it just the breaks?

When I called Diego, he knew by the words I spoke what had happened. And I almost lost it right there in the phone booth.

4/22/92

Yesterday, I was sitting on the steps of the church in the Piazza San Salvatore in Lauro waiting for Diego's mother. When this young woman (American?) came walking toward me arm in arm with an Italian. Fortunately, I saw her before she saw me so I had the advantage of being able to observe her unchecked. She was so fresh and pretty and happy. Cinnamon colored with dark brown, bushy hair.

Smiling, laughing, so pleased to be *here*. But when she saw me, something changed. She didn't speak. And she didn't look at me twice. She seemed to walk a half step faster to get out from under my gaze, to get out of my vicinity with her beau. Did I remind her that she wasn't as unique as her boyfriend's eyes told her that she was? Or did I inspire guilt over her newly acquired weightlessness or perhaps the brilliant wings clipped to her shoulder blades? Did she think I was a mean-eyed African? Or was it something else altogether? Nonetheless, she was uncomfortable—not hostile or antisocial, just uncomfortable. She seemed like she felt threatened. I could tell she was a tourist or at the very least a newly arrived Westerner. She wasn't accustomed to being studied on the street and she wasn't handling herself well.

4/29/92

This little son of a bitch Italian bastard just made a spitting sound behind me as I was walking by. I think he might have been feeling offended because I didn't address his smile. He may have been saving face in front of his friends.

The other day I was thinking that I'm so stupid to let these kinds of forces consume me. But then again, that's just me. I take things hard and dwell on them. The Italians are no more hospitable than any other people. Unlike Arthur, I stayed long enough in the Mediterranean to find that out, "long enough to be forced to put [their] good nature to any test" (*Just Above My Head*—James Baldwin).

4/30/93

Yeah, that's right. The freedom I felt when I first came here was partly due to language, the company I kept, and also the fact that I rarely went anywhere alone. Plus it was three and a half almost four years ago.

5/1/92

There have been riots in Los Angeles, San Francisco, Atlanta, and demonstrations all over the country in response to the Rodney King verdict. What's weird is that my sympathy goes out to the entire country—not just Rodney King and the people rioting and demonstrating in the streets (read—"the dispossessed" and "marginal[ized]"). It's not that weird of a thing that I feel sympathetic. But it's strange to me that I don't feel . . . I don't know—blind irrational anger or hatred toward "white" people anymore. I'm beginning to understand that "power, rooted in history, is also the mockery and repudiation of history. The power to define the other seals one's definition of oneself" (from *Just Above My Head*—James Baldwin).

But the funny thing I realized last night while watching the news in Italian is that when there's something big and racial happening in the States that makes international news, we come off looking like a type of South Africa. Blacks running in the streets, throwing bricks, being hosed down, breaking windows, being beaten, resisting arrest, being dragged into squad cars and police vans by white cops. Man the nineties are ugly.

5/7/92

I'm still trying to work through my reactions to the rioting. First, I feel great support for the rioters. Like, Right on! We've had enough of this shit. Show "the Man," etc. But then again I think: What a waste of energy. There is no revolution. Secondly, I feel great sympathy for those of all "colors" tragically affected by the rioting. And then I think it's easy for me to sympathize with everyone: I'm not there. Neither myself nor mine have been directly affected. How would I have felt if I had been there in the midst of it with my black ass on the line and been forced to make quick decisions? You're either with the program or you're not. Shit stinks and there are no guarantees you won't be flushed down the toilet when the handle is pulled. And third, I feel pity for all "the happy people of (my) country, who scarcely know that there is such a thing as history and so, naturally, imagine that they can escape . . . scot free." I feel pity mingled with some distaste (like saliva mixed with mint chewing gum) for those happy people who make a ruling like this one possible in the first place because they think "we are not paying (and that we will not pay) for our history" (both quotations from *This Morning, This Evening, So*

Soon—James Baldwin). And then on top of all that, I feel guilty for not being there. Like maybe it's socially irresponsible for me to be here "frolicking naked in the fields of green green grass." But it's not easy living here either. I haven't frolicked once. In fact, I haven't even seen those damn fields of grass (outside of in passing from the train window going to/from Ladispoli/Roma). I'm learning things I might have never learned in the United States. I always imagine that the human race will achieve civilization like that in *Stars in My Pocket Like Grains of Sand*—Samuel Delany. Terrific Book.

The nineties are brutal everywhere. No I don't think I need to be feeling any guilt. This isn't my moment. I'm only to blame if I waste this time, if I don't learn what there is to learn in preparation. What's important is how I come out of this, what I make of my time here. So that when my moment does come . . . But I'm honestly afraid that it won't or that if it does, I'll be too ignorant still, too scared, too slow or hesitant to seize it.

5/20/92

One of the ways racism manifests itself here is in terms of sexual harassment, sexual exoticism. Whereas in the United States a black women's sex is detestable, something that the mainstream culture wants forgotten. It is unthinkable, horrific, black sin. And people crusade against it, against us, as if their very lives depended upon our destruction.

Sometimes the men here look at me as if they would steal my youth away if they could, as if they would gobble it down in one mouthful like a hard-boiled egg or nibble at it delicately and stretch it wide with their hands like taffy, licking the stickiness away from their fingers and lips when they'd finished.

Bullet Holes of Resistance

SONIA SANCHEZ

In 1987, I visited Nicaragua with a group of Norteamericano poets. We had come to Nicaragua for the Rubén Darío poetry festival. The festival was in an outdoor stadium. The sun poured down on our heads. No mercy. But the people entered the stadium with their straw hats. They came to listen to poetry because they loved Darío and other poets. They came. Listened. Nodded their heads in agreement with the message and the beauty. Poetry for the people! Poetry for the children! Poetry for the country to live on amid attacks from Contras and other hidden enemies. They clapped and embraced our words as their own. And we were one. For a while. In between bullets and hunger.

Nicaraguan Journal

Jan. 17, 1987—Sat. nite

Nothing had prepared me for my arrival in Nicaragua. Not my trip to the People's Republic of China in 1973. Nor Cuba in 1978. Nothing had prepared me for the emotion i felt as i traveled up and down those roads, as i counted the bullet holes piercing a land full of resistance. And our bus hugged the road as if it were afraid of falling into a great wide hole. (Ah America. You will bring them to their knees. Starve them out. Huh???) i had come to this country from other countries. Footsteps walking from under my feet. i had arrived in Nicaragua after many hesitations: conflict of classes, illness, financial woes, a distance between H. and me. (i catch him staring into space. Someplace else. He encourages our distances i think.) Yet. Here i am/was on this January night. Inhaling these warm breezes erasing the cold studding my face. And the night felt easy. But i heard the city in guard against earthquakes. Contras. Blackouts. Hunger. Warships off its Atlantic and Pacific coasts. Hunger. Hunger. Hunger. And our bus moved toward our *hotelito* humming a sound that resounded with many silences. *La revolución es una chavala de cuatro años.*

MANAGUA. Riding on the bus to our hotel. What one sees in the Caribbean, Central America, how dark it is at nite. And the people, always congregating outside. Just as we did in Harlem. In the summertime, out of the dark, small, dingy houses that tried to restrict, reshape us into shapeless entities.

Sunday—January 18, 1987

And we came to Cuidad Darío: birthplace of Rubén Darío for the Rubén Darío Poetry Festival. What a day. Hot sun pouring down on our heads. Faces. Loud boisterous sun. With no manners. Doesn't know how to go home. Tomas Borge spoke. i shook hands with him. Told him i had seen him in Cuba in December 1984. Should have requested his autograph. Tom McGrath, Roberto Vargas, Carlos Rygbi read their poetry. And others. All very good! Musicians played. A group from Angola sang and played African instruments. *Muy bien.* Some of us read in the late afternoon. About 4:45—read my piece about "we are here for more reasons than history. . . ." Carlos translated . . . well received. On the way to Estoli. Near the Hondurian border. We walked in the streets. Saw buildings with huge bullet holes. Buildings destroyed by the war. Passed by a disco, loud American music emanating from the creases. The young people came out and looked at us. They were fascinated by Lamont's dreadlocks. They touched them hesitantly.

Estoli

The earth in Estoli sprang up as if seeking me out. i breathed borrowing this Estoli air that has had to heal its own bleeding children and women. i hold out my wounds.

Beautifully Ugly

ELEANOR SMITH

In 1979 at the Annual Meeting of the Association for the Study of African American Life and History, several women decided we were going to contribute to the void about the lives, events and contributions of black women by keeping journals. I decided I wanted to keep a record of my thoughts, feelings, accomplishments, disappointments, or whatever so that in the future scholars and interested readers would have available primary resources.

On January 28, 1979, the first entry in my journal was made and it was less than one page long. I wanted to write about things that would let the future readers of my journal know what a professional woman's life was all about and I wanted it to be a meaningful and pleasant experience rather than a task. Consequently, I have never written in the now six volumes on a regular schedule and sometimes the entry may be as long as ten pages. Since I have had the opportunity to travel to many parts of the world I also kept separate travel journals which number seventeen. This collection ranges from a special Trip Book to a writing pad and they come in all sizes and shapes. These journals share my thoughts and experiences about the scenery, culture, customs, and people of the countries in which I have traveled and serve as a memory source for the things I have learned.

However, after fourteen years of journal writing I find they have an added dimension I had not anticipated. I am able to look back over my experiences and realize how I have changed and grown and to see the things that have remained so much a part of my life.

One travel experience which had an enormous impact on me was my visit to South Africa which began in Johannesburg and ended in Cape Town.

October 10, 1989 — Cape Town

The hotel, Holiday Inn, is located in a "colored" area. Most of the time such areas are located at the fringe of the city or town. the whites live in the towns and cities. It seems that no matter where I visit the East Indians live very well. They have a very nice amount of space for each home and they are generally large homes.

Each racial group area has its own recreational area, hospital, centers, etc. However, the quality of such facilities varies based on race. The rural black areas have no recreational facilities, the schools are of the poorest quality and often there is no hospital—maybe a clinic. In one "colored" community in East London, they had a stadium which consisted of a field with seating for a few people. The goals on the field were in poor condition and there was little else. The "white" areas have large stadiums with seating for thousands. The "black" areas can be spotted because they don't have regular street lights. They are on extremely high poles and Margaret (a white whose name had been given to me to contact helps black children get a decent education by providing tuition funds) said this was to prevent the people from breaking them.

It seems to me that while some whites are trying to help the blacks, they have no respect for them. They talk about African time, how Africans do not follow through and generally believe Africans are irresponsible. Margaret gave an example of a man who worked for Jack's brother (Jack is Margaret's husband) on the dairy farm for years and knew all the things to do and did them well. The dairy farm was in Zimbabwe. When the land was taken from Jack's brother, he had to let most of his one hundred workers go. Prior to that he had provided everything for his employees and they lived in decent homes, had plenty of food, etc. This one particular man who knew all about cattle had several heads when he set out on his own. The brother later went to see how he was doing and found him sitting in front of a shack with a straw in between his teeth. His cattle were in terrible condition and he was not doing any of the things he knew to do and had done for him for years and years. The question was why wasn't he caring for his own cattle using the knowledge he had. He had been the best cattleman on the farm. Was it because of hopelessness and the deplorable living conditions? These are not easy questions to answer. Why when people take care of the homes of white people for years they don't do the same for their own homes regardless of the quality of the house. You don't have to live in filth because things are small. However, I do realize that things are complicated by the lack of sanitation facilities and running water in the home. I don't know how you can lift up thousands and thousands of people living in such poor and unhealthy conditions.

The lines are so clearly drawn between the quality of life for the different races that visually I can tell who lives where. I have seen no areas that could be called the slums for whites. There are areas in which one could designate as middle class or less affluent but the "white" area is decent and quality living is apparent. The white minority has the best of everything and the majority has the worst.

Margaret talked about how well the races got along and that at the hospital where she was a doctor, they worked side by side and race was not noticed. I commented that perhaps that is true but at the end of the day they depart for home with each going to separate group areas and the whites going to the choice areas. I asked her why didn't whites just ignore the laws and let the others move into their area. She said whites couldn't because they, the nonwhites, would be evicted. I suggested that if enough white areas did this the government couldn't possibly deal with a mass response. I think this kind of action doesn't happen because whites enjoy their privileged status and will not give it up until they have to and many, if not most, realize this will be happening soon.

One issue that will be difficult for blacks in terms of improving education is that most speak only their African language or dialect. The educational system will either have to teach in the different African languages or be prepared to teach English and/or Afrikaans. As it is now there are schools for whites in which either Afrikaans or English is the language used in the school. It might make sense to make English the national language. Again all these different languages complicate solutions to the problems.

My visit to Cape Town has not been as productive as it could have been because of two holidays. Monday was an American holiday and today a South African holiday.

I must say that I am looking forward to the end of this trip and wish I was leaving for the U.S.A. tomorrow instead of Harare, Zimbabwe. I know I will enjoy being there and then going on to Nairobi, Kenya. I am ready to sleep in my own bed, eat my food, and be in my own home.

When JM, an African American studying in Cape Town, got to the hotel for our luncheon appointment, he had forgotten this was a holiday and things were closed. So we had lunch in the hotel.

I learned a great deal about South Africa from his perspective. The first slaves of the country were imported from Indonesia and Malaysia. The Boers/Dutch could not conquer the Africans. There were two group of Africans who were in the area—one group were herders and the other gatherers. The land was sparsely occupied and the Xshotos were to the North. The Boers could do nothing with the Xshoto people and only the British with their heavy guns were able to handle them. This was in the mid-1800s.

The policy of apartheid was implemented in 1948 and the Group Act enacted in 1960s. The "colored" were living in Fish Hook and Solomon, where the navy base is located. They were living in the lovely homes on the side of the mountain overlooking the sea. The government came in and forced them out of their homes and the whites moved into them. They moved the blacks to the other side of the mountain on the Atlantic side and called it Ocean View. However, the ocean was nowhere to be seen.

I talked to him about black-on-black killings. He said they are fighting over resources, land, water, and such. They put blacks in areas and then provide one water tap for seven hundred people. The whites have done the same type of thing to blacks in the distribution of land. They end up fighting for enough space to graze their flocks and have their gardens.

He mentioned that gangs are formed so they can make sure they have access to water and to other basic needs. These gang leaders also go to factories and other workplaces to get the owners to hire their gang members. They will tell the owner they have twenty-five men for work and so they are able to recruit new members because they can get jobs and other services for them. Apartheid creates a situation which makes blacks respond to their needs by fighting each other. Apartheid has also made blacks feel inferior and lack a positive self-concept.

He talked about the poor whites "Afrikaner" areas he had seen. He said they were trashy and junky. These people are very hostile toward blacks. He also mentioned the majority of East Indians are not wealthy and whites love to show the wealthy Indian areas off and say aren't they industrious people.

The white South Africans talk about there being a first world and third world. JM thinks this is ridiculous. The so-called first and third worlds are one world with the difference created by apartheid. They are extremely dependent upon each other.

He said he was on the beach when Archbishop Tutu and others conducted a peaceful demonstration. The police were there with dogs, tear gas, chains, and whips. He said helicopters were flying very close to the heads of the people chasing them into the chains, whips, and dogs of the policemen. He said the most frightening aspect about the whole scene was the pleasure the policemen seemed to have beating old women and children. They beat them before they took them away. JM said, "I saw this with my own eyes."

Apartheid has negatively affected the lives of all the people of the country. The vision of the whites is so blurred with the skin privilege they have that they can't take charge of the situation they say they dislike. I think some consciously and others subconsciously live in fear of blacks. The rest of the races are human resources which are terribly limited and can't contribute to the welfare of the country.

Sanctions are affecting everyone in South Africa. The quality of life is declining for many whites. They can't afford the conveniences and other luxuries to which they have become accustomed. The economy is being negatively affected. Some whites have tried to tell me it was making the lives of blacks much worse but it can't get much worse for them and it can get much worse for the white South Africans. There is a 13.5 percent tax on everything and many items have gone up on cost. So they are feeling the crunch and several industries are having difficulty—e.g., the pineapple plantations.

When the white South Africans decided that the Natal area could support a sugarcane industry, they brought East Indians here as indentured servants to work the sugarcane plantations. Other Indians came as the shopkeepers and businessmen. It seems that white South Africans have never seen themselves as the labor force. They have created a financial and political system on the backs of others—people of color.

I had dinner with DJ, Director of the Institute of Race Relations. He said I had a choice of a Greek or Italian restaurant. Since neither is my favorite type of food, the Italian was the lesser of the two evils. The first restaurant we went to was very crowded and we were told we would have to wait a few moments. After waiting for some time, we decided to find someplace else which turned out to be another Italian restaurant.

DJ was very easy to talk with and we first discussed the Smith College South African Scholarship Program and his office. They offer bursars (scholarships) and an enrichment program for blacks. They have more than twenty teachers and teach classes on Saturday and holidays. They often start out with as many as two thousand students and about only five hundred end up sticking it out. The students have transportation problems and finding a decent place to study is difficult. Many have only candlelight to study by at night.

He talked about how the government came into the squatters' quarters and bulldozed the homes of the blacks down destroying all their personal belongings. The blacks finally built their homes out of plastic using poles to form the room. The area was all sand so they would put their sticks in at night and wrap the plastic around them so early in the morning before the police came they would take their home up. Finally, the police caught on and would dig up their poles and plastic and destroy them. Furthermore, they were building no homes in the black areas so there was no place for them to live. The cruelty with which these people enforce apartheid is unspeakable. How they can think the world is unfair by imposing sanctions is unbelievable.

. . . People stared at DJ and me and I am sure it was because he was white and with me. This sort of thing doesn't happen frequently. First of all the blacks don't go into the restaurants outside their area and a black woman and a white man together doesn't occur. At the same time I experience this kind of thing, people like Margaret tell me how well the races get along.

Needless to say this has been a most interesting and meaningful experience. I have learned much but I know I have only scratched the surface and I have accomplished my goals for Smith College. I must say I am not sad about leaving. It is one of the most beautiful countries, if not the most beautiful, I have ever seen. Yet it is the ugliest.

Showing Our True Colors

AUDRE LORDE

In the spring of 1984, I spent three months at the Free University in Berlin teaching a course on Black American poets, and a poetry workshop in English, for German students. One of my aims for this trip was to meet Black German women, for I had been told there were quite a few in Berlin. The appearance of Farbe Bekennen *fulfills the dream I had as I wrote these words of making the stories of our Black German sisters—and Afro-German history as a whole—available to English-speaking Diaspora.*

Who are they, these German women of the Diaspora? Where do our paths intersect as women of color—beyond the details of our particular oppressions, although certainly not outside the reference of those details? And where do our paths diverge? Most important, what can we learn from our connected differences that will be useful to us both, Afro-German and Afro-American?

Afro-German. The women say they've never heard that term used before.

I asked one of my Black students how she'd thought about herself

growing up. "The nicest thing they ever called us was 'warbaby,'"
she said. But the existence of most Black Germans has nothing to do
with the Second World War, and, in fact, predates it by many decades.
I have Black German women in my class who trace their Afro-German
heritage back to the 1890s.

For me, Afro-German means the shining faces of Mai and Katerina
in animated conversation about their fathers' homelands, the compar-
isons, joys, disappointments. It means my pleasure at seeing another
Black woman walk into my classroom, her reticence slowly giving way
as she explores a new self-awareness, gains a new way of thinking
about herself in relation to other Black women.

"I've never thought of Afro-German as a positive concept before,"
she said, speaking out of the pain of having to live a difference that
has no name; speaking out of the growing power self-scrutiny has
forged from that difference.

I am excited by these women, by their blossoming sense of identity
as they say, "Let us be ourselves now as we define us. We are not a
figment of your imagination or an exotic answer to your desires. We
are not some button on the pocket of your longing." I see these women
as a growing force for international change, in concert with other
Afro-Europeans, Afro-Asians, Afro-Americans.

We are the hyphenated people of the Diaspora whose self-defined
identities are no longer shameful secrets in the countries of our origins,
but rather declarations of strength and solidarity. We are an increasingly united front from which the world has not yet heard.

Despite the terror and isolation some of these Black women have
known from childhood, they are freer of the emotional dilemma facing
many white feminists in Germany today. Too often, I have met an
immobilizing national guilt in white German women which serves to
keep them from acting upon what they profess to believe. Their energies, however well intentioned, are not being used, they are unavailable in the battles against racism, anti-Semitism, heterosexism,
xenophobia. Because they seem unable to accept who they are, these
women too often fail to examine and pursue the powers relative to
their identity. They waste that power, or worse, turn it over to their

enemies. Four decades after National Socialism, the question still lingers for many white German women: how can I draw strength from my roots when those roots are entwined in such a terrible history? That terror of self-scrutiny is sometimes disguised as an unbearable arrogance, impotent and wasteful.

The words of these Black German women document their rejection of despair, of blindness, of silence. Once an oppression is expressed, it can be successfully fought.

Afterword

GLENDA P. SIMMS

This project intrigued me because the Canadian Advisory Council on the Status of Women, of which I am president, is in the final stages of producing a unique book entitled *Sharing Our Experiences*, a book of letters written by racial minority women of Canada. Both, *Life Notes* and *Sharing Our Experiences*, are designed to bring to the attention of the public the unique life experiences of women whose lives have not been the blueprint for the theories of feminism, womanism, and other schools of thought that purport to speak on behalf of all women. In *Life Notes* Black women speak clearly of their concerns in a most unique and personal way. Their voices ring out to me, telling me how much we have in common, how much our lives overlap, how profoundly our black experience crosses geographical, class, and cultural boundaries.

Every Black woman can recognize the themes that have been recorded in these personal writings. When our sisters' journals reflect our own lives so closely we are forced to stop, to listen, and to think. We need to stop and take stock of self and of others. We need to listen to the inner voices that get drowned out by the external clutter of irrelevant and distorted ideas about our Black womanhood. We need to think about how we can strategize to move beyond a recognition of the forces that present us with opposing views of ourselves, to a state of consciousness of how we must take control of our personal and group lives.

As we record our experiences we see the critical paths established by the oppressive forces of racism, classicism, and sexism. We face the differences created by these aberrations, and, in facing them we find ways of uniting, not just around our race and gender, but around the energies of liberation that both our foremothers and our contemporary sisters generate. For in the final analysis, Black women's lives are the "real stuff" of the universal human experience. This came home to me as I read through the many accounts in *Life Notes*. I was engrossed in the events described. I found it difficult to stop reading. I needed to know what came next. I feared coming to the end. I wanted the stories to go on and on. Why? Because the life experiences of these women were running commentaries of my own personal journey from childhood into womanhood, from the mountain village in southern Jamaica to the isolated northern extremes of western Canada and eventually to the power-brokering capital city, Ottawa.

The close patterns of identity between my experiences and many of those expressed in *Life Notes* is an indication of the interconnectedness of the human spirit. As Black women we need from time to time to stand back from our personal histories and make decisions about how we can either heighten the effects of our actions or change the trajectory of our life forces. If, in fact, we are products of our particular socialization and history, then we must intelligently decide to take control of those aspects of our lives that are self-directed: our education, relationships with others, attitudes toward self, feelings about Blackness and feelings about being women. In short, we need to grapple with our internal demons in order to ward off the demonic forces of the external. Indeed, we must acknowledge that our lives are conceptualized not by the negative forces (slavery, colonialism, neocolonialism, imperialism, racism, sexism, and other marginalizing historical forces), but by the detailed recording of the positive outcomes of our lives as individuals. These outcomes are testimony to the enduring truths about our ability to reshape our destiny, to find peace in war zones, to seek friendship among enemies, to find shelter from the wind and rain, to preserve our soul in a soulness climate—to survive against all odds.

The life experiences of Black women need to be moved from ideas about the ordinary and the mundane. *Life Notes* has done this. It has shown us in a unique way that Black women can validly be seen as microcosmic figures, encapsulating and representing the lives and struggles of all women, and also the struggles of all suffering humanity—male and female. In exploring what it means to be Black and female, we are presenting to the world mirror images of self and the other. In these lives, written by women who are marked by race and gender as objects and symbols of oppression, there is much to be learned, by women of other races and by all men, about the nature of survival—the principle of life itself.

Contributors

FAITH ADIELE was raised in rural Washington State and currently resides in Cambridge, Massachusetts. Part of her memoir-in-progress, about growing up with her Scandinavian mother and then traveling to Africa to find her Nigerian father and siblings, has appeared in *Radcliffe Quarterly* and *Coloring Outside the Lines: Writings by Mixed-Blood and Multiracial Women of Color.*

AI is the author of five books. Her latest is entitled *Greed* and will be published by W. W. Norton. She lives in Tempe, Arizona, with her Siamese. She loves to shop.

ANNE ALEXIS BENNETT ALEXANDER, younger sister to Jenniffer, is a thirteen-year-old who likes to write poetry, draw, talk on the phone, and have fun.

JENNIFFER DAWN BENNETT ALEXANDER is fourteen years old. She and her sister, Anne, live in Athens, Georgia.

BRENDA FAYE BELL, younger sister to Patricia Bell-Scott, is a writer, homemaker, and an English student at Chattanooga State Community College in Tennessee. She is also a foster parent and grandmother.

PATRICIA BELL-SCOTT, professor of child and family development and women's studies and adjunct professor of psychology at the University of Georgia, is principal coeditor of *Double Stitch: Black Women Write about Mothers and Daughters*, cofounder of *SAGE: A Scholarly Journal on Black Women*, and coeditor (with Gloria T. Hull and Barbara Smith) of *All the Women Are White, All the Blacks Are Men, But Some of Us Are Brave: Black Women's Studies*. She recently returned to the South—region of her birth—to nurture her creativity. She hopes that *Life Notes* will affirm and encourage Black women's personal writings.

DAWN D. BENNETT-ALEXANDER is an attorney teaching law at the University of Georgia's Terry College of Business. She has written the first employment law textbook for colleges of business and is working on a book about the chicken processing plant fire that occurred in Hamlet, North Carolina, on September 3, 1991. The inspiration for all she does is the women and her ancestors who have gone before her. She is also the mother of two adolescent contributors—Jenniffer and Anne.

CARROLL PARROTT BLUE's film, *Nigerian Art-Kindred Spirits*, was initially broadcast in the 1990 PBS series, "Smithsonian World." Her other credits include producer of the program "Vision" for the 1994 NOVA PBS series, "A Natural History of the Senses"; field producer for Marlon Riggs's 1993 *Black is . . . Black Ain't*; segment producer for *Eyes of the Prize, II*; and producer of *Varnette's World: A Study of a Young Artist* and *Conversations with Roy DeCarava*. She is also an associate professor of telecommunications and film at San Diego State University.

MÉLINA BROWN was born in France and raised in the Midwest. She now lives in North Carolina where she is completing graduate studies in library science.

PAULETTE M. CALDWELL is a writer, attorney, and professor of law at the New York University School of Law.

ALBERT CHONG, whose work is featured on the cover of this anthology, was born in Kingston, Jamaica, of African and Chinese ancestry. A graduate of the New York School of Visual Arts and the University of California at San Diego, his works have been exhibited at the Museum of Modern Art in New York and the Museum of Fine Arts, Boston. He has received several artist awards, including a National Endowment for the Arts Fellowship in photography.

PEARL CLEAGE is an Atlanta-based writer whose works include the book *Mad at Miles: A Blackwoman's Guide to Truth* and plays *Hospice* and *Flying' West*. She is the mother of one daughter, Deignan.

RISÉ COLLINS, a dark being of light (and sound), is in the process of writing her way to self-realization. She wants her words to carry consciousness, power, love, and medicine.

MIRIAM DECOSTA-WILLIS teaches comparative Black literature at the University of Maryland Baltimore County. She is editor of *Blacks in Hispanic Literature* and coeditor of *Erotique Noire/Black Erotica, Double Stitch: Black Women Write about Mothers and Daughters,* and *Homespun Images: An Anthology of Black Memphis Writers and Artists.* She is also a member of the editorial collective for *SAGE: A Scholarly Journal on Black Women.*

TOI DERRICOTTE, an associate professor of English at the University of Pittsburgh, has published three collections of poetry, *Natural Birth, The Empress of the Death House,* and most recently *Captivity.* She is the recipient of two fellowships from the National Endowment for the Arts, the Lucille Medwick Memorial Award from the Poetry Society of America, a Pushcart Prize, and the Folger Shakespeare Library Poetry Book Award.

R. H. DOUGLAS was born in Trinidad, West Indies. She currently lives in New York. Her works have been included in *Erotique Noire/Black Erotica, Creation Fire: Anthology of Caribbean Women Writers, The*

New Voices Literary Journal, and *Editor's Choice: Spirit That Moves Press.* She believes that keeping a diary from the past eighteen years has saved her from madness and stagnation.

RITA DOVE was born in Akron, Ohio, in 1952. Author of four poetry books—most recently *Grace Notes* (1989)—a collection of short stories, a novel—*Through the Ivory Gate* (1992)—and a verse drama— *The Darker Face of the Earth* (1993), she was awarded the 1987 Pulitzer Prize in Poetry for *Thomas and Beulah.* Other honors include Fulbright and Guggenheim fellowships as well as grants from the National Endowment for the Arts, the National Endowment for the Humanities, and the Mellon Foundation. She has received the Academy of American Poets' Lavan Award, a General Electric Foundation Award, two honorary doctorates, and the Literary Lion Citation from the New York Public Library. She is Commonwealth Professor of English at the University of Virginia and was recently appointed Poet Laureate of the United States.

GWENDOLYN J. DUNGY is a community college administrator who has a doctorate in administration and a master's degree in English literature. Private writing is her constant companion.

QUO VADIS GEX-BREAUX lives and writes in New Orleans. Her poetry has appeared in several journals and anthologies and she is presently editing a book of poems, *Jazz Rain.* She has three sons.

MARCIA ANN GILLESPIE is editor in chief of *Ms.* magazine and former editor in chief of *Essence* magazine. During her tenure at *Essence,* her intensely personal editorial columns titled "Getting Down" were a form of public diary.

BELL HOOKS is a professor of women's studies at Oberlin College. A feminist theorist, cultural critic and writer, she has authored eight books; the most recent is *Sisters of the Yam: Black Women and Self-Recovery.*

CATHARINE SMITH JONES is author of *Songs for My Sisters*, a collection of short fiction, which has been distributed in U.S. and British markets. She teaches creative writing at Emory University.

JAMAICA KINCAID was born in St. Johns, Antigua. The recipient of several literary awards, she is author of three highly acclaimed books of fiction—*At the Bottom of the River, Annie John*, and *Lucy*.

AUDRE LORDE, Black feminist lesbian warrior poet mother, died in November of 1992 of cancer. She authored nine volumes of poetry and five works of prose. The recipient of many distinguished honors and awards including the Honorary Doctorate of Literature, Hunter College (1991); Walt Whitman Citation of Merit (1991); Honorary Doctorate of Letters, Oberlin College (1990); Honorary Doctorate of Humane Letters, Haverford College (1989); the Manhattan Borough President's Award for Excellence in the Arts (1988). She was named New York State Poet in 1991. Her personal writings are a source of inspiration for women around the world.

LOIS FLORENCE LYLES received her Ph.D. from Harvard University. She teaches English Renaissance literature and contemporary American literature at San Francisco State University. She was invited to present her story, "Easy Riders Got to Stay Away," about the civil rights movement in Mississippi in 1964, at the 1993 National Twentieth-Century Literature Conference at the University of Louisville, Kentucky.

ANN LYNN is an attorney living and working in Atlanta. She continues to keep a journal, attend support meetings, and find beauty in her life with the help of close friends.

CAROLE STEWART MCDONNELL, a Christian Black woman, writes all it fully implies. She writes movie reviews and is presently putting the finishing touches on a novel, *Black Girls Have Always Loved Cowboys (and Other Oreo Blues)*.

DEBORAH E. MCDOWELL is professor of English at the University of Virginia and author of the forthcoming *The Changing Same: Studies in Fiction by Black Women* (Indiana University Press). She is editor, with Arnold Rampersad, of *Slavery and the Literary Imagination*, and author of numerous essays on African-American literature.

TIJUANA MURRAY is a free-lance writer living abroad in Rome, Italy. She received a degree in English with emphasis in creative writing from Trinity College in Hartford, Connecticut. She is currently at work on her first novel, *Through the Looking Glass.*

TINUKE OLUYOMI, an elementary school student, attends the New Capital School in Abuja, Nigeria, and hopes to become a medical doctor. Her hobbies are writing, reading, and debate. She makes friends easily and enjoys meeting people.

HERMINE PINSON teaches at the College of William and Mary. She is the recipient of awards and fellowships from the National Endowment for the Humanities and the Ford Foundation. She has authored one collection of poems, *Ashe,* and her poems and short stories have appeared in *Callaloo, African American Arts Review, Konch,* and *Tribes.*

YIN QUILTER—unfortunately because of the nature of her piece, a pen name—is a lawyer, quilter, professor, and writer who has many publications to her credit. She wishes fervently that her children will grow up so that she can use her real name when writing pieces such as this. She feels that sharing their lives is the best way women can help each other.

VIKI RADDEN lives and writes in Woodacre, California. She is completing her first novel and working on short fiction and her memoirs. Her works have been published in *SAGE: A Scholarly Journal on*

Black Women, The Abiko Literary Quarterly, Sojourner, and *Women Travel.* She was recently awarded the Hawthornden Fellowship for writers in Edinburgh, Scotland.

SHAMARA SHANTU RILEY is a first-year graduate student in American politics at the University of Illinois–Urbana/Champaign, where she received her bachelor's degree in 1992. She is a founding member and president of Black/Out, a campus organization for Black lesbians, gays, and bisexuals. Her first published essay about the contributions of Black women to the environmental movement, will be published in the forthcoming anthology *Ecofeminism and the Sacred.*

BELVIE ROOKS lives on California's Pacific North Coast. Her previously published works have appeared in *Double Stitch: Black Women Write about Mothers and Daughters, Essence, The San Francisco Review of Books, San Francisco Chronicle,* and *Women's Voices.* She is a book publicist and coeditor of *Paris Connections: African American Artists in Paris,* and *Paris Connections: African and Caribbean Artists in Paris.*

SUSAN J. ROSS is a photographer who lives in Atlanta. Her work has been featured in a number of publications, including the book jacket for *Double Stitch: Black Women Write about Mothers and Daughters.* Photography is her way of keeping a journal.

EVELYN C. ROSSER grew up in Valdosta, Georgia, and now lives in Athens, Georgia. She teaches language arts at Cedar Shoals High School and writing for the Upward Bound Program at the University of Georgia. She received her B.S. from Fort Valley State College and her M.Ed. from West Georgia College. She is currently working on a novel.

ANDREA BENTON RUSHING teaches in the departments of Black studies and English at Amherst College and coedited with Sharon Harley and Rosalyn Terborg-Penn, *Women in Africa and the African Diaspora.* She is currently working on two manuscripts: the autobiographical "Rape: The Invisible Wound" and "Speaking in Tongues" (based on color photographs she has taken in Nigeria), which both decodes Yoruba women's attire and demonstrates ways it challenges contemporary Euro-American fashions and feminisms. (These projects have her collection of short stories, "Birthmarks and Keloids," *way* on the back burner.) She is also blessed to be the mother of an extraordinary twenty-three-year-old daughter.

SONIA SANCHEZ holds the Laura Carnell Chair in English at Temple University and is author of thirteen books, including *Homecoming, We a BaddDDD People, Love Poems, I've Been a Woman: New and Selected Poems, A Sound Investment and Other Stories, Homegirls and Handgrenades,* and, most recently, *Under a Soprano Sky.* A recipient of a fellowship from the National Endowment for the Arts, the Lucretia Mott Award in 1984, and an award from the Pennsylvania Coalition of 100 Black Women, she also won an American Book Award in 1985, the Governor's Award for Excellence in the Humanities in 1988, and the Peace and Freedom Award from the Women's International League for Peace and Freedom in 1989. She has lectured at over five hundred universities and colleges in the United States and has traveled extensively, reciting her poetry in Nicaragua, Cuba, England, Norway, Australia, Africa, the Caribbean, and the People's Republic of China.

SAPPHIRE is a poet, writer, and performance artist. Her work has appeared in numerous anthologies and journals. A collection of her prose and poetry, *American Dreams,* was published in 1994 by High Risk Books/Serpent's Tail.

AMA R. SARAN is a Spelman College sister of the Sixties; currently residing in Seattle, Washington, and happily ensconced in the building of a chapter for the National Black Women's Health Project. Having completed her master's in public health at the University of Washington's School of Public Health and Community Medicine, she is completing her dissertation chronicling African-American women's magic and religion in the time of AIDS.

JUDY SCALES-TRENT is a professor at the State University of New York at Buffalo School of Law. She writes about the interaction of race and sex in American law, and the intersection of race and color in her own life.

ELAINE SHELLY is a poet and performance artist who finds life-sustaining energy in writing. She practices these life revivals almost daily in St. Paul, Minnesota.

GLENDA P. SIMMS was appointed by the prime minister of Canada as president of the Canadian Advisory Council on the Status of Women (CACSW) in December 1989. She is an acknowledged advocate of women and minority groups, whose unique vision of an inclusive feminism continues to guide research, policy, and staffing decisions at the CACSW. A teacher in her native Jamaica, Simms moved to Canada in 1966. She began her teaching career in Canada in northern Alberta, among the Metis and Cree Aboriginal peoples. Her commitment to Canadian Aboriginal issues has continued throughout her career.

MICHELE L. SIMMS-BURTON is a writer living in Alexandra, Virginia, a Ph.D. candidate in American literature, and university fellow at George Washington University. She is the mother of one son, D. Malik Burton, and wife to David L. Burton. She began keeping journals at age ten and has continued to do so to the present.

BARBARA SMITH is a Black feminist writer and activist. She is coeditor with Gloria T. Hull and Patricia Bell-Scott of *All the Women Are White, All the Blacks Are Men, But Some of Us Are Brave: Black*

Women's Studies and editor of *Home Girls: A Black Feminist Anthology*. She is a cofounder and publisher of Kitchen Table: Women of Color Press. She lives in Albany, New York.

ELEANOR SMITH is a higher education administrator and currently vice president for academic affairs, provost, and professor of African-American studies at William Paterson College, Wayne, New Jersey. She has published numerous articles on the African-American experience, particularly African-American women. She also has a music degree, having studied piano and voice at Capital University.

PAULA OBE THOMAS is a poet/short story writer/artist/photographer who lives in Trinidad. She explores the theme of feminism and social issues in her work. She has recently started working at Servol Life Center as an adult development program officer. Her work has been published by *New Voices, CAFRA Newsletter, TIANO Covering Columbus*, and other poetry anthologies. She is also involved in popular education.

VALERIE TURNER now claims the name **VALERIE JEAN.** She is a poet, undeniably Black and woman, writes as much as she can while raising an eighteen-year-old daughter. She teaches creative writing at Essex Community College in Baltimore County, Maryland.

ALICE WALKER, prize-winning author, has written numerous essays, several volumes of poetry, two collections of short stories, and five novels, including *The Color Purple, The Temple of My Familiar*, and *Possessing the Secret of Joy.*

DAKOTA WELLS is an associate professor of clinical psychology. She has found peace and is entering into joy through a passionate engagement with the Spirit, her family, and her work.

DOROTHY WILBANKS, a retired telephone operator from South Central Bell who lives in Chattanooga, Tennessee, is mother of Brenda Faye Bell and Patricia Bell-Scott. She is sixty-four years old and now works part-time at Sears.

Credits

Ai: Excerpt from "Arrival," from *Contemporary Authors: Autobiography Series*, vol. 13 edited by Joyce Nakamura. (Gale Research, 1991.) Copyright © 1991 by Ai. Reprinted by permission of Ai.

Carroll Parrott Blue: "Sometimes a Poem is Twenty Years of Memory," from *SAGE: A Scholarly Journal on Black Women*, spring 1987. Copyright © 1987 by Caroll Parrott Blue. Reprinted by permission of Sage Women's Educational Press, Inc.

Paulette M. Caldwell: Excerpt from "A Hair Piece: Perspectives on the Intersection of Race and Gender," *Duke Law Journal*, 365. Copyright © 1991 by Paulette Caldwell. Reprinted by permission of Paulette M. Caldwell.

Pearl Cleage: "Jive Talk and Random Thoughts," from *SAGE: A Scholarly Journal on Black Women*, spring 1985. Copyright © 1985 by Pearl Cleage. Reprinted by permission of Sage Women's Educational Press, Inc.

Rita Dove: Excerpt from "The House That Jill Built," from *The Writer on Her Work*, edited by Janet Sternburg (W. W. Norton, 1991). Copyright © 1991 by Rita Dove: Reprinted by permission of Rita Dove.

Quo Vadis Gex-Breaux: "Night Raid," Copyright © by and reprinted by permission of *Xavier Review*.